Double Happiness

One Man's Tale of Love, Loss, and Wonder
on the Long Roads of China

Tony Brasunas

TORCHPOST CREATIVE

DOUBLE HAPPINESS
is a publication of

TORCHPOST CREATIVE
1612 Bay Street
Alameda CA 94501

First Torchpost Creative edition 2013

Trade paper: ISBN 978-0-9911662-4-4
Casebound: ISBN 978-0-9911662-9-9
E-book: ISBN 978-0-9911662-1-3

www.Torchpost.com
www.DoubleHappy.be

BOOK DESIGN BY JOEL FRIEDLANDER
Cover photos courtesy of Damian Spieckerman and Jordan May.

To my mother, Lynne,
for her optimism, her curiosity,
and her dedication to growth throughout life.

不上高山不顯平地

If you do not climb the mountain,
You will not see the plain.
—CHINESE PROVERB

Contents

Prologue

"Do you want to tickle the dragon?" My father was calling up to me. I was curled near the ceiling in a carpeted cubby he had built as a loft space. Lying on my belly like a snake, I sorted golden rivets into piles: long, yellow brass ones; shorter, reddish copper ones; dull, gray steel ones. It was fun and important work, but I could never resist tickling the dragon.

I climbed down the ladder and stepped onto the sooty concrete floor. The smell of coal hung in the air around my father's brick forge. I grabbed hold of the wooden peg on the giant black wheel and pulled it down. The wheel began to turn. Because I wasn't tall enough, I let the wheel spin the peg back up, and I caught it again as it came down, pulling again so the wheel began to turn faster. Heat radiated in intensifying waves from the hole in the center of the forge, and embers of hot orange and gold flew from the hole. The dragon was breathing!

"That's it," said my father. "Good. He's awake." In iron tongs he clutched a long piece of black steel that maybe, finally, he would make into a sword instead of a horseshoe, triangle, or fancy gate.

But I had to watch from above. He sent me back up to the loft, and I let my head hang over the edge so that I could watch as my father held the steel in the dragon's breath. The fierce heat now exhaled constantly and turned the steel purple, red, orange, and finally a bright golden white. The flames held my gaze. *Is there really a dragon down there, under the concrete floor?* I wondered. *Does it actually eat the coal we give it every morning?*

He pinched the white-hot steel with the tongs, set it on the anvil, and with a heavy iron hammer, he struck the glowing metal, once, twice, three times, and sparks flew: Long, hairy fragments of orange shot everywhere in an inverted waterfall of light.

✿

THIS WAS the end of the 1970s, on a commune in West Virginia. Twelve years earlier, before becoming a blacksmith, my father had been one of the first long-haired hippies at MIT in Boston. He swore he would never wear a tie, and he leapt into the civil rights and peace movements that were sweeping through the country like wildfire.

Soon he changed course and elected a more personal path to fixing the world. With the woman who would become my mother, he traveled to England and lived for a year in a spiritual community west of Oxford. They learned meditation techniques from the community's leader, John G. Bennett, a wise and well-traveled man. Bennett determined that the time had come to start a community in the United States, and an estate called Claymont, in West Virginia, with four hundred acres of hilly forests and fertile farmland, was chosen for the purpose. At Claymont, my father turned an old concrete storehouse into a forge while my mother worked in the bookstore and the vegetable gardens. I helped in the forge and attended the three-room school, studying math, French, and art in the mornings alongside the two dozen other children; in the afternoons, our teachers would take us into the loam-smelling woods or down to the gurgling waters of the fish farm.

After a mere nine years, the commune faltered, rudderless. Bennett's unexpected death had robbed the experiment of its visionary, and efforts to replace his leadership had largely proven fruitless. My parents had ushered my sister and brother into the world, and they consulted an astrologer for a new path. "Telecommunications" was divined in my father's future, and he concocted a short resume, tied a tie to his neck, and landed a phone company job in a nearby town.

I went a different way, breaking with my strange hippie parents and attending a faraway college, exploring a freshness I found in political and cultural conservatism. But the dragon's fire that I fanned as a young boy was something that I had also lit deep inside me, and an interest in travel, a love of languages, and a curiosity about China that my father, through his secondary role as the school's occasional geography teacher, smoldered in me—and these coals did not die. Math, computer science, and, finally, Chinese drew and held my attention. After my college graduation, I left the United States for the first time. I flew alone to the other side of the planet, and at twenty-two arrived in China with but a few bags and a handful of wild expectations.

The year was 1997, just before international travel became dominated by the omniscience of smart phones, ATMs, and email—before Google, Twitter, Facebook, Wikipedia, and the technologies that would replace them, before the ubiquity of blogs on every imaginable subject. In China, it was an exhilarating and confusing time. The nation's political isolation was thawing rapidly but unevenly: Many towns and regions were open, but others remained verboten to foreigners, and the motives of Americans in particular were suspect. The excitement was palpable: Hong Kong was reverting to Chinese rule after 157 years of British colonialism, the economy was heating up like a blacksmith's forge, a building boom featuring modern glass and steel was transforming cities small and large, and formidable international honor from things like the Olympics had become more than a gleam in the eye of well-placed officials. It was before 9-11, before the "War on Terror," before American invasions of Iraq and Afghanistan; in many ways it was a simpler time for Americans to travel. In every other respect it was just like today.

❁

THE STEEL glowed in the flames as if coated with honey-hued neon. My father pulled it out and flipped it over on the anvil.

High-pitched notes rang off the walls as his hammer pounded, metal-on-metal. Sparks leapt through the air, danced across the floor, vanished. Slowly the steel cooled under the transformative blows.

Could it be? I watched the steel flatten, lengthen, darken.

He dipped the steel into a barrel of water beside the anvil, sending clouds of steam hissing into the air. He motioned that I could climb down.

"Are you making a sword?" I asked.

"What else are you going to be carrying—if you find a dragon that isn't friendly?"

I stepped towards the blade.

"Let it cool," he said, a hand on my shoulder. "It will be yours soon."

CHAPTER 1

Heart of an Empire

The way of the superior man is threefold,
But I am not equal to it.
Virtuous, he is free from anxiety;
Wise, he is free from hesitation;
Courageous, he is free from fear.
—CONFUCIUS, *ANALECTS* 14:28

THE FIRST promise of dawn paints a watercolor on Tiananmen
Square. An old man dressed in navy blue flows quietly through
the circular movements of tai chi; a woman on a bicycle tows a young
girl in a red wagon. The canvas of this painting is the broad square
stones beneath my feet, stones that murmur nothing about parades or
riots, joy or mania, blood, the toes of leaping feet, tears. The moment
holds only peace. Long stone buildings form the painting's frame: The
Great Hall of the People stands to the west, the People's Museum of
the Revolution is on the east, the granite-gray Frontgate towers to the
south, and Tiananmen Gate stands at the north, guarding the countless golden roofs of the Forbidden City. On every stone cornice, eave,
and column, the air hangs silent and still, as if waiting between earthquake beats of time.

Out of place amid all the stone is an electronic billboard in front
of the Museum of the Revolution. "147,988 seconds," announce its red
digits, precisely measuring the earthquake beats of time that remain
before the *huíguī*, the handover of Hong Kong, in a bit less than two

days. The four dark squares to the left of the decrementing digits suggest that the billboard has been counting down for years, perhaps even for all thirteen years since Margaret Thatcher first pledged to return the colony to China. In any event, it's June 29, 1997, and there's little time left for the British to change their minds. Decorative flags hang everywhere, drooping patiently in the quiet air: Half are the familiar, scarlet Chinese banner; Half are the future flag of Hong Kong, which is also red but with a single white Bauhinia orchid succinctly replacing the British crown.

Three young women clutch miniatures of the two flags in their fingers, and they skip the scoreboard and stroll up to me. "Be in a picture?" one asks boldly.

I nod, and two of them stand beside me, tentatively touching me just at the moment the third snaps a camera. Then they're gone, as always.

My steps carry me further across the paved plane, past Mao Tse-tung's enormous mausoleum, to a towering granite obelisk called the Monument to the People's Heroes. As Hong Kong's seconds tick away, I sit on the monument's steps, my royal blue backpack beside me, and I feel the liquor of freedom and the terror of utter isolation mingle in my body. The sun's early rays throw inky shadows from the monument and cast the rest of the world in a glistening stark light, as if this painting is but moments old and its painter has only just set down his brush.

Hundreds of pigeons swoop and alight nearby. A small boy dashes at the pigeons, gleefully hurling handfuls of yellow bread. Green-uniformed schoolchildren rush over in a horde, bouncing their own fistfuls of dough among the heads of the hungry birds. Hungry myself, I reach into my backpack for a breakfast of leftovers: a red apple and some crumbling crackers. Sleep didn't come well or easily during the thirty-four hour train ride up from Guangzhou, and my eyelids struggled to stay open as we rolled into China's capital city at 5:15 am. The bus driver announced Tiananmen Square, and the place seemed to call to me, so I got off.

Now I'm here and eager—despite inadequate sleep and food—to do what's next: call Colt. He handed me a phone number months ago, before leaving Guangzhou, telling me he'd be staying with the family of his mother's San Francisco acupuncturist. But it is hardly proper to call a Chinese family I've never met at the crack of dawn.

Thirty minutes pass, and the need to move unseats me. Energy pours through my veins from every direction, gathering in my chest, running to my limbs, tapering at my fingers. I enjoy the feeling as I move, letting it kick out the kinks in my knees and ankles from the two-day ride. I walk all the way to the south end of the square, Frontgate, the oldest edifice here; Frontgate was once the one and only portal among thick walls that immured royal palaces, back when entrance was forbidden to the public. Now, abandoned and denuded of its walls, vestigial Frontgate quietly gapes outward, southward, across a boulevard of speeding cars, to its motley young neighbors: McDonald's and KFC.

The patio outside McDonald's is already crowded with locals at 7:45 am. To the overjoyed children, hip teens, and businesswomen in skirts, this restaurant, this endlessly replicated plastic diner is a symbol of modernity, a hot spot for social climbers, a place to see and be seen. To me, when I open the doors, the picture flips into its opposite, like a photographic negative, and a world that was strange turns suddenly familiar: the subzero air conditioning, the synthetic yellow and red décor, the plastic imitation wood tables, the particular stench of special sauce. Here *I* know the mores, *I* know the words, *I* can be the one who laughs. I order in English, and lickety-split, orange juice, eggs, and a hash brown puck land on a brown tray. I sit on a red-orange bench and consume morsels of a syrupy grease I haven't tasted in these ten months. I look around me, return the stares for a moment, and smile comfortably to myself. The audible words, phrases, and conversations, however, still fly at me from this peculiar Mandarin universe that has callously lost and found me so many times through these many moons that I often feel deaf, dumb, and stupid. On the table, beside my plate of eggs, I thumb open my scarlet pocket Mandarin dictionary and build vocabulary the hard way, word by word. I learn that I mispronounced the term *gètǐhù*—individual street vendors. *Gètǐhù*, called China's newest capitalists, typically *xiuli shǒubiǎo* (fix watches), *mài bàozhǐ* (peddle newspapers), or sell hot *ròu chuān* (meat kebabs).

Leaving *Màidāngláo* (McDonald's) and returning to *Zhōngguó* (China), I spot a few *gètǐhù* right here in the heart of the communist *shǒudū* (capital city). A barrel-chested man fries sweet-smelling wheat bread on a black griddle; an old woman knits socks behind the counter of a magazine stand. The woman eyes me as I approach and reach for her red telephone. 8:45 a.m. seems sufficiently polite. "Local call?" she demands, in Mandarin. I nod and extract a purple half-yuan note from my belt pouch, and fling it coldly onto the counter, as the Cantonese do. The receiver emits clicks as I press the buttons, and then it rings and rings. No answer. I check the digits, the date, the time, the city. I dial again, but again it only rings and rings without response. Retrieving my money, I walk over to a concrete bench, needles suddenly shooting through me. *He forgot? He lied? He changed his plans? He met an untimely death in the Mongolian hinterlands?* I stare at my backpack, its soft blue nylon skin shining in the sun. I packed lightly: four T-shirts, four pairs of socks, two pairs of shorts, one pair of pants, and one long-sleeve shirt. I brought a camera, a journal, a pocket dictionary, and the securely rigged belt pouch Lu Lan helped me buy in Guangzhou, which is stuffed now with cash, traveler's checks, permits, and two forms of ID. The day before I left Guangzhou (the people are *Cantonese*, but no one calls the city Canton anymore), a package from my father arrived containing Herman Hesse's *Narcissus & Goldmund*, and I tossed the novel into my pack. And that's it, that's all I have here—that bag and my solitary self. My guitar and all my other worldly possessions will hopefully, peacefully, remain safe and sound in my teacher's dormitory at Peizheng Middle School until I return.

The crowd thickens before my eyes. Chinese tourists, cameras in hand, arrive in busloads. I am about to call out to Lu Lan, but of course it's not her. A girl in a group of college students smiles at me, waving those same two miniature *huíguī* flags. Witnessing the flags in happy hands again and again, I feel as if I've crashed an enormous wedding, as if the flags are party favors, symbols of a bride and groom, and the crowd represents a million guests converging on a church. *Who will sing the wedding song, the song I sang in Guangzhou, the canticle of the tortured lovers,* Aobao Xianghui?

I return to the phone stand and dial the same numbers. Fruitless again. I hoist my backpack onto my shoulder and cross back into the square. Face after face stops to watch the seconds tick away on Britain's freewheeling colony. They also watch me, even point at me, or ask me to give their photos a cosmopolitan touch. Meanwhile the sun blazes hotter and hotter as I try Colt's number every half hour. At 11:00, I confront reality: I'm alone, solo, *yìgèrén.*

I continue walking, gazing skyward at the kites brought by wedding guests. *Is it too late to go back to the train station, to go back to Guangzhou, to just go home, as everyone else—Byron and Lauren and Paige—did?* The kites overhead are eagles and diamonds and rainbows, and they soar to and fro against swaths of ivory cloud in baby blue.

CHAPTER 2

All the Myths Are True

不入虎穴焉得虎子

One must enter the tiger's lair to see a tiger cub.
—CHINESE PROVERB

I SIT IN a small chair, its plastic seat and back the color of sunlight shining through honey. Two thousand teenage boys and girls surround me, seated in the same small chairs, row after row of them on a vast field of sepia gray dirt. The kids are in uniform—bleach white with royal blue trim. Overhead, a loudspeaker crackles to life with brassy orchestral music that must be China's national anthem. The teenagers rise one row at a time and march in formation across the field, performing drills and turning their young faces towards me and away, in unison. The anthem rises to a crescendo. Then the music goes silent just as the students retake their seats.

A man in a tie strides across a concrete dais to a microphone and clears his throat. With a garble that makes his words nearly unintelligible, at least to me, he begins orating in official Mandarin Chinese. "It is September 2, 1996," he says, formally opening the school year here at Peizheng High School, Guangzhou, Guangdong Province, China. The principal's voice saws on and on. Squeezed into my tiny student's chair and sweating profusely, I catch only occasional phrases about achievement and the importance of hard work. Far above us, a fat tropical sun arcs through the city haze. I've been in this land, this empire, this hulking city, a whole week, but everything still scares me and exhilarates me—just breathing what's in the dirty air, eating what's on the bountiful plates, wandering through the crowded, crumbling streets. All the myths are true: the interminable noise, the nondescript clothing, the inscrutable faces. And now these two thousand silent, attentive teenagers.

"Our foreign teachers," the principal announces, reading our names out one by one. Byron. Paige. Lauren. My name, Tony Brasunas, is mispronounced last. I follow my compatriots over the dirt and onto the dais. Mrs. Yuan, a woman wearing an absurdly formal, pink, Western-style gown, hands us navy and burgundy neckties embroidered with the school's official crest. I glance nervously at the assembly, at the two thousand pairs of hands clapping. One boy's face catches my panning eyes: His smile radiates innocence and curiosity. The principal continues orating, declaring that we Americans have arrived "not only to teach English," but to inspire the students, to "uplift the nation."

Uplift the nation. The words ring in my brain. Returning to my chair, I examine the necktie and its golden crest, which features communist-looking stars, sheaves of wheat, and the year 1889. The Qing Dynasty was still teetering along in 1889. I wonder how this school survived the 1911 revolution, the 1949 communist takeover, and all of the other violent upheaval I've heard about. I wonder whether I'll survive a single year.

The students rise and march again. The loudspeaker intones a staccato count, and they drill like soldiers in the morning heat, weaving in circular exercises, intersecting, and nodding as one. American high-schoolers would never march with this kind of discipline, I decide, gazing half-hypnotized at the faces.

When it all ends, each student lifts a golden chair and carries it back across the dirt field, towards the three high-rise buildings that hold their classrooms. *Our* classrooms. I stand, and a boy darts in, grabs my chair, and hurries off with it. The other three foreign teachers and I follow the students at a distance. Lauren, a blonde from Connecticut, walks alongside me cheerfully. "Time for action," she says, taking my arm.

"The moment is here," I nod, hoping to hide my anxiety. I translate the principal's words for her. "We're not just here to teach. We're here to 'uplift the nation.'"

"Let's lift it up!" she smiles. "You ready?"

"I guess. I've just never done anything like this."

"You can do it," she jabs a finger into my arm. "Just go for it. All in, heart and soul."

CHAPTER 3

An Old Summer Palace

Eighteenth century China had no Ministry of Foreign Affairs.
Relations with non-Chinese peoples were instead conducted
by a variety of bureaus and agencies that, in different ways,
implied or stated the cultural inferiority of foreigners,
while also defending the state against them.
—JONATHAN SPENCE, *THE SEARCH FOR MODERN CHINA*

ALONE, BATHED in bright noontime sunshine, I thread through crowds of wedding guests. My feet carry me the length of Tiananmen Square, past two-story-high Chinese characters that scream at passerby the same phrase that decorates the rivers in Guangzhou: "Celebrate the Glorious Victorious Return of Hong Kong!"

Past the tall banners, I reach the north end of the square. Tiananmen Gate itself stands before me with its five vermilion archways, seven bridges, and the perch whence emperors once surveyed the masses. Today, an enormous portrait of the most recent emperor, Mao Tse-tung, hangs above the portal, smiling into an incessant fusillade of adoring camera flashes. I take out my own camera, aim, and fire.

In search of respite from the heat, I eventually wander off the plaza and cross the heavily-trafficked eight-lane Boulevard of Eternal Peace. I take a seat in the shade on the steps of the Great Hall of the People, China's national legislature. I pull out *Narcissus & Goldmund*. The book's cover features a sensual mélange of faces, young and old, male and female, in a collage that seems to promise a disturbingly fluid universe. Its first page transports me to medieval Germany, to a boys' school run by monks, where a young boy named Goldmund is enrolled in school and then abandoned there by his father. The boy studies piously, but before long he sneaks out at night, wanders through rolling countryside to a nearby village, and there meets a girl and experiences his first kiss. He lacerates his cheek on a rosebush while racing home in the darkness. Narcissus, a cool, intellectual monk, cares for young Goldmund, nursing the boy's guilty conscience and fevered body back to health.

I look up from the book, back across the boulevard, and the square is now full, holding thousands upon thousands of Chinese visitors. Plus the occasional big nose. A white guy walking alone wears a burgundy shirt that reminds me of Colt.

He's looking around, weaving back into the masses. I'm rushing blindly across the street, calling to him. By pure heavenly providence, not one of the many cars or bicycles run me down.

"Colt!"

He turns, looks around. "Wow!" He flashes his goofy, good-natured grin. "It's you!"

"What happened?" I blurt out. "How'd you know I'd be here? Why didn't you pick up the phone?"

"Yeah, sorry! Long story. I finally… came out looking for you."

"I gave up," I say, practically tackling him in an embrace. "I figured you'd died in Mongolia or something."

"The woman I'm staying with locked the phone in her bedroom and went to work. I just sat there listening to the phone ring every—"

"I just came to Tiananmen out of curiosity," I interrupt him in amazement.

"I was wondering how to find you. I eventually figured this place was worth a try."

"Incredible, in a city of thirteen million people!" I lead him across the street, through the cars and bikes, to my backpack.

"Fate," he says, glancing around and running his fingers through his short, curly brown hair. "So, have you checked out the scoreboard?"

"I think I've posed there twenty times. I was thinking of setting up a business—a little *gètīhù* on the side."

"Awesome," he laughs. "Clever." He wants to check it out, so we walk over and take our own photos as the clock strikes 130,000. "It's like the Fourth of July, Christmas, and New Year's all rolled into one around here," he says. "The official bash, *huíguī* day, will be here, at Tiananmen, tomorrow, with fireworks, concerts, and confetti. Not that it matters—we won't get in."

"Couldn't we sneak in? It's such a huge place."

He smiles. "Let's not tempt fate, not after this. There will be walls of soldiers. How close do you want to get to the People's Liberation Army?"

❁

A DUSTY DRAGON roars up, gobbles up Colt and me and hundreds of others into its snaky body, and whisks us all west. The Beijing government built what would be nicknamed "the Underground Dragon" for military purposes in the 1960s and opened it as a subway system to the public in 1977. In 1980, permission was extended to *dà bízi* (big noses).

Colt and I surface in a residential neighborhood, blinded by the summer sun. We turn our noses down a quiet *hútòng* alley where the air stinks of rice vinegar and motor oil. Conversations in courtyards on the other sides of gray brick walls are easily audible. Three young men pedal by us, ringing their bicycle bells.

We take a left, then a right, and then Colt stops in front of a plate metal door. He has a key, and he lets us into a dingy concrete courtyard. The furnishings include a metal dining table, a two-burner gas stove, three clotheslines, and several large red flowers blooming lustily in ceramic pots. An assortment of wooden tools lies in a corner. "That's the sister's bedroom," Colt points to one of three doors. "The phone's in there, but she's always at work and leaves it locked." He points to another door. "The brother's always in that room, watching TV." He opens the final door, and we enter his room, the storage room, where a bed is jammed between two towering bolts of fabric, a giant birdcage, and a stack of dusty chairs. "At least it's cool in here," he says, shrugging, squeezing past the birdcage and falling back onto the bed. "You know, it's a nice traditional Beijing home. Not bad at all."

While nodding my agreement, I attempt to mentally calculate how much my perspectives on comfort have changed in a year.

Colt says that the brother and sister are planning to renovate this room with money remitted by their parents, who are acupuncturists in California.

Back in the courtyard, he knocks gently on the brother's door. Already ajar, it creaks open to reveal a small television playing an old Chinese movie: Actors in black scholars' robes sport two-foot pony-tails. Then Zhong Wujia, pudgy, middle-aged, shirtless, fills the door-way. He offers me a hand and smiles vacantly as we shake. "How long are you in Beijing?" he asks in Mandarin.

"A week," I reply.

"Have you seen the Great Wall?" His eyes cast about.

"Not yet, maybe in a few days, after the *huíguī*." Behind him, on a table beside a bed, a kettle exhales puffs of steam. His tea water is ready.

"No, tomorrow. You must see it," Wujia says. "The Great Wall!"

"Should we go to see the section at Mutianyu or Simatai?" I ask.

"Eh? Take a bus, maybe an hour. You take a bus. And up there above the restaurant are the large horses. The green ones—"

"He has a problem," Colt murmurs in English. "It's not you. He's already told me about the Wall three times."

"—from the top," Wujia goes on, "look, West, you can see all the beautiful horses—"

"We're going out to lunch," Colt interrupts. "Do you want to come?"

"Eh? I already ate. You can eat in here, watch TV."

We thank him and decline. Back out in the *hútòng*, Colt steers us to a neighborhood diner. He orders for us, and his Mandarin is smooth, far more fluent than mine, but I think—and hope—that my pronunci-ation is better; he seems able to understand everyone perfectly, but his tones sound awkward and American. I'm utterly unable to understand the waitress, and for a moment my body freezes in some kind of anxi-ety. *What am I planning to do exactly? Wander across this empire alone?*

She brings our food as expected. Even our drinks are right—a lemon-honey Jianlibao soda for him and a cold local Yanjing beer for me. Colt recounts Wujia's story. The young man was happy and happily engaged to a woman back in February, but then a bus careened into an icy intersection and ended her life. And his too, it seems. He had a good government job, like his sister, but he fell quickly into some sort of catatonic depression. "The sister works seven days a week now," Colt adds. "She seems resentful and angry. He muddles around, watches lots of TV. They receive money from their parents every month. Hopefully he'll snap out of it one of these days," he shrugs. "Hopefully."

After eating, to cheer ourselves up, we leave the quiet web of *hútòng* capillaries for an arterial boulevard and its deafening clamor. Eggshell-hued wisps of exhaust hang in the air as buses queue up like beads on an abacus. We shove our way into one headed for the Old Summer Palace, a park built around the ruins of Emperor Qianlong's 17th century palace. Our bumpy and crowded journey ends right at the park's gate, which is decorated for the *huíguī*: Red flags snap imperiously in the breeze; longer green, pink, and yellow banners flutter around the flags like an endless cascade of confetti; and gargantuan, Hong Kong-style dragons coil around the gate. We slip through the gate and thread our way past a colonnade of crumbling stone pillars. Even amid swarms of picnickers, the ruins have a stoic, pensive beauty. A large placard greets us: "The merciless imperialists of France and England slaughtered countless innocent people here and burned down our beloved palace."

We continue on to a secluded marsh to evade the heat, crowds, and placards. The grass on the marsh's bank looks inviting, but no one sits on the grass in Chinese parks. We find a rare vacant park bench under a willow, and I confess my admiration for his language skills at lunch. He chuckles. "You'll pick this up—all of it—it just takes a little time." He says ordering our meal was nothing compared with what he accomplished in Inner Mongolia. He delves into a story about living in a dirt-floored yurt with a family of Kazaks, a people ethnically distant from the nation's dominant Han. After several weeks there in the yurt, he hiked further, out to a barren part of the grasslands where the horizon is an endlessly long, endlessly straight line, and the fertile grass is swallowed up by sandy yellow nothingness.

"It was amazing, the desert appears suddenly, from nowhere," he recalls. "On the bus out there I had met two guys: a bearded cross-country runner from Oregon and a weird Canadian who sat there memorizing Karaoke songs to sing to Chinese girls in bars. The three of us traveled together through Xinjiang and out to the Lake of Heaven. The Canadian dude took off, probably because there were no bars out there, but Roy from Oregon and I trekked on. One day we ran into a creek that was swollen with snowmelt and had risen above the bridge. I got drenched crossing it, so Roy tried to jump. He took a running leap but slipped where he landed on the bank and went down howling in pain. I pulled him up onto the bank so that just his foot was in the water, to reduce swelling and everything, and I ran to the nearest village of yurts. But they spoke only Kazak and couldn't understand 'doctor.' So I said, 'money for horse,' and they ran off into the fields to get one. Roy was lying there in shock, shivering and muttering, but I put him on the horse, and we rode that way. It was a long road, many miles. We had to rent a boat to cross a lake, and then get on a truck, and finally we arrived at a hospital."

He closes his eyes remembering the difficult time. "The hospital had gravel floors and only two rooms. The doctor was smoking! X-rays were just two yuan each, but there was no lead padding, nothing. The doctor just puffed on his cigarette and flashed the X-ray on all of us. He told us nothing was broken and recommended that a healer rub some warming herbs on the ankle and 'pop it back into place.' This sounded reasonable to me, but Roy was like, 'Hell no. Get me home!' So I lent him 1000元 for a plane ticket back to Beijing."

"Very nice of you."

"Yeah, I barely had enough cash, but I made do. I even managed to travel around further out there and drink a ton of nasty Uyghur yak butter tea."

"Did you try Mongolian hot pot—the real stuff?"

"Definitely, it's delicious. We had the big platters of raw meat, the mushrooms, and greens, and a large bowl of boiling soup. You cook the raw stuff in the soup before popping it into your mouth. But I was near starving half the time, so anything tasted phenomenal."

He hasn't heard from Roy, so I agree to loan him 830元 ($100) for the remainder of his trip—back to Guangzhou and home to San Francisco. In return, he loans me something I hadn't thought of—a travel guidebook. "The *Lonely Planet*," he says. "It's a bit out of date and short on detail, but it helps." Relinquishing the cash feels scary, but something about holding the guidebook in my hands feels assuring. I want to see places I know nothing about, I tell him. "An urge is pulling me west. I'll stay here in Beijing a few days, then head out west to Xi'an, then take the Silk Road and see where it takes me. Maybe I'll reach Jiuzhaigou or even Tibet. I want to see the religious and spiritual parts of this country—the Muslim lands, the Tibetans, the Buddhists."

He smiles. "You should check out Xiahe, an amazing town nestled up in the foothills of the Himalaya. It's shared by Hui Muslims and Tibetan Buddhists." He visibly lights up. "There's this café in Xiahe beside the Tibetan monastery with a veranda behind it. It's really something. You can watch the monks chanting from the roof."

We stand and stroll alongside the marsh. Two seated men hold fishing rods tirelessly in the brackish water. Beyond them, towering on the far bank, is a replica of Hong Kong's skyline, a miniature painted steel model of the city. It's as if the colony in its last days has literally drawn near to Beijing. Huge red characters stand in the water, making grand proclamations. "Hong Kong Returns to the Motherland! One Country, Two Systems! Glorious Victorious Chinese Feelings!" *Something will finally be reclaimed from the merciless imperialists.* Yet the replica is unreachable: The path doesn't cross the marsh, and the distance between the *Beijingrén* fishing and walking here and the splendor of Hong Kong feels immeasurably vast.

CHAPTER 4

Uplift the Nation

耳聽為虛眼見為實

Trust what you see, not what you've heard.
—CHINESE PROVERB

T HE SUN rises higher in its arc through the tropical haze, the morning air is cloyingly humid, and I'm alone. Five flights of concrete stairs take me up to the top floor of Classroom Tower C, and I stop where Mrs. Yuan instructed, at a door labeled—in English and Chinese—"The Reading and Listening Room." With the back of my hand I catch a bead of sweat rolling from my hair down my forehead. My hair is newly buzzed to a quarter-inch, about right for this sweltering heat. The heat must also be the reason that all the buildings here have outdoor hallways, like American motels.

The key that Mrs. Yuan gave me fits the lock, and the door swings inward. The dark room exhales dust and still more heat at me. I step in and pull red strings dangling overhead until fluorescent lights blink on and reveal small golden desks and more of the golden chairs, all frosted with white dust. The rusty blades of ceiling fans don't respond to any of the strings, so I push open metal windows one by one.

I step up behind the lectern at the front of the room, preparing to teach the first class of my life. I assume a responsible posture, or what hopefully will pass for one. My empty stomach clenches, remembering the breakfast that I was handed before the opening ceremony but barely touched: a warm, three-month-old carton of milk and a doughy white bun that squirted a salty red bean paste onto my tongue.

Voices echo on the hallway, a cacophony growing nearer and nearer. Thirty ninth-grade boys and girls arrive, no longer marching, no longer attentive, no longer quiet. They are gaping at me, pointing at me, pushing each other into the room, and arguing over the least dirty chairs. Unsure how to intervene, hoping to look confident, I nod at them. Every student, regardless of gender, has short hair: bowl-cuts for the boys, crop-jobs with bangs for the girls. Each student is wearing a white buttoned shirt embroidered with the school crest and royal blue pants. They finally do sit. Each face gazes at me.

I inhale. "Hello."

"HELLO!" they roar back. The word washes over me like a wave, reverberating off the dry walls, drenching the torrid air, uniting all of us in some unfamiliar satisfaction—as if we'd just passed a test we'd studied for all our lives.

I inhale again. "How are *you?*"

The wave smashes on dark, jagged boulders. Some voices answer while others repeat the question. Desperate, I look upward, appealing to the motionless overhead fans. "My name is Tony," I say. "T-O-N-Y." I write the letters on the board. Silence falls as I explain in excruciatingly slow English, underscored with hand gestures, that I don't know how well they speak or understand English, that I will speak slowly. "You should always tell me if you don't understand something." My white shirt bunches at my armpits. I look from face to face, and it feels like a miracle when they nod.

I tell them to tear squares of paper from their tiny notebooks and write down their English names—the names they selected during their first year at Peizheng, seventh grade. "Write big," I say, rewriting my name on the board in giant letters to demonstrate. "Fold your nametag like this." I demonstrate making a little paper tent.

I survey their tents, and they're not bad. "Yes! Good!" I say. "Let's do introductions."

The first boy stands up when I call on him. "I am Raymond," he says, before sitting back down.

The next boy's nametag reads "Bwen," and Bwen stands too, but he only mumbles inaudibly before sullenly dropping back into his chair.

His neighbor stands quickly. His hair is a mess and his fingers casually clutch his nametag. "Hello! My name is Sandoh. Welcome to China!"

The class erupts in applause.

"Thank you, Sandoh," I say, impressed but suddenly anxious about his confidence. He sits back down, pleased. The rest of the teenagers generally handle the drill competently, and they seem to stare at me curiously, as if expecting… something.

I write the alphabet on the board, letter by letter. Then I write a list of words below it, point to each word, draw arrows, and rearrange the words. They gaze at me silently, so I assume they get it—alphabetical order—and I launch my master plan: Alphabetically Assigned Seating. I hope to impose some order on my classes by learning their names and where they sit. I explain all this as they whisper to each other, and they seem to miss the concept completely.

I write a new list of words on the chalkboard, this time using their names. Chalk coats all ten of my fingers by the time I have erased and rewritten a second list of their names. I underline and point, but they don't follow and begin to chatter quietly in Cantonese.

I spot a girl surreptitiously change her name from 'Sally' to 'Alice,' and it dawns on me. She gets it. She wants to avoid sitting with a group of boys. She's fourteen years old, and she's afraid of the opposite sex. Shocked, I appeal to the fans again for help, but no help is forthcoming. *They're pretending not to understand me! They're deceiving me!* My wrist aches, and I look down at my watch. I've gone five minutes over. "Th-Thank you," I stutter. "OK. Class over. Goodbye."

"GOODBYE!" they roar, jumping up and grabbing their pencils and notebooks. They wave to me on their way out and dash chaotically back into the day. "Thank *you*, Teacher Tony!" Sandoh grins.

O N T H E outdoor hallway, I command a view of the campus below me. There are smallish buildings, made of orange brick, and huge five-story classroom towers encased in baby blue tile. The athletic field, where this morning's ceremony took place, is an expanse of ashen dirt. In the space between the classroom buildings, the athletic field, and several basketball courts, most of this walled dominion is paved with concrete sidewalk tiles, between which grow large, happy, unruly tufts of grass. Palm trees and banyan trees, all painted waist-high with white insect repellent, cast oases of shade.

Beyond the walls of campus, interminable ramshackle neighborhoods of the city unfold in a sea of crumbling brick walls and corrugated steel roofs. Jackhammers pounding in the distance give the impression that not just a city but an entire continent is under construction around us. What we hear is that any day now billions of yuan in investment money will transform Guangzhou from a slapdash, crowded backwater into a shiny, modern urban marvel. All I can tell for certain is that thick gray construction dust coats everything, and I'm inhaling it with every breath.

I step back inside, take my position behind the lectern, and try to ignore my stomach's intensifying growls of hunger. *Uplift the nation.*

Teenagers stampede through my door with energy that astonishes me in the heat, and I watch as they jostle and push and finally settle on seats. For a moment they gaze at me, and I can taste their curiosity and anxiety and delight. Or maybe those thick feelings are all mine. There are ugly faces and pretty faces, well-groomed achievers and ragged troublemakers, confident athletes and nervous nerds. "Hello," I say.

"HELLO!" comes the thunderous response.

I lead them through creating nametags and enunciating introductions, and this group seems smarter than the first class. I expect them to get alphabetical order easily.

I'm wrong. Everything slows down and traps me again. *Did they get a tip-off from the other class?* In frustration, I walk around the lectern and stand in the middle of the aisle. I ask them all to stand up in a single line down the aisle. There I have them reorder themselves alphabetically by their English names. This they do loudly but quickly. Apparently, without the danger of sitting beside someone uncool or of the other gender, they really are smart.

And that's it, I'm done. *I did it.* I taught a class. I look at them, and they look at me, and I look down at the lectern, then at my wrist. My watch says fifteen minutes remain. I look at my students again, and for a moment we just stare in curiosity at each other, as if to indulge a craving. *Who are you?*

"So—" I begin and stop, racking my brain for something, anything. *Why wasn't I told about this, what to do, how to prepare?* I look back at the board, chalk up new words, erase them. Finally, hoping to impress them, I go with a colloquial dialogue. I call on two obedient-looking kids.

"What's up, Rina?" reads Keive, glancing at Rina's nametag and inserting her name smoothly.

"Hey, no-, not much, Ke-Keive," Rina stutters. "How's it go-going?"

"OK," Keive replies, "Peizheng is cool! See you."

"Take it ee-easy."

I nod. "Good," I say, with a conspiratorial smile. "Don't use this greeting with your other teachers. They won't understand."

Two girls smile at me before they begin, either enjoying the informal greeting or perhaps amused by the weird pale animal winking and stumbling around before them. They giggle and blush as they struggle through the dialogue and finally collapse back into their chairs.

The next boy doesn't stand up at all. "Peizheng is not cool! I *hate* it," he says. His shirtsleeves are rolled rakishly past his elbows. Everyone laughs and looks at me. I do a double-take at the tall block letters on his nametag.

"Hitler," I read. "Please stand up."

Hitler rises to his feet, shrugging, glancing out the window.

"You don't have to like Peizheng," I say slowly. I think what to say next, wondering exactly how they chose their English names, who supervised, what they were thinking.

"Hitler is a *bad boy!*" calls out Thomas. Everyone laughs.

Hitler says nothing, smirking at me as he sits again.

"Who's your girlfriend?" calls out a boy named Ban.

I shake my head, refusing to answer, trying to stay cool. The students laugh and chat amongst themselves in Cantonese, and I notice I've gone late again.

They'll never listen to me. I was wrong this morning—about them, about the discipline, about the myths. It's all a lie. I can't uplift this nation.

"Do you have a gun, Teacher Tony?" calls out Thomas.

CHAPTER 5

One Chinese Home

是謂微明柔弱勝剛強

The subtle wisdom of life reveals this:
The slow and soft overcome the fast and hard.

—*TAO TE CHING*, 36

T HE SKY blushes periwinkle, and the air finally cools. Colt and I leave the ancient grounds of the Old Summer Palace and return to the Zhongs' courtyard home. At the plate metal door, we're greeted by Fujin, the sister, who is more slender than her brother and sharper in the eyes. She is charming and gracious but curt as she introduces herself. She's an official at the Beijing Commission on Elementary Education, she says.

Colt casually mentions my phone calls this morning, and Fujin's glance shoots past him. "Wujia *never* answers the phone."

As if on cue, Wujia emerges from his room, and she says something harsh to him. He nods and mutters as he takes a seat at the courtyard table. She tells him we went to the Old Summer Palace.

"The Old Summer Palace?" He looks from Colt to me. "Did you go to the Great Wall?"

Silence hangs in the evening air. Fujin sighs and rolls her eyes before turning to me. She invites me to stay for dinner, but having learned the decorum, I refuse. She insists, but I refuse again. She asks the crucial third time, and I assent. Her face lights up like a lantern; she ducks under a clothesline to fetch another chair.

Colt and I sit at the courtyard table next to Wujia, who is obviously confused. He asks us again about "the beautiful horses." This time for some reason Colt plays along, telling him we did go to the Wall and did see horses.

Fujin returns from a kitchen nook that I hadn't noticed before, carrying a large steaming bowl of ginger soup. Barely a minute later, she brings out more: sour, fish-sauced, hot-peppered pork; steamed sides of red snapper with mushrooms and garlic; and bittermelon with bony hunks of beef. She rejects our effusive gratitude with a small laugh and finally sits to dine alongside us. After a few bites, she asks us about the American educational system, and Colt explains preschools and kindergartens to her, the age ranges, the curriculum.

"Children should remain at home," she interrupts, "with their parents, until they're at least six."

Colt chopsticks a bit of beef into his mouth. He replies that women often work in the U.S., and that grandparents live separately, and so there's generally no one to stay at home with the children. "Sometimes children start preschool at age three."

Fujin shakes her head. "That's wrong. That's definitely too early."

Wujia is staring blankly at pork bones that he has sucked clean. Fujin looks at him reprovingly, as a mother might, then rises and returns to the kitchen nook. She fetches a Beijing summer delicacy: sliced watermelon.

My belly is sweetly stuffed so I just watch as Wujia bites into a juicy slice, swallows, and awakens for a moment. "America has very bad racial problems and discrimination," he says. "But in China we don't have these problems."

It turns out that neither of our hosts has actually seen, in the flesh, anyone with skin significantly darker than their own. I speak up, pointing out that ninety percent of China is Han Chinese, and that the other ten percent live in small, distant pockets. "So you don't have any problems. But if a hundred thousand Americans arrived in Tianjin or Dalian and started taking all the jobs..."

Fujin nods without showing interest. She begins carrying dishes to the sink, refusing our help. Wujia retreats to his room.

Colt looks at me, and speaks in English. "You have a different personality in Chinese."

"With the race thing?" I ask. "Was it too much?"

"No, well I don't know if what you were talking about is racism, but I think you're more cautious in Chinese, more pensive. You have poise."

"Poise? It's just my lack of confidence with Chinese, and my small vocabulary." I pause. "Or maybe the language is a reflection of the culture, and this culture is just that way—more considerate, more reserved."

"Right," Colt chuckles. "Reserved. I've been harassed, yelled at, ridiculed, chewed out, and insulted in Mandarin more times than I have been in English—and I've only been in this country a year and a half."

"Maybe I'm concentrating on the tones, trying to say things just right."

Fujin hasn't invited me or said anything about staying the night, and I don't want to overstay my welcome or in any way loose strife in the household. But Colt says there's a straw mat I could sleep on, and when the offer comes, I'm too ridiculously tired to refuse. In Colt's room, we toss the mat on the other side of the birdcage, and lie down to sleep, discussing the morning—the dawn of *huígui* day.

I suggest we go for it, make an adventure of it, and visit Tiananmen Square.

"Fujin said July 1st is the work holiday," he says. "Not tomorrow. No one's supposed to go to Tiananmen. We're not going to tempt the PLA, remember?"

I see them in my mind's eye—the army—standing, performing, marching. I see myself there, watching, feeling, listening. *Why wouldn't we go?*

"You really want to sneak in?" he asks. "What for? No one's going to protest. It's Hong Kong's glorious victorious return to the Motherland, remember?"

"Don't you want to know? What this place is really made of? What this *world* is really made of? A few centuries ago at the Forbidden City the price of admission was death."

He smiles at me. "True." He hesitates a moment. "OK, Why not?"

I look at him, surprised I've really convinced him. "OK," I say. "We're doing it."

He nods and drifts off to sleep mere moments later, but my long day stretches before me, and I lie there, staring up at the dusty rafters. My mind slips backward to the morning's vast solitude, and images play over and over before my eyes. I take out *Narcissus & Goldmund* and place the book in a shaft of moonlight. In the cloister, in medieval Germany, Goldmund chastises himself for his transgressions. He regrets sneaking out to the village, indulging his curiosity, feeling the sensuous longings ignited by the girl's kiss. The teacher Narcissus hears Goldmund's confessions, and rather than reproving him, he calmly explains to the boy the duality—the battle of heart and mind—that can torture men. Halfway down the page, exhaustion pulls on my eyelids and softens my focus, and I put down the book. I pull the scratchy wool blanket over my shoulders to protect my skin from mosquitoes. My arm instinctively touches the pouch that is belted around my waist containing my scant links to other worlds: a passport, money, permits, and a health record. My eyes set like suns, and the night's sweet oblivion overtakes me.

CHAPTER 6

A Grand Total of Ten English Words

見怪不怪其怪自敗

Face a strange thing without fear,
And its strangeness will disappear.
—CHINESE PROVERB

"APPLE PIE!" cries Sandoh. I write *Apple Pie* on the chalkboard, under the heading *Desserts*. "Let's have some side dishes," I say.

"Pizza!" shrieks a boy who's forgotten his nametag. "Pizza Pizza Pizza!"

"Ice cream!" yells another.

"Side dishes," I repeat.

"Doughnuts!" "Chocolate cheese!" "Fried chick!"

I add a few sides myself to broaden the menu. *Rice, Salad,* and *French Fries.* I slide two desks across the floor and push them together to create a miniature restaurant. I tap Sandoh and Leon as customers, and Jenny as the waitress. "It's your turn first," I say to Sandoh, as he sits at the table. "You order what you want to eat."

"French fries!" he calls out. "And I'll have a milk shape."

"And you're the waitress," I say to Jenny.

"OK," Jenny mumbles, standing beside him.

"Sandoh, those are good choices," I say. "But everyone must choose something from the 'main dishes.'" I tap the words *Main Dishes* on the board.

They look confused. "*Zhǔyào de cài*," I say, translating, offering my first-ever words of Mandarin to the class.

The room explodes with applause, and a wave of pride washes over me. But it becomes confusion as I observe faces who have looked lost listening to my snail's pace, parrot's complexity English. How am I going to communicate with *them*? What little authority I have will evaporate if I employ my patchy Mandarin. "Main dishes," I repeat, returning quickly to English.

"What would you like? A man—main dish," Jenny turns to Sandoh.

"Nooooooodles!" he croons gleefully. "Nooooo—"

Laughter rings from all corners. A handful of boys slap hands and call out jokes in Cantonese. A quieter boy in the back row hops up and prances strangely to the back of the room.

"Sit down!" I call out, my eyes rising to my friends, the rusty ceiling fans. The boy drops anxiously back into his seat. "The spaghetti?" I ask, pointing to the board again in frustration. The word *Noodles* does not appear. "Choose something off the menu."

"Yes," he nods. "Spa-gah-ETT," twists uneasily off his tongue.

"Spa-ghet-ti," I enunciate for him. "It's a noodle dish from Italy." I look to Leon, who sits quietly across from Sandoh.

Sandoh whispers to him in Cantonese. Leon orders a cheeseburger.

Jenny pretends to bring out spaghetti and a burger. "Eat that," she says.

"Good," I nod. "More often, the waitress will say, 'Enjoy your meal.'" I write the phrase on the board, and they all repeat the words, blankly, the way they probably do in their other classes. Some copy the words down into their notebooks. "Remember," I say, as the next three students sit down at our restaurant, "speak only English in this class."

"We want the Pepsi!" Money informs the new waiter, George.

"Yeah, we want the Pepsi," Alice repeats.

I suggest the chicken and the rice, and the girls whisper in Cantonese, then Money says, "Pizza." They leave the restaurant and return to their seats, done. *A grand total of ten English words.* I sigh at the fans. *And only if I count repetition.* It doesn't work, what Paige and I devised—this lesson plan. It doesn't work. *Bù xíng.* It doesn't go.

"Goodbye," I dismiss the class.

"GOODBYE!" they cry out with undiminished enthusiasm. Sandoh is out the door first, as if his "Spa-gah-ETT" is burning on a stove somewhere.

Paige awaits me on the outdoor walkway. Her classroom is one floor below mine, but she's up here to confer with me, or perhaps for a better view of the student soccer game on the athletic field. We're partners in a sense, each taking half of standard sixty-child classes, so it makes sense for us to teach the same lessons. "We got a great menu," she says, with a wry smile. "But they got really upset when I told them Americans eat vegetables."

I chuckle. "They're not interested in a balanced diet. Mine went crazy, yelling out 'Pepsi,' 'hamburger,' 'milkshake' faster than I could write."

She nods, running fingers through her long hair, holding out tresses of umber for her own contemplation. "I keep saying to myself, it's *Welcome Back Kotter, the Peizheng Years*." She laughs. From Seattle, fluent in Chinese, quite funny and not unattractive, Paige's penchant is for black clothing and cutting sarcasm. *Not my type*, I'm thinking, as I try to express to her my doubts about the lesson plan.

"Tony," she eyes me. "We're teaching each class *one* forty-minute lesson per week, and we have *twelve classes*—you're not going to 'captivate' many kids."

Her words ring in my mind. I want to engage my students, all of them, in order to help them experience the thrill of learning a language, to teach them English better than I was taught Chinese. It's what I'm here to do. When Mandarin seemed impossible, I fantasized about this, the other side of the coin, about helping people in China grasp the basics of English.

"Why do you always run late?" she asks. "Don't you hear the bell?"

"Bell?"

She nods, eyebrows raised. "There's a bell."

Paige returns to her classroom downstairs, leaving me to endure the callous heat. My next class arrives and swims around me, royal blue pants and white shirts soaked with sweat from soccer, basketball, jumping rope, table tennis, and track sprints. The noise grows as their invasion of my room approaches completion. I enter and immediately begin to yell, sounding feeble even to myself. "Kobe Bryant!" Kobe looks up with a startled grin, letting go of Hitler's shoelaces. Hitler whacks Kobe on the head, telling him in Cantonese to sit down.

"Quiet! This is your chance to learn English." I try to be stern. "I am a native speaker, and you can learn things from me that you cannot learn from your other teachers. You could study, you should listen." I look from face to face. I explain the menu, but my only piece of chalk shatters and rolls all the way to the door. They shout and laugh as I retrieve it, and this time my voice dies in my throat. *Why can't I have quiet, control, discipline? Why can't I do this—teach them, guide them?*

Some of the students seem to have forgotten their nametags, perhaps intentionally. But many nametags are here, and some names are already easy to remember, like Raymond and Alex, and the oddballs Zark and Keive. Some names, like Kobe Bryant and David Beckham, have clear inspirations, but others appear misspelled, like Angle and Jrace. Others seem downright strange, like the boy named Iceboy, and the girl named Sucky. I can't even keep a straight face when I scold the boy named Donkey.

Betty, Ban, and Keive—three of my more attentive students—respond to my summons, and we manage to serve a meal in the embattled café. Keive flawlessly orders a double cheeseburger "with mustard and tomatoes." The next group, however—Hitler, Alex, and Rina—is a nightmare and class disintegrates into laughter and uproar. No bell whatsoever, and it's seven minutes late when I remember the existence of my watch.

"Hot dog!" Kobe Bryant yells, as he gives me a high-five and struts out into the day. "Hot hot hot dog!"

CHAPTER 7

The Glorious Return to the Motherland

勝人者有力自勝者強

He who conquers men has force,
He who conquers himself is truly strong.
—*Tao Te Ching, 33*

THE SUN scorches Tiananmen Square, all thirty-four acres of its paving stones. Festive scarlet lanterns dangle from wires and gyrate in a light breeze. I'm adrift in a sea of happy Chinese faces in the middle of the vast plaza. Prohibited or not, the people have come: thousands crowd around me.

"Soldiers!" someone cries out in English. It's a young man perched on a concrete lamppost five feet above the masses. He has Asian features and wears a forest green T-shirt.

"What's going on?" asks a friend on the ground.

"There are soldiers—in rows—forming lines—they're about to march!"

I ask, "How many?"

"Hundreds," he says, and looks down at me. "I don't see any tanks."

Everyone knows the date. June 30. At midnight tonight the gray fortresses surrounding us will finally take control of a wealthy, world-famous little renegade island a thousand miles from here. Precisely 31,202 seconds remain, according to the red digits on the billboard. I look up again at the man on the lamppost.

"He shouldn't be up there," mutters a smallish woman.

"He shouldn't?" I turn to her, surprising her with my Mandarin.

"It's not safe." She eyes me warily. "He could fall."

"I think he just wants a better view."

She shakes her head. "Are you American?"

"How did you know?"

"Your Mandarin is very good."

"You're flattering me. It's still really bad."

"No, it's standard. Like a politician's."

"How do you feel about Hong Kong returning to China?"

"Mm," she pauses. Her eyes drift past me. "It's been too long. A hundred fifty-seven years! Hong Kong has always been a part of China."

"Have you been to Hong Kong?"

"Not yet."

"It's very wealthy and developed, fast and modern. No one speaks Mandarin."

"Cantonese, eh?" she chuckles. "I don't understand Cantonese at all."

She'll never be allowed to visit Hong Kong. I know it, she knows it. But it's been so long, so eternally long, since China has enjoyed international honor.

"He should get down," she turns back to the young man on the pole, whose T-shirt reads *Dartmouth*.

"What's happening now?" I call up in English.

"They're going to march," he reports. "Oh no," his voice drops. "Two are coming over here—right now! The People's Liberation Army is coming!"

Two men in the olive drab of the PLA push past me, their eyes on the pole-climber, and I imagine their thoughts. *No proper Chinese would single himself out, so this one must have succumbed to the spiritual pollution of the West, he must be a* huáqiáo *(overseas Chinese). He must be naïve.*

My foreign opinion screams silently, How does this harm anyone? It's blindingly hot, the crowds are mashed together, sweating, laughing, taking photographs, and everyone's just hoping to take part in history.

34

What's wrong with securing more air or a better view? But they're pulling him down. He's a *huáqiáo*, and regardless of how many years he's spent in, say, America, or whether he considers himself, say, American, he is still Chinese to the Chinese, and they still expect Chinese behavior of him. Run-of-the-mill *dà bízi* (big noses) like me cannot possibly be expected to know right from wrong—it's astonishing if we can put two words together in Mandarin—but *huáqiáo* should know better.

I move on, cutting through the masses to the front of the square, where PLA soldiers stand in rigid double-file. They wear coats with bright brass buttons and dark green pilot's hats with red stars; they stare straight ahead with an almost haunting motionlessness. I walk up to the two soldiers at the front, surprised to find that one is a woman wearing a beret instead of a pilot's hat. Armed with my camera, I capture a hundred dead-still, perfectly aligned shoulders decorated with epaulettes. The faces look young and nervous, reminding me of how my students looked doing oral reports.

"Hey!" calls a voice behind me.

I turn, and Colt shoots. He steps closer, twisting the lens of his camera. "You look like a general inspecting his troops!" he laughs. After arriving with me, he struck off on his own.

"A little eerie here, isn't it?" I ask. "The army watching dumbly, the people sitting peacefully on blankets."

"Thinking of 1989?"

"It's impossible not to," I say.

"No, the people today are celebrating, not protesting. Look at all the miniature red flags in everyone's hands. I just talked to a vendor who couldn't care less about Hong Kong; he just hopes to sell enough *huíguī* yo-yos to buy his family a refrigerator."

"Get any glorious victorious shots?"

"Yeah, I got up on those scaffolding towers—the guards saw my white skin and didn't ask any questions."

Looking around, taking it all in, we try an estimate: 80,000 people.

Two lines of soldiers goose-step across the street, and continue marching towards us across the square. Double lines that face us soon stretch the entire width of the square. "It's almost 3:30," Colt observes. "It's about to get interesting." The soldiers link hands, forming a giant phalanx, and Mao's portrait hanging over the five arches of Tiananmen Gate behind the soldiers seems to survey us confidently.

The soldiers stand stock still for minutes on end. Colt and I weave back into the crowds. On the stroke of four o'clock the soldiers step towards us. Time seems to stop, the moment engulfing us like an ocean. *Now.* I see it before I feel it: A wave pushes everything south, away from Mao and the gates. The wall with green legs takes another step. Colt and I stand thirty yards from the double chain, feeling the human barrier impel confusion and bodies at us. The people on blankets stop munching. The wall takes two more steps, unleashing another wave, and it seems to sweep my feet an inch off the stones. My breath catches in my throat. *Now.* Two more steps, pause. Everyone rises, moves, yields. Two steps, pause. Young and old, in jeans and dresses, they all stream past me. A small boy, his head craned backwards, walks straight into my leg. Whipping his face around, he gapes up at me before a man and woman grab him by either hand and guide him away.

"Want to go?" Colt asks, but I barely hear him.

This might be the best symbol of China, right here. A great wall. Colt repeats his question. "No," I shake my head. "Let's see what happens." *What is this barrier, this authority, this blunt force? Who are these young men?* I lose count of how many small backward steps I take, but I begin to see the individual faces. The young soldier coming straight for me has a square face, as if his natural face was pushed flat. Two steps, pause. Two steps, pause. Two steps, and he's at arm's length, right in front of me. His expression is impassive and reminds me of my students marching on the athletic field on Peizheng's opening day: dutiful, focused, innocent. *Innocent.*

"You're going very slowly," I say, in Mandarin, looking at the young face that mystifies me. His eyes widen, but he presses his lips into a straighter line. I hear myself pushing the conversation. "Do you want some help?" He clenches his neighbors' hands and looks past me. The line comes to a standstill. Twenty yards to my left, some folks hesitate before standing, but there's no organized resistance. "I speak English," I continue. "I could help you with the foreigners. I'll call out: 'leave the square, big noses, go home!'"

A good-natured smile, there it is. He doesn't nod, but his eyes betray curiosity. The wall steps again. Two steps, pause. "What do you think?" I ask. "I'll help you."

And with that, I turn and stand before them. I become them. I take two steps with the PLA. Two steps, pause. Two steps, pause.

"We don't need your help," says the neighbor.

I look over my shoulder at him just as the shy, younger soldier bashfully utters English. "You go home."

I feel a strange warmth as I reply in Mandarin. "Your English is better than my Chinese!"

"Yes, I study English," he replies. Two steps, pause. "My high school teacher was American."

"Really? I am a high school teacher in Guangzhou."

Two steps, pause. "Guangzhou?" asks the older soldier. "Have you been to Hong Kong?"

"I have. A beautiful city, on an island, tall buildings right beside the sea."

"What do you think? Of Hong Kong returning to China?"

"Today is a happy day for China," I say. "An extraordinary moment."

We come upon an obstinate group of picnickers. I speak first. "Get up!" I say in Mandarin. A young woman looks at me and bursts out laughing. I look at her and laugh too. "Are you ready?" I ask.

She nods and stands up, and the group leaves with her. An intoxication washes through me as I watch them—the masses—retreating before us, granting our wish, heeding our whim. I feel connected to it all, to both sides, somehow.

Alone, these soldiers around me are nervous, curious, weak schoolboys; united, they're omnipotent. I walk with them fifty more steps, and then I say goodbye. I stride off, faster, in front of them, fleeing just like everyone else.

CHAPTER 8

The Chinese Word for *Carrot*

Wherever you go, go with all your heart.
CONFUCIUS, *SHU KING* 5:9

THE FOUR of us, the American teachers, first met in Hong Kong, where we foolishly took air conditioning for granted. Two days of confusion and jetlag in a plush hotel ended abruptly when we climbed aboard a train and rumbled away from the modern metropolis, north through undulating green hills, up Kowloon peninsula, across the border, and into the People's Republic of China. We passed through the border city of Shenzhen, and soon flat brown farmland unfurled all the way to the horizon. Half an hour later a city sprouted around us like a maze: sprawling junkyards, concrete highway overpasses, and row upon row of pastel green apartment towers. This was Guangzhou. We'd arrived.

In an immaculate yellow business suit, her hair a perfect black triangle behind her ears, Mrs. Yuan greeted us on the platform with dainty handshakes. The concrete station around us was filthy, and the August day sucked us into a suffocating, tropical warmth from which it wouldn't release us for months. But we didn't know that yet. An uneasy smile crossed Mrs. Yuan's face, as if she were lying to us about something. She showed us to a white Hi Ace minivan, where the driver laughed at us and called us *gwailo* (foreigners) as he eagerly jammed our large load of luggage into the back. He piloted us through the city and took the women—Lauren and Paige—to a drab off-campus apartment which we would soon call comfortable. Byron and I were then delivered to campus. We were dropped at a dormitory that featured prison-like bars enclosing the windows and porches. Mrs. Yuan accompanied us to the top floor, the third. "Boys live on the first floor, girls on the second," she explained, saying nothing about our floor. I watched her for clues. *And dangerous foreign men on the third?*

She opened a barred gate and brought us to door 302, which gave way to reveal a cell with white walls and bald concrete floors. She crossed the concrete floor, pointing proudly at our two great luxuries: a pale green refrigerator squatting in one corner and a dusty television perched on a rickety desk. It was as hot as an oven, and I felt numb. She led us into our other room, a bedroom furnished with two more rickety desks, two narrow plywood wardrobes, and two sidewalk-hard beds hidden under thick mosquito netting. Our one window faced a large apartment tower. A jackhammer was destroying something nearby. "Welcome to your home," she called pleasantly over the clatter. We followed her into a five-foot-by-six-foot box of white tile—the kitchen—and Byron turned the sink's single knob. Out came… a sucking sound. Fortunately we weren't thirsty. "The proletariat shall go without water," Byron smiled at me, "to test their commitment to the Revolution."

"Boil water first?" Mrs. Yuan told us. "Before drinking?" She didn't seem comfortable in any part of the English language. She was our liaison with the school, she told us, and then she left.

I'd taken three semesters of college Mandarin, and Byron didn't speak a word of any Chinese dialect, so we decided quickly that if we were to survive, we'd have to divide our labors: I'd become our shopper, our maverick in the marketplace, the one attempting to distinguish the edibles from the poisons at the local bazaar, and he'd be the cook, experimenting with the obscenely enormous wok, antique kettle, and hefty meat cleaver waiting there in the kitchen.

THE MOMENT soon arrives, the time, the day, the hour, after my befuddling classes have finished for the afternoon. I'm hungry. My first expedition to the market can wait no longer. My mind kicks into gear, dazzling me with visions of exotic Casbahs overrun with Hollywood's swarthiest criminals. I'll get cheated, robbed, kidnapped. I'll have to haggle for carrots. I prepare mentally some self-defense moves, contemplate bringing a weapon, and practice a few Chinese phrases. *I don't even know the Chinese word for carrot.* I settle on a pocketknife, a backpack, my red pocket dictionary, and a mass of brightly colored notes amounting to 200 yuan, eight of which could make a dollar on the other side of some vast ocean.

The campus reclines under soupy sunlight. Students are playing table tennis on scattered concrete tables and jumping rope on a dirt volleyball court. I pass the dilapidated swimming pool and the three naked concrete basketball courts. After the baby blue classroom towers, I pass the tree-shaded, ancient-looking orange brick administrative building, which holds Mrs. Yuan's office. The campus gate spits me out, onto narrow Yandun Street. It's a river of cars, bicycles, and motorcycles, and the flow of vehicles pushes the stream of pedestrians up onto tiny sidewalks and nearly inside the shops that make do without front walls.

I join the stream, threading my way on a sidewalk, letting other bodies push past me: a dark-skinned peasant man balances two wooden buckets of cabbage on a long beam over one shoulder; a business woman in teal hurries along the crumbling sidewalk in high heels. I squeeze by peddlers of chicken kebabs and faux leather wallets. I pass small, packed restaurants that exhale fabulous aromas of plum sauce and sautéing garlic, and faces everywhere follow me, like sunflowers tracking the sun. Involuntarily, I ensure that I'm wearing pants. *Pants, check. Must be something else.* In a nook between two cafés, three men squat and munch on white ears of corn. They stare at me. I stop and smile, and there we are, sharing approval of something, something that I can't quite put my finger on but that a voice calls *ridiculousness*—the notion that the rare species *gwailo*, long-nosed and pale-skinned, is here, out of its habitat.

The food smells are pierced by odors of garbage and chemical floor cleaners. I pass an alley of apartment towers with balconies like metal

cages: bars imprison the residents while restraining lush fruit bushes
and suspending wet laundry. I pass a shop selling stationery and pens,
followed by another, and then another, and it makes me think that perhaps shopkeepers here aren't bent on putting their competition out of
business. What I don't see is a Casbah, a market, a busy bazaar, and I
stop and reach for my dictionary. A balding man in a brown tank top
sits on a stool, half inside and half outside the third of the four stationery shops. His arm rests on a bright blue ice cream freezer, and his
eyes—and those of two men in the next shop—are on me. I inhale.

"*Qǐng wèn, shìchǎng zài nǎr?*"

"Eh?" he squints.

This is supposed to be your language, old man. I try again, since it's
all I've got, even if every word I learned in college was wrong. "*Shìchang
zài nǎr?*" Where is the market?

"*Shìchǎng ah?*" He smiles knowingly. He tells me what might be
his entire family history, and I think back to college, Amherst, where
I spent all of my sophomore year and half of my junior year fumbling
like an impostor through Mandarin Chinese language labs. He's still
talking and I haven't caught a word. I can't even tell if it's Mandarin
or Cantonese. He points down the street, and waves left. I thank him
(*Xièxiè*).

He laughs and waves me off.

So I press on, passing a tiny toy store jammed with racetracks and
video games and boys and men playing together, zapping, steering, and
punching. The synthetic sounds spill out and mingle with the honking
cars and growling motorcycles. A horn screams in my ear and I leap
into some kind of medicine shop as a blood red taxicab careens by.
The other pedestrians and bicyclists adjust their trajectory and evade
the cab by inches. I turn and smile awkwardly at the man behind the
counter as a glow flushes his face; he laughs at me; he point to the jars
of roots, berries, and powders behind him; the air carries scents of fish
scales.

Back on the street, Michael Jordan stands in front of a shoe store,
his life-size cardboard simulacrum propped against a wall. I touch

the cardboard basketball pinned between his arm and hip. The street opens into an enormous plaza walled in by billboards, and pedestrians stream throughout the space, filling the entire area, shopping, jostling, queuing for a handful of idling buses. Behind a newspaper stand, a woman cries out the name of a paper: *"Wanbo, wanbo!"* I push through the crowds and turn left—as the old man instructed—uphill, towards the fierce yellow sun. A huge cartoon chicken perches above a Western-style fast food restaurant. Glancing inside, I spot several kids in Peizheng uniforms sitting on molded plastic chairs, using plastic forks on oily fries and fried chicken. Across the street, a pet store with live ducks and rodents in cages on the sidewalk turns out to be a traditional restaurant. The scent of roasting soy sauce wafts out as I watch a young couple point thoughtfully at a black rabbit, then pause to gaze at me and my white nose. The animals seem to eye me too, and my mind is lost in a memory of our fast food chains, with their posters of hamburgers and hot-fudge sundaes. Here it takes a stronger type of advertising—real flesh and blood—to tempt passersby.

Cookies and biscuits fill bowls on two street-side tables. I spot the caramel chip cookies I loved in college, and I signal to a saleswoman who's busy wrapping up four coconut-topped buns for a gray-haired woman. *"Duōshǎo qián?"* (How much?) I point to the cookies.

"Wǔ kuài yī jīn," she snaps, too busy to gape for more than a moment. Five yuan for something.

"Wǒ yào liùge," I say. I want six.

She hands me a paper bag, and I place six of the golden brown cookies inside. From my pocket I extract a brown five-yuan note that features the heads of two smiling Tibetans. I'd buy bread too, but I don't see any loaves among the buns and yellow biscuits. The saleswoman returns, grabs my bag, sets it on a scale. *"Yī kuài sì máo qián,"* she barks, pushing up a shirtsleeve energetically in the heat. I hand her my 5元 note and she drops 3.60元 into my palm. Two little girls laugh at me from across the street as I reach into the bag and continue up the street, thinking *six big cookies for twenty cents!* Recalling pleasant autumn afternoons in Massachusetts, I gobble half of the tan cookie into my mouth. It's all wrong. Egg yolks and burnt pork and weird sour spices stick to my throat, choking me, and I heave, hacking it up right onto the street. *Not cookies.* I manage to swallow what remains on my tongue of the nasty, hard snack biscuit and squeeze the remainder of it into an overflowing green trashcan. *Not caramel, not college.* I shove the bag into my backpack thinking Byron might like them.

An alley opens to my left, a passageway flanked by slaughterers and festooned with a thousand hanging hunks of meat, and a menagerie of animal heads. The alley teems with people, and I realize I've arrived. I push through, into the dank market, my sandals sticking to the ground. Flies buzz on long duck carcasses that hang from rods above raw, pink slabs of flesh. My foot slips on something, and I land on a knee, and my face is inches from a leathery pig's face. Suspended there, open-eyed, dried mud slung across its round left nostril, the head rests there, waiting, bodyless, in a silver bowl. A salesmen behind it busily hawks its chopped and diced muscles, its organs, feet, and skin on a long plank. Strings of scarlet red intestines—sausages?—hang overhead from nails. The air stinks of sawdust and blood.

"*Gwailo!*" A man in a blood-smeared green apron calls cheerfully to me as I wade onward. He holds up a plucked, pitch-black chicken. I nod, giving my approval, uncertain why its skin is so dark. Blood pours over the gleaming, silvery scales of fish heads as a man decapitates live fish, enthusiastically shoving one at me as I pass his stall. Behind him, two women pause and smile at me, then resume chopping at juicy hunks of something. Yesterday Byron mentioned what I'd been unwilling to confess—I'm terrified of falling ill—and we decided to eschew cooking meat at home, at least for now.

I forge on, to still tinier stalls that sell dried goods: rice, beans, noodles, mushrooms, nuts, spices; everything is on display in sacks, buckets, tanks, jars, and bottles. In a stall redolent with tangy, sweet, earthy smells—mushrooms, anise, ginger—I screw my courage to the sticking place and ask the young shopkeeper about soy sauce. His eyes go wide, taking me in, pointing to a bottle with a fancy yellow label. I nod, and say, "Good?" He replies happily, and I think he's agreeing with me, so

I accept a bottle. I also select flat squares of dry yellow noodles, white rice, coarse salt, and shelled peanuts. Things I recognize. He fills a bottle of cooking oil from a tall metal vat. "38元," he says, chuckling at me. I pay him and leave, hoping my second purchase will prove wiser than my first.

A pale blue strip of sky floats overhead between six-story build-ings. *I understood that guy!* Perhaps the two of us are the same age, and maybe at heart we're not so different—I could be the soul born here, scooping rice and noodles, and he could be the soul faraway, explor-ing and working in a foreign land. *Or perhaps he just slowed down his speech for me, something no one else here cares to do.* Maybe he's from elsewhere and his first language is Mandarin. Originally the Beijing dialect, Mandarin was declared four decades ago China's *pǔtōnghuà* (common tongue), and all teachers and television reporters are now required to use it. Still, around here, common folk speak mostly the lo-cal dialect, Cantonese, and while they understand and speak Mandarin when necessary, they don't employ its gentler syllables casually.

The sea of bodies engulfs me again where a collage of colorful mounds covers the ground: fresh scallions, purple cabbages, husky carrots, green peppers, apples, garlic, bok choy, and red and brown fruits I don't recognize. I crouch down in front of an ancient-looking man, feeling a drop of sweat roll over my ribs as legs brush by my back. The man smiles at me, his dark cheeks creased with diagonal lines. I thumb open my dictionary and finally learn the Mandarin for carrot.

"How much for the *húluóbò?*"

"*Qī kuài wǔ yi jīn*," he reveals, toothless, speaking Mandarin, his eyes sparkling. I think he means it's 7.50元 for a *jīn*, which is a Chinese weight measurement slightly heavier than a pound. The *húluóbò* are enormous and the most brilliant orange I've ever seen. He holds open a little white plastic bag and I stick a huge carrot inside. After two more, he places the handles of the plastic bag onto a hook on the end of a long stick and slides a metal weight along the stick. "26.50元." This tells me that carrots here are giant-sized and go for more than a dollar apiece. I point to his potatoes. "*Bā yuán qián*," he says, oddly making a gun with his hand. It sounds like 8元, so I ignore his gesture and select two fist-sized, dirt-encrusted tubers. Green peppers find their way into my backpack too, and it all comes to 43元. I thank him warmly and move on.

A sweet rose fragrance wafts by my nostrils as I pass an incense vendor. Beside his scarlet sticks, a young woman stacks dozens of pale green gourds, each the length of my arm. I crouch beside her cloth and ask what they are. She looks shyly over my shoulder, to a woman selling mangosteens, bananas, and persimmons, and they exchange rapid bits of Cantonese. I squeeze one in my hand, trying to look intelligent, and it feels like a cucumber, only lighter and harder. She smiles but doesn't speak. I select two of the gourds and employ my other well-worn phrase: "How much?" She tells me the price and inexplicably breaks into laughter as I pay. A neighbor of hers, a quieter woman, sells me garlic, oranges, and yellow onions.

At the end of the alley, salesmen lean languidly behind huge barrels of tofu. Then there's a fish market, where long trout-like specimens swim about in giant pans. At egg stalls, people take eggs of all sizes and colors and hold them up to naked light bulbs before buying. I turn for home, and my nylon backpack chafes my shoulders in heavy, sweet, sweaty proof of my accomplishment—*I did it!* I smile, thinking about this commerce, this simple buying and selling that defies classification, that is neither communist nor capitalist, that is owned by no one era, land, culture, or nation.

Our dormitory awaits, stolid and forbidding. Gazing at its cage-like bars and gate, I realize I forgot my keys. A teenager is locking the metal gate. I approach hastily, and I realize he is actually unlocking the gate. *For me.* He waves me under the stairs to a room where he apparently lives, and he pulls a manila envelope from a stack of letters. The envelope is addressed in English—to me—and the envelope behind it is addressed to Paige. I take them both. He says nothing. He's too old to be a student, and I finally get it—this is his job, he's our gateman. I thank him.

Upstairs, I knock on our door and Byron, shirtless in the heat, lets me in. His long brown hair is pulled back with a rubber band. I tell him about our gateman as I unload the goods, shoving the veggies into our diminutive fridge. The manila envelope contains a Dave Matthews guitar book that I remember—with a sigh of pleasure—ordering for myself weeks ago from my faraway other world.

The bathroom smells of mildew and urine, but it's time for a shower. The showerhead points directly onto the bathroom floor, and in one corner is a drainage hole big enough for small creatures to crawl through. The heater, despite a fat orange gas tube snaking towards the kitchen stove, doesn't work, so the spray is a single unsoothing blast of cold. I shudder and bear it, remembering to let no drop pass my lips.

Byron goes to work in the kitchen. By the time I'm dried and dressed, he has the mini-stove fired up and a yellow pool of oil popping at the bottom of our emperor-sized wok. "Is oil supposed to smoke?" he asks, as thin black wisps climb heavenward. He dumps sliced onion into the oil, and the POP-POP-POP is replaced by a pleasant sizzle. I look at him and shrug. "Smells good!"

For a novice, Byron's vegetable stir-fry turns out better than just edible. The green gourds are as bitter as dandelion stems, and we pick them out, but the mixture of carrots, onions, and peppers doused in the deluxe soy sauce blends delectably. We dig in and celebrate, toasting cups of boiled water. *May it not poison us*, I pray, as we swallow the fluid of this strange new earth. We fire up our television, and there are four Chinese channels and—lo and behold—an English channel! We watch a young American Superman save a faraway suburban world in an episode of *Lois and Clark*. Next up on our little screen, as worlds far and near collide, is the evening news, and it's Chinese Secretary of State Qian Qichen declaring that some islands near Japan are—BEEP! The screen goes white. Byron and I look at each other. *Censorship?* I return to the wok for seconds, and Byron launches into a political lecture of his own. "This is a Hong Kong station we're getting," he decides. "Across the border in Hong Kong they get to hear what the Secretary of State says, but you think there's any chance they will get to after the handover in June?" He goes on, and he tells me more than I really wanted to know about censorship and propaganda and Marxism, about how philosophy once guided the Chinese Communist Party but now, "in the face of globalized capitalism, Marxism languishes. Now the socialism is just in the propaganda, covering up what's going on, so that the people don't realize their government is changing and leaving them behind."

The screen blinks on again, and it's a news story about ostriches at the zoo.

❀

A FEW DAYS later, when we've finished our mediocre leftovers, Byron begs our one neighbor to teach him how to cook. The other apartments on our floor all seem empty, but yesterday on the walkway we ran into a visiting English teacher, a Chinese woman from a rural village. With the two of them chopping onions inside, I sit out on the open hallway, playing guitar, singing a Dave Matthews tune from the book. "*Could I have been a millionaire in Bel Air?*" I sing. "*Could I have been anyone other than me?*" Across a courtyard from me, barely a stone's throw away, in the window of a crumbling jam-packed ten-story apartment building, a woman is stir-frying dinner.

A tiny girl in a bright yellow outfit bolts down the hallway towards me. She halts, four feet away, and her mouth falls open. She gazes at my foreign eyes. I blink twice at her to get her to smile. "*Nǐ hǎo,*" I greet her. We met Tingting, our neighbor's daughter, yesterday too. She spins on a toe and launches into her own Mandarin song, carousing up and down the hallway.

Spicy, mouth-watering fragrances—*là jiāo* peppers, garlic, fish sauce—waft out from our kitchen, and the smells penetrate deep inside me, triggering a sigh. I'm *here*. I live *here*. Relaxation settles across my shoulders, drips through my back and down the bones of my spine, down through my hips to the muscles and tendons of my legs. I witness the world around me, swat away a mosquito, and open my journal.

September 5

The myths and stereotypes I brought with me now seem ridiculous, or descriptive of some other land I haven't yet visited. The market is chaotic but not in any scary way. People, humans, buy and sell food—to eat and to have enough to eat— and a sense of respect and friendliness permeates the haggling. The streets are packed, but there aren't any kung fu masters or Buddhist sages wandering about, nor are there regiments of Communist automatons patrolling the streets. What other lies have I been believing? May I find out, may I discover, may I be open to the truth.

CHAPTER 9

The Atom Bomb

If you want to understand today,
you have to search yesterday.
—PEARL S. BUCK

THE WARM night buzzes with summer insects and celebration. Fireworks explode like red and white pottery against an asphalt black sky, but they're low, near the horizon, since Tiananmen Square is now a mile away. I leave the crowded sidewalk, dart into the center of the boulevard, and snap a photo of the glowing pyrotechnics. The *huígui* is ending, China has prevailed, Hong Kong will belong perhaps to some other country in one hundred fifty-seven years, but for now it's a part of the Middle Kingdom. A policeman's hand lands on my shoulder. I turn to him, "May I take one more glorious, victorious photo?" He shakes his head, missing my humor, sending me swiftly to the curb. His job is to ensure a single file of cars trickle down this broad street. Red *huígui* flags and lanterns dance overhead, and I think about Tiananmen, about the concerts and the dances and the grand international convention of officials and Communist Party bigwigs. I long with an unfamiliar intensity to be there, to experience it all, to penetrate or to conquer this force opposing me.

Colt finds me, and together we peel off the busy avenue and weave our path through the *hútòng*. Wujia's television screen is exploding with fireworks, better ones—brilliant greens, purples, and golds— from a scene at Hong Kong's majestic Victoria Harbor. "I guess we'll do what everyone else in this country is doing," shrugs Colt, his face lit up by the flicker of the screen. "Watch it on TV."

"Maybe we should've gone to Hong Kong," I wonder aloud.

"We were at Tiananmen until the PLA made us leave," Colt informs Fujin. "There were thousands of people there. Tony helped the PLA."

"What?" She looks bewildered.

"I walked with them," I admit. "I helped them. I asked some people to leave."

"Why?"

"I don't know. I wanted to see what would happen." I look at her. "I wanted to know what it's like to be in the army. I wanted to understand what in this world… you can trust."

She chuckles the nervous, arms-length chuckle. "You're a foreigner."

"Prince Charles is speaking," Wujia cuts in. The scene has shifted from the harbor skyline to a cavernous auditorium. Prince Charles is smiling thinly, enunciating carefully, giving away a colony—another one, after so many toys and trinkets, so many wildly different, graft-ed-on fingers and toes have been stoically surrendered by his British Empire. "China tonight will take responsibility for a place and a people which matter greatly to us all. We shall not forget you."

The camera cuts to the Prime Minister, Tony Blair. The television commentator declares with impeccable certainty: "Chinese all around the world are celebrating this glorious day." Of course Colt and I know that Hong Kongers are in fact extremely worried that their new con-stitution, the "Basic Law," won't mean a damn thing and that great green walls of PLA soldiers will start marching through their streets tomorrow. I begin to say this aloud, that this is all untrue, false, another myth, another lie, but I swallow my tongue as I look from Fujin to Wujia. New Chinese President Jiang Zemin rises woodenly on the dais and proclaims triumph. "'One Country, Two Systems' is the brilliant conception of Deng Xiaoping," he declares to the world. "Hong Kong's glorious return to the Motherland will assist China's development and be a blessing to all Chinese."

Wujia gazes at the screen with an intensity that propagandists must covet; Fujin looks at Colt, then down at her lap. Just before midnight, she rises and makes tea, and the four of us happily toast Hong Kong's final British minutes with tea, that delicacy that has always been Chinese but for a while seemed quintessentially British.

An hour later, bitten anew by curiosity, I convince Colt to take a cab with me back to Tiananmen. We ride down to the Boulevard of Eternal Peace, but again, we can't get very close. As we turn down a side street, I ask the driver his feelings about the *huíguī*. He gushes happily. "It makes everyone proud. Everyone. We all now hold our heads high! The British dominated China and made us second-class citizens. But today the world can hear a new voice rising—the Chinese voice." He looks at me. "You know the—" he uses a word we don't understand, so I consult my dictionary. *Atom bomb*. "Mm," he assents. "You're American, right? It restored your national honor. For us this is like that time, when you dropped the atom bomb on Japan."

CHAPTER 10

Celebrity *Gwailo*

*The most outstanding characteristic of Eastern civilization
is to know contentment, whereas that of Western
civilization is not to know contentment.*

—HU SHI, 19ᵀᴴ CENTURY CHINESE DIPLOMAT

I T'S A strange buzzing, an angry bumblebee. My ear perceives it, adjusting to its pitch and timbre, even amid the howls of laughter at Adam, a boy whose white uniform is fraying badly at the neck. The bell is ringing.

I close business at our embattled café on time, and the students spring up and flee through the door. On their way out, three students who didn't yell at all during class, who paid attention, who ordered sushi at the café, pause at the lectern. It's Jrace, Winnie, and Iceboy, and they gaze at me as if starstruck. Jrace giggles nervously as she speaks. "Can we take a picture... with you?"

I nod, and Winnie clutches tightly to Jrace's forearm as the two girls step around the lectern. The two of them wear a less common version of the uniform—round-collared blouses and navy blue skirts—and they stand close to me, grinning, holding out two-fingered peace signs. Iceboy clicks the camera.

"Do you have the pictures of your family?" Winnie asks, blinking, still gripping Jrace's arm like a life preserver. She has trouble with 'v' and 'th' sounds, as do nearly all of my students, and her question comes out: "Do you how fruh picksha fyo fammee?"

"Yes," I reply. "One. I can bring it to class."

"Great!" she cries. "I would like to see it."

Jrace is staring at me, and she speaks quietly. "Do you love China?"

"China," I pause, observing the three of them in turn. *They actually want to practice English.* "China… is good. It's better than I expected."

"OK!" they dash back to grab their books. "Bye bye!"

Strolling home, I gaze up into the overcast sky. *Good? Better than I expected? Is it true?* I didn't expect all this concrete and construction. I expected pandas, bowls of rice, pretty screens of bamboo, and respectful children studying like machines. The only pandas I've seen are on the kids' pencil boxes; rice is served, but primarily at the ends of banquets; I've seen bamboo, but only in the ubiquitous construction scaffolding; and precious few students study like machines in my classes. *I brought myths and myths and more myths.* I had another expectation too—that I would be told what to teach. I've taught two full weeks of these classes now, and neither Mrs. Yuan nor Mr. Guo, the head of the English Department, have given me any instruction whatsoever: no guidelines, no dos and don'ts, no textbooks, no supplies, not even permission to photocopy the few materials I brought. I am blessed with academic freedom or abandoned to the student hordes, depending on my perspective. Perhaps we *gwailo* teachers are trusted completely here, or perhaps some tacit Chinese communication is lost on us. At banquets we've been treated as important, prestigious members of the English Department, but then last Wednesday our classes were inexplicably and secretly canceled, so each of us sat in our classroom waiting as the afternoon drifted by; Donkey and a few other students finally swung by to let us know English class was cancelled because a big biology test was occupying the students.

As for Princeton in Asia, the organization that sent us here, no directions have been forthcoming from them either, perhaps as a liberating and terrifying form of benign neglect.

The gateman spots me coming and opens the gate. I ask him the customary Mandarin greeting: "*Nǐ hǎo, nǐ chī fàn le meí yǒu?*" (Hi, have you eaten?)

"*Chī le,*" he nods and smiles. No mail for me today, he apologizes when I ask. Mr. Chen lives in the room under the stairs with an adorable toddler, Bo, whom I sometimes see waddling about in open-butt pajamas, mooning me or reaching for my nose. I haven't yet seen Bo's mother.

Byron is home, and he's wedging the tea kettle, still steaming, into the fridge. "We'll have cold, drinkable water by tomorrow morning," he says with a smile. He grabs a shirt and we leave together, as planned, on a tourist journey. We cross campus and strike out through Peizheng's gate, hike down bustling Yandun Street to the plaza, and wait at a bus stop for the #17 bus. Our destination is the tomb of Sun Yatsen, the man called the founder of modern China. His tomb isn't far from campus.

A bus squeals to a stop in front of us, and with two dozen other desperate souls, we push purple half-yuan notes into a rusty box and squeeze on. There are few seats, I notice, probably because more people fit standing up. The furnace of bodies is so tight I don't even need to hold on. "Where go?" blurts an old man at my shoulder. I respond first in English, then Mandarin, but his transfixed eyeballs never wander. We careen around a corner, and a man in a beige shirt covered with red insignias smiles at me from eighteen inches away, pronouncing every syllable: "Hello. Where are you come from?"

"I am from the USA," I reply precisely. "*Meǐ Guó*."

"*Meǐ Guó*," he repeats and laughs. "*Meǐ Guó*! You speak Chinese?"

"*Wǒ huì shuō yì diǎn*," I reply. I can speak a little.

"*Hěn hǎo!*" he cries. "*Nǐ shuō de hěn biàozhǔn!*" He's either praising me or asking if I'm spreading poisonous American ideas among the people. He introduces himself as Dun, a police officer, and asks our ages. He asks if I like China, twice, and I say yes, twice, trying not to stare at the sweat on his forehead, before realizing I'm confusing the word *xǐhuān*, which means "like," with *xíguàn*, which I don't recognize. "You teach me English?" Officer Dun asks. "You be *lǎoshī*?"

"I'm sorry," I say, relieved not to be getting arrested. "I can't be your *lǎoshī* (teacher)." The older man grabs my wrist, twisting it, waving at the window, at a gigantic blue pagoda tower. "I'm very busy," I apologize to Dun, extricating my hand and joining Byron as he hastily slips off the bus.

In front of the blue tower is a gate and a ticket booth. Admission prices are painted on the booth's wall:

LOCAL VISITORS - 2元
FOREIGN FRIENDS - 10元

"Five times the Chinese price?" I ask the ticket lady, twice.

She eyes us both silently, like a frog watching flies.

"Discrimination!" I say to Byron.

"We need a Tourist's Bill of Rights," he declares, alluding to that faraway place called *America*. "It's only $1.25," he calculates.

"What's your salary?" the woman snaps in Mandarin without blinking.

"1,800 each month," I reply, when I finally understand her.

She grimaces. "American dollars?"

"No!" I say. "*Rénmínbì*! We're not that rich."

"*Rénmínbì*?" she shakes her head in disgust. "You should get more."

Still, she won't give us the locals' price, so we hand over 10元 worth of Revolutionary People's Money, also called *rénmínbì*, and we pass through the gate. A vast compound of gorgeous manicured lawns surrounds the attractive memorial, which is an impressive tower of blue tiered roofs and burgundy colonnades. Flower-lined walkways lead toward the memorial, and elderly couples relax on benches under enormous trees with ancient, unruly roots. The odor of chemical fertilizer hangs in the air, and the hue of the grass lawns is a bright sickly green. The air smells slightly better when we reach the memorial itself, which was erected in 1931 "by Sun's many overseas friends," according to a plaque. A statue of Sun gazes past us, frowning, as if in reproof of all this attention. I point out Sun's expression to Byron, and he tells me that Sun Yatsen is considered China's first revolutionary because he was the leader of a rebel movement that brought down the Qing Dynasty in 1911, long before the word "communism" was even a whisper in Beijing. Sun was also a *Guǎngzhōurén* (Cantonese), and his organizing cemented this area's reputation as a hotbed of heresy and rebellion.

"His frown might betray his disappointment that his Revolutionary Party never amounted to much," Byron says with a chuckle. He did end the empire, inspire the masses, and usher in the era of the Republic, but his dreamt-of union never materialized, and it was the Communists who finally united China three decades later, in 1949.

Byron drifts away, perhaps having tired of me or having tired of talking. Hailing from upstate New York, between semesters studying philosophy at Princeton, he spent a year at Oxford, learned to row a warship in Turkey, and had a love affair in Greece. He frankly seems unworried about adjusting to China and its ideologies, chemicals, and extortion. What surprises him is that this is my first time abroad, and that I've read so little political science or philosophy. I studied computer science, music, art, and Chinese, and while I've long yearned to leave the U.S., to me it didn't seem strange that my first trip abroad would be to China.

Entering the memorial alone, I find a long hall with glass cases that hold faded photographs and bilingual captions: "Comrade Sun and a revolutionary comrade at the train station of Shanghai." "Comrade Sun with factory comrades in France." Between the cases stand stacks of dusty books, and topping one stack is Sun Tzu's *The Art of War*. Whether or not touching the books is permitted, the coincidence of finding China's two most famous Suns united under one roof is too much for uneducated me. I flip open the tome and struggle to decipher the poetic lines of military advice. "All warfare is deception," one phrase surrenders to me. "Water flows according to the nature of the ground." My mind on its own reels in another of his famous epigrams, and then there it is: "*Zhī bǐ zhī jǐ…*" "Know the other, know thyself, and you will always succeed." I repeat the words to myself, smiling as they ring through me, as if they are what I've been looking for all along. *This is why I'm here, why I'm teaching, why I made this long journey. To know and understand China, to know and understand Chinese students, and to know and understand myself. Teaching is another form of learning.* I gaze at the portrait of Sun in France for several minutes, and appreciate that he too was a traveler.

Double Happiness

September 18

Three weeks that feel like a lifetime. For the first time, maybe ever, the world seems to be slowing down around me—somehow here in this strange land I can live moment to moment and examine my thoughts and feelings patiently. I teach a class or two a day, and then whole afternoons spread out before me, open and without agenda. Sometimes, in the middle of an evening, I simply observe the present—the now. Now is here. And now is also…here. Now is also my last day in Guangzhou. I know that 46 weeks of different nows will come, go, stop, fly by, ramble beside me, and then now will be time to leave. Now will be time to return to that other world.

This now, I'm at home, in this concrete dorm, it's nighttime, and I'm lying under my canopy of netting. A few mosquitoes perch on the outside of the netting and look in. I wonder what now feels like to them. I wonder if they realize I'm not taking any of the anti-malarial drugs. Byron, as reticent as ever this evening, reads in the chair beside the desk. To his right is my guitar, above which hangs a Monet poster I brought—Impression: Sunrise—and to its right are our flimsy wooden wardrobes, and then the large window with its prison-like metal bars securing us from unimaginable villains.

❀

O
N NATIONAL Teachers' Day, a holiday in honor of the Republic's weary instructors, Mrs. Yuan escorts the four of us American *lǎoshī* to another banquet, this one hosted by our English Department. A gorgeous hostess in a skintight red *qípáo*—a side-slit dress that Mao Tse-tung criticized as licentious—floats up on high heels and leads us down a strip of red carpet. The only furnishings in the chamber are enormous glass jars that line the walls, jars that contain a watery liquid and… coiled snakes. Pythons of spotted black, striped green, and murky patchy white. Dead, or at least sleeping. A man hurries by us toting a wire mesh cage of live, writhing ophidians.

The hostess takes us further, into a private room fit for royalty that features a black leather sofa and a towering Karaoke machine. On the walls are elegant paintings of orioles on blossoming dogwood branches. I sit beside Mrs. Yuan on the sofa. "Snake makes the man feel very strong," she says, without turning to face me. "Especially the snake's blood." She issues a strange, high-pitched laugh. "Many men come to a restaurant like this one, because the snake is flexible and so fast, and they will feel very strong."

"Yes, sometimes I feel weak," I joke, falling into stiff English, realizing again that even these English teachers don't fully comprehend the language. "What do women like?"

"I like Beijing Duck," cuts in Mrs. Liu, a slender, bespectacled teacher who sits down on my other side. Her demeanor is warmer. "I am from the North. Do you know Shanxi province?"

"No," I reply, looking from her to Mrs. Yuan.

"It is famous," Mrs. Liu says. "Very famous. You can see the Great Wall."

"Will you see the Great Wall?" Mrs. Yuan asks.

"I don't know. I do want to travel."

"Do you know '*Bú dào cháng chéng, huài hǎo hàn*'?" she asks.

"No."

"It is a famous saying," She giggles abruptly again. "It means, 'If you do not see the Great Wall, you are not a real man.'"

Lots of manhood at stake tonight. "Yes, it is famous," I acknowledge. "I should see it."

"Maybe for Chinese New Year?" she asks.

"Maybe," I nod, turning to listen to Byron, who is asking about traditional snake remedies. Principal Wu, up close, turns out to be an affable man with a thick mop of hair and a bulbous nose; he laughs and answers Byron with growling English reminiscent of Bobcat Goldthwaite. Paige has secretly christened him Wu-cat. "The liver bile," he says. "It slides down easily, uh, slippery. Good for cold."

Mrs. Yuan cuts in. "We Cantonese people are famous. There is a saying: 'A Cantonese will eat anything with four legs except the table.'"

Lauren looks at me with an incredulous smile, as if to ask whether I can believe all of this is happening.

"And snakes too!" blurts Wu-cat.

Bowls containing inky liquid arrive on the table, and we all rise from the sitting area to claim red-cushioned chairs around the table.

I sit, and immediately, from behind my shoulder, a waiter with a long spouted copper kettle arches a long, smooth stream of hot tea into my white teacup, not a drop landing on the tablecloth. Mr. Guo, a wiry English teacher sitting on my right, watches the perfect tea land in his cup too, and then he takes a turn with me. "Tony, do you know your way in Guangzhou?" He dips his chopsticks into what turns out to be turtle soup, and as he secures a shell-covered chunk of meat, I say yes, since it's been almost three weeks now. He gnaws on the morsel he finds. "Can you do shopping?" he asks.

"Yes," I declare. "I just bought vegetables on Wednesday." And without deciding to, I slurp up a big spoonful of hot broth. It's earthy and bitter, with a dose of ginger and an aroma of earthworm.

"Did you pay too much?" Mr. Guo asks. I consider this as other dishes arrive: beef tripe with shredded mushrooms, bony chicken cutlets with fish sauce and snow peas, a whole open-eyed blue jay glaring at me, leaves of vegetables sprinkled with oily chunks of garlic, spicy tofu with chipped pork and acerbic bamboo shoots, and innumerable other permutations on pork. In Mandarin, the word *meat* implies that it's pork. I sample a tough bit of pork cooked with an oily, bitter melon. Inedible. I gnaw through my first cow stomach, finding it harder work than the beef muscle, but still palatable. Mr. Guo is still looking at me, so I ask him to clarify. "How would I know if I paid too much? How much are carrots?"

Our conversation is interrupted by the main attraction. Two beaming waitresses carry in a silver tray on which a long snake reclines in a sinuous curve on a white platter. Everyone *oohs* and *aahs* as the splendid serpent makes its way around the table. The diverse members of the Peizheng English Department partake with delight.

"Carrots?" Mr. Guo chews loudly on a length of snake. He glances around the table, noticing that everyone is chewing and listening to us. He looks back at me. "Well, how much did you pay?"

"7元 per *jin*," I reply.

He bursts into laughter. "No, really?"

I repeat what I've said, and he gapes at me. He repeats in Cantonese my words, in case anyone missed them, and now the whole table is laughing.

Mrs. Liu explains to me that carrots should cost about 1.20元. I nod, feeling stupid, and then more than that—like a fraud that's been shamed, mocked, and finally exposed. *I can't teach English, I can't speak Chinese, I can't even handle buying carrots.* I finally just bite down into the snake. The texture is tough and sinewy, making me imagine a spinal cord, maybe my own. The flavor is rocky and salty, slightly smoky.

"Do you like the snake, Hero of the Market?" asks Lauren. She meets my eye. "It's good for your health."

"So I should be feeling more manly now?" I look down at the jagged, half-eaten bit of snake sitting in my bowl. "Somehow that's not happening." Countless other organs and parts of the snake are brought before us, and we learn that it is Chinese custom to eat any prized entrée in its entirety, from hind to hair, from tongue to tail. I refrain from snake eyes and most everything else, but I take a tiny gulp of the blood. My belly quickly churns. I inhale deeply as the sauces, flavors, and textures collide inside me in a bizarre mélange that is nothing like "Chinese food" back home. What I saw at the market hanging from rusty, bloody hooks—well, that's what we're swallowing here. First ripped off, now poisoned. *Where did that snake live? And the turtle? Did it have filariasis, malaria, Dengue fever? What is Japanese encephalitis?*

A waitress brings yet another tray. This one holds eleven slender shot glasses of a yellow-green liquid. Mr. Guo clears his throat: "It's a drink made from the snake's—how to say—?" Everyone takes a glass, and Mrs. Yuan throws out speculative English translations for the source of the liquid. Gall? Kidney? Spleen? "It is the bile from the liver," she decides, "mixed with *baíjiŭ*," China's most famous liquor, a vodka made from sorghum.

"In college they called Byron a fish!" says Lauren.

"Shark," Byron corrects her, eyeing the fluid in his glass. "And *baíjiŭ* wasn't exactly my drink."

"*Gānbēi!*" Wu-cat calls out the Mandarin version of "bottoms up," raising his glass.

Lauren raises her glass to me, winking.

I shake my head. "No one knows what this actually is!"

"*Gānbēi!*" echoes off the walls and they all hoist the *baíjiŭ*-bile combo. I leave mine untouched. Maybe I'll *gānbēi* next time if no one gets sick. Maybe if I'd had more snake's blood, I'd feel more manly. Maybe someday I'll eat anything with four legs but the table.

CHAPTER 11

Barbarians at the Gate

為者敗之執者失之
是以聖人無為故無敗

He who fusses over anything spoils it,
He who clutches onto anything loses it.
—*TAO TE CHING*, 64

COLT AND I check windshields for the famous words. We're in a chaotic stretch of street where buses dash to and fro like frenzied ants. He calls above the din to a driver, and the young man nods: He does go to *Cháng Chéng*. Colt asks how much. The man shoves a finger at a minibus and looks past us. "30元. Get in!"

"Simatai?" Colt asks. Does our pilgrimage to the ancient miracle begin here?

The man nods. "We leave, ten minutes, get in." Colt tells me a joke in Chinese that crosses the language barrier: Foreigners buying tickets here are like apples at Mid-Autumn Festival. "Ripe for ripping off." Yet

30元 is what the *Lonely Planet* guidebook says, describing this spot as a bus station for daily transport to Simatai, the remote section of *Cháng Chéng* that we want to explore.

The minibus is a ramshackle affair, with rusty metal seats covered hastily by threadbare cloths. A dozen men with cigarettes occupy the seats, but we find space on the front bench, next to the only man not smoking.

"Wasn't it strange that Wujia didn't even seem excited this morning—after insisting so many times? Now we're actually undertaking his quest," I say. Two teenage boys duck in and take seats behind us. "Actually, I feel bad talking about him."

"Yeah, it's a scene over there." Colt winces strangely, twists in pain, and suddenly darts to the door. "Gotta hit the bathroom. Don't leave!"

The young man to my left steals glances at me as I calmly examine the items in my bag. I have my dictionary, my camera, a bottle of water, *Narcissus & Goldmund*, the LP guidebook, and a question. *Am I a traveler or a tourist?* I carry only the money I saved as a teacher, I like to haggle, and I speak the local language; yet here I am going to the Great Wall of China. I feel compelled to understand this land as deeply as I can, to imbibe its every sight, sound, and smell, to sleep in its homes, to march with its soldiers, and yet I use a guidebook and I broke bread at McDonald's. The driver starts the engine while people continue to cram in. With an elbow I protect Colt's seat. Suddenly he's there, collapsing beside me. "Man!" he groans. "*Lā dùzi* (diarrhea). Must've been the *yāoguǒ jīdīng.*"

"I had a bad run-in with chicken myself," I say.

He manages a smile. "I remember the story."

The city streets funnel bicyclists, motorists, and pedestrians around us, and we can only inch along before merging, at long last, onto a pleasant oak-lined highway and picking up speed. Interspersed with the ubiquitous *huíguī* flags I spot communist hammer-and-sickle banners fluttering red against the sky. The hammer and sickle is something I simply never saw in Guangzhou. The billboards we pass are more familiar—ads for new housing developments. "Visit the Happiness Acres, an Elite Community for Sophisticates."

Colt writhes beside me. "Stop the bus!" he yells in Mandarin. "Big convenience. *Lā dùzi!*"

The driver nods and pulls off onto the shoulder. Colt shoots out across the road, down a hill, and out of sight. I step down too, worried, and for a "little convenience." I urinate between two willow trees, gazing across a vast meadow of leafy green crops blossoming with white flowers. Colt staggers back across the road. He's still pale, and as we board together, people tease him, jabbering, chuckling, and complaining about the "weak *dà bízi*" and "never getting to Nanhua."

Fifteen minutes later he gasps, and the scene repeats.

"That's it," he sighs, reboarding and nodding at the derisive laughter. "I hope. It's cool that the driver didn't leave us. Three weeks ago, in the middle of nowhere, on the way to Lanzhou, I had to get off and run for the bushes. The driver decided he'd had enough and just tossed my bag off the roof and drove off."

And this is my plan—to travel out into the middle of this land—with these kindly folks—alone? We roll into a dusty parking lot, and I crane my head out the window at a sign: Welcome To The Town Of Miyun. As everyone gets off, I eye the driver, inquiring whether we're at the Great Wall. He turns. "You catch another bus here." I try to confirm with him that we've already paid, but he smirks. "You get off here." And perhaps to show us weak *dà bízi* what he means, he hops to the ground and walks away.

"What?" I turn to Colt.

Colt, looking much improved, glances at me as we step down. "Honesty with foreigners isn't exactly in the Chinese bus driver's code of ethics. Remember, apples at Mid-Autumn Festival."

The lot is crawling with local travelers. Peddlers hawk hot tea, fresh fruit, soft drinks, potato chips, frying bread, ice cream, pots of hot sweet beans. We purchase a bunch of bananas from an old woman who tells us that there's another bus, one that does go to Simatai; she eventually nods at a bus bouncing into the lot. We approach its driver, and he waves us on with familiar words. "Get in!" We take seats in back and peel bananas. Two men load huge crates of watermelons into the aisle, packing the bus wall to wall. A woman sits down beside me, cradling an infant in her arms, and the little boy reaches out as if to touch my big foreign nose, giggling when I hand him a bit of banana. As I lean down close to his face, he yanks on my *dà bízi* like a door-knob, left, right. I pull back, and the boy cries out and grabs handfuls of my shirt. His mother praises my Mandarin and plies me with questions. "Aren't your parents worried about you? How did you teach in English?"

The driver revs the engine as two more people rush aboard: *dà bízi!* Colt and I stare at them along with everyone else. It's a white couple—our age—Americans, judging by their gear and the sweet ignorant confidence stamped across their faces. They can't find seats, and although people make room for them, the girl refuses to squeeze in; instead, she berates the driver in decent Mandarin for selling but not saving them seats. They finally flop down on the floor and lean against the crates of melons.

The bus lazily meanders into the hills, picking up passengers and dropping off others. Grassy slopes and rocky crags close in on either side as we ascend. The fare collector asks passengers for 6元 or 8元, and then demands 25元 from us, but we pay up without whining or questioning. Half an hour later he turns to us as we pull over where no one is waiting. "Great Wall," he announces.

"Where?" I ask.

He points at the window without looking. "Here. You get off here."

I survey the rolling meadow. "Where?"

He gestures backward, behind us, to a diverging dirt road. "You go over there."

Colt and the other two *dà bízi* climb down to the ground. I stop. "No! We each gave you 25元, right?" I ask.

"Mm."

"I said, 'Does this go to the Great Wall?' You said 'yes, the Great Wall.' Now where are we? Are we at the Great Wall? No! You're trying to trick foreigners. Shameful!" Anger charges through my veins, and for what feels like the first time in forever, I don't suppress it. I'm not stupid, and I'm not handing out gifts anymore. "Where? How do we get to the Wall?"

"Down that road," explains the mother with the infant. "You catch a bus."

"Let's go," Colt urges from outside.

"Another bus?" I ask the driver. "*Another bus!* Why would you say, 'We go to the Great Wall' when all you go to is this nothing? You're a… trickster," which is about the worst name I can conjure. My clumsy Mandarin amuses many, but I also sense sympathy. Finally, looking from face to face, I grab my bag, squeeze down the aisle, and switch to sarcasm: "'We go to the Great Wall.' What does this mean? You swindle foreigners. I'm a poor teacher, not some capitalist-roader or rich nose or big nose." I climb down and stomp over to the others. The bus rolls away.

"Last damn time I pay anyone *anything* before actually arriving," I say.

"Ridiculous," agrees the girl. We introduce ourselves and start down the dirt road. They're from Columbus, Ohio. Cathy is studying Mandarin in Beijing and her companion is her younger brother, Brad, who is here visiting her. Colt tells his joke about the apples again. A motorized tricycle wagon appears, and we come to terms with the elderly driver and hop on back—but don't pay. The road zooms by and as the wind whips through our hair, I peer up at the green peaks, still seething. With my eyes, I follow the high undulating horizon, and I welcome a deep breath. Haggling has brought assertiveness, and I trust my instincts more. *So why am I so angry? We sought out an unspoiled section of the Great Wall of China—of course it's difficult to get here.*

We roll through a crease between huge mountains, and on the tops of the peaks—along their spine—tiny stone towers are linked together by a golden thread. We roll to a halt in a parking lot, pay the motor tricyclist, and then pay an admission fee at a small booth. From there, we set out walking on a dirt path that winds past farm huts and around a large lake. Fresh air floods our lungs, and lapping water whispers in our ears. The path climbs the mountainside, and the grassy, moist red earth turns gray, rocky, and dry. I catch sight of the ancient stone, and it makes me wonder: *Why do people visit this thing?* Thousands died to construct it, and it didn't even serve its purpose: Barbarians—an epithet for anyone not Han Chinese—invaded repeatedly, even after its completion. But now we barbarians pay homage to the brutal barrier; it was built to keep us out, but today it is what draws us here. The steep path stops right in front of it. The Great Wall of China. I draw my hands across the roughly hewn orange stone, massaging it through a light film of dust. It feels cool under my fingertips. According to Mrs. Yuan, I'm now finally a man.

CHAPTER 12

Playing Chicken and Losing

吃一塹長一智

Knowledge comes from falling in a pit.
—CHINESE PROVERB

"HELLO!" THE saleswoman shouts to me cheerfully. She crouches over a neat mound of jumbo carrots, obviously eager to rip me off. The other vendors are already observing me, so her English words signify little. "Hello!" I echo, but my sarcasm disappears into the culture gap. For a moment I miss supermarkets and their simplicity, their price tags, their neon-light clarity.

I lower myself beside her, over a large mud puddle, and use my best, quiet Mandarin. "How much are the carrots?"

"*Liù kuài yì jīn,*" she says, smiling at her neighbor.

I understand! 6元 per *jīn*. Yes, last week I was betrayed, ridiculed, taken to the proverbial cleaners. That old guy smiled at me so warmly because I was paying him five times his normal price for potatoes! And that giggling cucumber girl. They all had a grand time.

"Too expensive," I say. I think for a moment what to say next. "How much is the Chinese price?"

"Eh?" She eyes me. There's a pause. "4.50元. I need to eat too."

I turn and walk off, comprehending their game. They're just laughing at the big nose, plotting to fleece me. *Let them keep their damned vegetables.* I step into the shop with the young shopkeeper, my kindred soul, who also heartily overcharged me. The vat of the best cooking oil

71

draws my eyes, and I smile at the shopkeeper, realizing there's a choice here. I can be angry, or I can view the prices I'm quoted as an opportunity to give charity to my neighborhood vendors. Rather than handouts to the rare beggar, I can give gifts to poor women selling carrots. It's patronizing perhaps, but if they feel a need to hoodwink me, I'm certainly entitled to treat them as devious children. The government may even encourage them to overcharge *gwailo*—everyone certainly thinks we're filthy rich. I move on through the stands and stalls, listening more, nodding less, laughing more wisely with the young woman with the cucumber gourds. I offer her eighty percent of her prices and fill my pack with round mottled asian pears, emerald-leafed bok choy, husky heads of garlic, and the finest gargantuan carrots.

The smell of burning sugar wafts out from a small bakery on my way home, and I step inside. The chairs and tables are small and a bright, childish orange. In the glass display case are sweet buns and honey-hued breads. The place actually has price tags. But there's a different problem: I need to avoid the odd pork pieces and red bean paste that seem to hide inside every doughy roll and bun. A girl in an orange-striped uniform catches my eye, and I point to a roll. "What is the... inside-this-thing?"

She laughs, but not like the market vendors. Her chuckles betray a different, softer amusement.

"Is it the hóng doù (red beans)?" I ask.

She's helpful, and we stumble together through each of six different kinds of sweet buns. I say *xièxiè* (thank you) many times and walk away with a sack of eight assorted buns.

Back on the street, I try another wild experiment and open a freezer. A Magnum Bar—a real vanilla ice cream bar coated with chocolate—draws my eyes. Ice cream freezers purr all over these sun-baked sidewalks, but I know dairy isn't a traditional part of Chinese culture or cuisine, so I've hesitated ever since that nasty carton of milk on the first day. *Ah, what the hell.* I buy one, tear open the wrapper of the imported Hong Kong treat, and lick the silky chocolate. Delight charges like electricity along my lips, up my tongue, awakening my taste buds like rain on parched land. In a flash the pleasure overwhelms me, telling me its secret: I am changing, I am transforming, I am adapting—to this dirt, to this heat, to this food, to this language, to this confusion. Part of me is starving, but I am surviving. For now, as my eyes slide closed, I savor the cold, sharp, exotic sweetness.

❀

SAPPING LIFE even from the leaves of the trees, the afternoon heat counsels sloth, but I forge ahead with my plan. Paige is continuing with a "multicultural awareness" lesson that we devised together, but for me it's been a failure. It feels like holding water in a fist just trying to maintain my students' attention, let alone connect in any meaningful way over something as cerebral as *multiculturalism*. It's Thursday and I'm with my favorite class, Tenth Grade, Class IV, the one with Iceboy and Jrace and Winnie. I'm going it alone.

"Hello!" the students roar. As always, they're laughing, whispering, yelling, or gazing silently, and the ones who remember their notebooks are copying down the new words I've written on the board. They listen to my instructions on the future tense. Adam stands and shouts: "*I will* watch the NBA tomorrow!" Then he fills in the other blank: "*After* I go to McDonald's, *I will* watch the NBA tomorrow." Two more stand and deliver, performing well, tossing out cultural references with spurts of fluency. This is a smart class, I decide. Iceboy could be the smartest student in any of my classes. He says: "*Before* China becomes a modern country, it *will* ruin the environment like America did." A boy without a nametag says he can't read the words on the board, and I skip him, but the next two students copycat, feigning innocence, smirking, and they don't listen to my explanations; everything hurtles downhill, as if my students suddenly conspired to do absolutely nothing useful.

"Donkey, what *will* you do?" I hear my voice rising in frustration. "Yes, but what *will*—" The bell rings. They know I hear it, and they don't even wait for me to dismiss them. I scold them: "*Before* you come to my next class, you *will* improve your English."

They're leaving, filing out, and I sigh, trying to let it go.

Downstairs, to the dormitory, through the gate, and I'm home; it's 2:45, two hours before I'm meeting a woman whose business card my father gave me ages ago. He never met her, but her telecommunications company and his formed a joint-venture. Her name is Xie Ran, and a few days ago I fumbled with a telephone long enough to ask her to shop with me at the market. Hopefully she'll instruct me a little on navigating Cantonese life. I take out my dictionary, check on a few words, and then lie down for a rest.

My eyes fly open. Sweat clings to the back of my neck and my head is swimming. The hands of our pale green clock point to 4:10. I climb out of bed and stagger to the toilet. Nausea and cramps, and my gut gives out. Light-headed, I slowly return to bed, dizzy. The ceiling drops in close, as if to strike me. Like a fist to my stomach comes a realization: I am unfathomable journeys away from anyone who cares.

Some time later I hear the front door.

Byron walks in. "Hey, what's up?"

"I'm sick," I mumble.

"Really? With what?"

"Sick. Headache, dizzy, just bad. Could you go meet Xie Ran at the front gate? I'm supposed to meet her, but tell her I'm sick. She speaks good English. You can go shopping with her if you want."

"Well I—OK, I'll bring my backpack. I'll go. I hope you feel better. I'd say I'd call a doctor, but...I don't know any." He laughs alone. "We can find one if it gets bad." He leaves. My cheek drops back down onto the hot pillow, and the dirty white walls and fluorescent lights spin freely. I roll over and clothespin the netting, sealing myself off. My eyelids sink shut. The blood pounds inside my skull rhythmically, making the bed sway. *It's those tenth graders,* I'm thinking, *their infuriating noise.*

I hear talking and the clink of plates, but I can't see. It's suddenly night. My stomach is churning and I need to get to the bathroom. The netting grabs me like a web but I manage to struggle to my feet. I stumble across the dark room, palming the wall to steady myself. I step through the door, into the light, and past the table. Byron and Xie Ran look at me, then I'm in the bathroom. I collapse on the toilet. My head and stomach fly against each other. My bowels slam into my stomach, and I almost keel over, feeling my body ripping apart. *It's too much.* In a vision, my body is drawn and quartered by horses; my torso surrenders, explodes.

I manage to clean myself up, and somehow I'm back in bed with a cramping belly, a throbbing head, and the knowledge that I'm dying. This is not just sickness, illness, bad luck; this is an exotic, lethal, belly-ripping, incurable, invincible monster.

A hazy vision of Byron's face appears and asks something, and then Xie Ran materializes and also speaks. I close my eyes. I'm leaning on Byron down the stairs and out of the building. Saccharine air and a red taxi sit there, where no road goes. We drive around on campus, on the sidewalks, on the basketball court, and my head lolls back. The window is open and the gusting air reminds me of life. It's suffocating, and it's going to make me vomit. We park and Xie Ran and Byron help me into a gray box of a building, and I collapse on a small yellow chair. The floor is red and black tile, chipped, dirty. People around me wear masks of pain and fear and desperation. The old woman on my right writhes, sighs, and moans as a young boy crawls on her. Her cheeks are swollen like a feasting squirrel's.

Hours slip by. Byron takes me into a room with several beds, each obscured with a circular curtain pulled tight. *To hide dead people. We'll all soon be dead.* I lie down and close my eyes, and a doctor unbuttons my shirt. I whisper, "No needles." I have to repeat myself until Byron finally hears. Maybe Xie Ran will translate. I try to pray—to Jesus, to Buddha, to Sun Tzu, to new gods floating above me wearing wild crimson robes. The doctor leaves and comes back with tongue depressors. He feels my bare chest and shoulders. *If I survive, I'll leave this land, I'll go home. If I survive.*

My feet land below me, and I'm handed a metal bowl, tissues, paper cups.

"Stool samples," says Byron from some faraway place. "The bathroom is downstairs. I'll show you." He leads my feet down a corridor where people are seated on the floor, along the walls. A boy with a garish, raspberry-hued face watches me. We pass through a dark doorway, onto large stone steps, down, down, down. One hand on the stone wall, I descend into a damp dark dungeon. "In there," Byron points into an archway. "Knock 'em dead."

I step in. The air stinks thickly of mildew and feces and I barely discern a trench cut into one stone stall. Energized somehow, I set down the metal bowl and the paper cups and squat over the trench. Not to disappoint, the rest of my stomach streams out. The room spins and my breaths come short as I pour from the bowl into the cups. I hear and then find the drip-drip-drip of a broken spigot and rinse my fingertips in the stinking water. I struggle back upstairs, carrying my disease in the flimsy cups.

Byron greets me at the top of the stairs. "Over here, follow me. It's good... Xie Ran is here... I don't know..." A doctor takes the warm cups. Xie Ran says they'll do tests to see about dysentery, and the word *dysentery* means that she really does speak English. I long to lie down, but I drop into a chair and my eyelids descend. Xie Ran is talking, "Not dysentery... the tests... days... Western or Chinese medicine?" My stomach ties new knots. A taxi cradles me, and I hope my body will hold together a moment longer, a minute longer, so I can enjoy this miracle that God grants us—that our bodies ever hold together in the face of this immense need to explode.

"Paige can take your classes tomorrow," Byron says. I nod and my bed swallows me whole.

✿

I WAKE UP late, sweating in the afternoon heat. Byron says that they got me Western and Chinese pills. Both are covered in Chinese writing, but the Western pills are a stark white and are packaged in detachable plastic bubbles. I study them. *What a fool I am, an idiot. I knew if I dropped my guard for a moment the demonic local germs would infiltrate my flesh and snap their jaws around me.* It's a Chinese illness, I finally realize, it needs a Chinese cure. With a gulp of boiled water I swallow two yellow pills.

Evening brings gentle breezes and mercy from the heat, and Xie Ran visits with two bottles of 7-Up. I finally manage to introduce myself, hoping my grateful words make up in sincerity what they lack in vigor. *You were my savior.* She shares some good news that saddens me: Her company is sending her to Shanghai for an eight-month business course on Internet marketing that will set her up for a promotion. Feeling abandoned, I wish her luck.

But by Saturday I'm well enough to recant my hospital oath, and I choose to stay in China. The snake, the ice cream, the bad pastries, the smelly chicken—whatever it was—matters little. My worst fear came true. I was an idiot, I tore up my belly, I died in a Chinese hospital. And I'm still here.

A Chinese illness needs a Chinese cure.

CHAPTER 13

A Child's Drawing of the End of the Earth

道生之　德畜之　物形之

All beings are expressions of the Tao,
Born in virtue, and shaped into matter.
—*TAO TE CHING*, 51

A STONE STAIRCASE leads up into a tower of roughly hewn orange stone. From within the stone tower, a second staircase takes us up and out and onto the Great Wall of China. We stand on it, at an incline. In one direction the tremendous wall plummets down all the way to the glistening lake, crosses it like a dam, climbs up the far side, and then arches like a great serpent over angled crests as far as the eye can see. We turn the other way and hike up, into the warm windy sky.

Built two thousand years ago, the stones of the Wall remain well cobbled, and between the crenellations the Wall here is quite broad— wide enough for passing horsemen. The drop on both sides is precipitous however, and we tread carefully. A slip would become a long somersault all the way down to the grassy meadows of the south side or down to the no-man's land on the north side. As we continue our upward hike, my eyes are drawn like magnets to the beauty of the north, the barbarians' side. Small hills stretch like wrinkled brown blankets all the way to a hazy horizon. I wonder if it is the Wall's monstrous size or the spellbinding grandeur of the view that is lodged so fiercely in

Wujia's mind; despite his reveries and recommendations, there are no green horses to be seen.

A tranquility settles into my mind as I inhale the fresh wind. That outburst on the bus must have been triggered by my anxiety—about traveling, about weakness, about loneliness. *It's all here.* I take a deeper breath.

"Look," Colt stops me. "You'll be able to take a ride up instead of walking."

I follow his eyes to a row of pink poles that appear to be a half-built ski lift.

He chuckles. "No beautiful historic site that couldn't use some pink plastic."

Simatai will soon be like the touristy sections of the Wall found closer to Beijing, I decide. Brad, adjusting his scarlet Ohio State cap, gazes at the poles. "But it won't make it quite all the way up," he observes. "The slope's too steep."

"Don't underestimate these people," counters Colt. "If steepness were enough to stop them there never would have been a wall here at all."

We reach the next tower and scramble up into it, shimmying through a crumbling window. We discover other humans inside—four Japanese tourists, sitting quietly in the cool darkness. I remove my tan cap to let my forehead cool, and I peer back through the window, admiring how the Wall rides the peaks' undulations like a cowboy on a bronco.

"Drinks?" A short, bronze-skinned woman appears, her lined, weathered face upturned. Three big leather satchels of beverages and snacks are slung over her shoulders. Colt declines for us, and he and I discuss the stones beneath our feet—the precision with which they're laid, the way the Wall perches on the very apex of the mountain. "How were the stones carried up here?" Colt asks the stooped lady in Mandarin.

She grimaces as if she remembers. "There were ten thousand strong men. It took one hundred years."

Nice round numbers.

"Cool water? Cola?" she asks. We shake our heads. She doesn't seem interested in the Japanese tourists and she insists. "Soon you'll be hot and tired and want something to drink."

"We're strong," Cathy replies, and turns towards the doorway.

"Americans?" she asks.

Cathy nods, and perhaps that's the reason the woman follows us.

We reach another tower, and then another. Breezes kiss my neck and a biting heat rushes into my thighs as we climb higher. The incline grows steeper, probably impossible for horsemen, and the chunky orange bricks fit together less snugly. I fall behind and chat with the drink lady. She smiles a toothless smile when I ask her why she's still with us. "Soon you will be very thirsty," she says. She wears a tattered brown jacket and her black hair hangs long and ragged about her bags.

"But aren't your bags heavy?" I ask.

"It'll be lighter coming down," she says. She isn't answering my real question—how she does it at her age.

Water from my own bottle wets my throat. "I'm not going to buy any of your drinks," I say. "But why don't you let me carry some?"

She looks at me, and without argument hands me two of her sacks. Honored, I sling the honey sodas, bean milk, bottled water, and herbal health concoctions over my shoulder. She tells me she's here every day. "I live down there." She points down to the barbarians' side, to a small village with a dozen tiny houses. The houses and the Wall are of a similar shade, and between breaths, I ask her if they are the same stone.

She nods. "People often take stone to build their homes."

"Are you married?" I've gotten the hang of asking this question the Chinese way, without hesitation.

"Yes," she assents. "My husband is a—"

SLAM! A stone gives way beneath me, and I slip. The edge of the Wall rushes up to meet me... The drinks crash around me. I'm clinging to the very edge of the crumbling Wall.

"Be careful!" the drink lady scolds me. My heart pounding, I dust myself off and carefully stand up. I nod to her, watching her recover her sacks. She climbs on steadily, not slowing down, not appearing upset.

We pass two more towers, and then the Wall disintegrates. It collapses to a mere path that threads its way through mounds of dilapidated orange stone. There are no rails, and we step slowly. Cathy removes her glasses to mop her brow. "Our sherpa," she points to the lady. "She says the crumbly cliff up ahead is Wangjing, the highest part of the Wall around here, but it's at least another hour to get there." Colt and I smile at each other and shrug; Brad says he's up for it.

So we forge onward, upward. Silence envelops us like gauze. We can see for miles. I want to capture the experience entirely—the sounds of dislodged stones; the warmth in my thighs; the way the cool, gusting wind gently stings my lungs—but my camera just crops the magnificence, and the effort feels futile. This puny instrument captures only a small slice of the visual, I remember, shoving the thing back into my bag. *It's best to forget the future.*

The Wall folds back on itself to reach Wangjing, a peak that looks like a child's drawing of the end of the Earth. The mountain, with the Wall along for the ride, goes up and up to a crumbly spire, then ends. We clamber up the grass and dirt and jutting stones, scrambling, grasping, pushing. Finally we reach it, the peak, Wangjing. It's a marvelous summit. We see that the Earth *does* go on, on and on and on, a boundless kingdom of dimpled hills and wispy clouds. A grinning fool, I use the camera to capture what I can. And of course we buy refreshment from our clever barbarian vendor, our indomitable drink lady, our sherpa who knew us better than we knew ourselves. I uncap a fresh bottle of water, put it to my lips, and a river of joy runs over my parched tongue. In delight I witness my companions, these heroes who sighed and sweated along with me; and the Wall, slithering in midair, suspended between heaven and earth.

CHAPTER 14

Six-String Lǎoshī

知彼知己勝乃不殆

Know the other, know thyself,
And you will always succeed.
—SUN TZU, THE ART OF WAR

September 29

I survived. The horrible hospital saved me. Or something did. This strangeness I call "normal" has resumed. I teach and read and play guitar and live the now. It's all so mellow and regular. And yet there's something new: an impatience, as if my worries over dying were just myths, like Kung Fu masters and automaton students, and now I see through them. I want to experience the real China now, whatever it is. The Moon Festival holiday is next weekend, and I'm not going to travel with my fellow gwailo lǎoshī down to Hong Kong. I plan to stay here alone and cook and wander the streets, to explore the alleys and find the places that beckon to me as if they're waiting for me, as if my destiny will unfold only once I discover them.

My students ramble into my classroom, fresh from afternoon basketball. I open my long black case, fit the strap around my back, and turn to face them. They applaud eagerly. In the ensuing moment of stillness, all twenty-eight pairs of eyes seem to shout in unison: *We're finally getting the real show!*

I strum my acoustic guitar, launching into John Denver's "Leavin' on a Jet Plane." Before class I chalked up the lyrics, and so I proceed to belt out the whole song, verse-chorus-verse-chorus, and my audience watches as if hypnotized.

Afterwards, I begin to go through the lyrics line by line, speaking slowly, asking for them to repeat after me. "All my bags are packed. I'm ready to go."

"No, just you again," Donkey says, clapping again. "You again."

But before long, he and all but the shyest few pronounce the lyrics. "Kiss me, and smile for me." I pucker my lips, kiss the air, and smile while gesturing to my heart. There are a dozen giggles. Finally, we hit it in concert, and it feels fantastic, a roomful of blue-and-white-clad boys and girls singing a love song.

I write lyrics to another classic on the board, "This Land is Your Land," and we sing it all the way through. "From California to the Gulf Stream waters, this land was made for you and me." I erase "California" and "New York Islands" and ask the students for places *in China*. At first they're confused and suggest streets in Guangzhou, but soon they get it and name places like Tibet and the Great Wall. We sing the song for China. Finally, leaving behind every country's imperialistic aspirations, we choose places and nations from around the world, and we sing for the whole planet. "From Argentina to the Japanese islands..." rings through the open windows and out over the soccer field, and I feel my chest hum with a new pleasure. *We're singing the same song, smiling the same smile, as if we're all made of the same stuff.*

I'm teaching China to sing.

I'm uplifting the nation.

The bell buzzes, and the air goes silent. Most of the students dash out into the day, as always. Jrace and Winnie stop at the lectern. "You play really well, the guitar," says Jrace. She giggles nervously.

"Do you know Cantonese?" asks Winnie.

I shake my head and sigh. "Not yet."

"Your Mandarin is so great," murmurs Winnie.

This confuses me. I haven't spoken Mandarin in class since that first week.

"Do you want to learn some Cantonese?" Jrace asks.

I nod, and the girls proceed to teach me. "Thank you," Jrace instructs. "*Mgoi.*"

"*Mgoi?*" I ask.

She corrects me, and I repeat after her.

"*Duo chieh,*" Jrace says next. "This is also 'thanks,' but it means thanks for a gift." I get that one too, and she applauds my pronunciation. "Try this one: *ngo moi nei.*" I repeat this phrase many times, but the girls keep asking me to say it again.

Jrace smiles bashfully. "This means 'I love you.'" She and Winnie laugh mischievously.

"Do you have a girlfriend?" Jrace asks.

"No!" I laugh too.

"I told you," Winnie whispers to her.

"Can we take another picture with you?" Jrace stands next to me, holding two fingers out in a V. I smile as Winnie snaps the camera.

They rush out, leaving me alone to pack up my guitar.

Out on the hallway, a bronze-skinned man with a crew cut awaits me. "Herro?" he greets me.

"Hello." I nod, locking up the classroom, mopping my forehead, preparing to meet another curious *Guǎngzhōurén.*

"I hear you play the guitar," he says. "Very good!"

"Thank you," I take the compliment the American way. Then I try the Chinese way: "No, actually I play very badly and the students laugh at me."

"It is good," he decides. "Maybe you can teach me." He's the picture of a healthy Chinese man: squat, robust, an easy smile, and a typical outfit of navy pants and buttoned white shirt. His only flaw seems to be a squinted left eye, as if in a permanent wink. A fraying black guitar case leans beside him. *Why not?* "Sure, come on," I finally say, and motion him to follow me home.

"Oh, I can't today," he stops. It seems odd, and I sense it's a required formality. I insist, glancing at his guitar case, but he still shakes his head.

"Just for a little while," I repeat, and on this third entreaty, he concedes and follows along. *The third time.* He follows me to my dormitory, and I introduce him to Mr. Chen. He introduces himself as Li Song, a history teacher.

"You're a history teacher?" I ask, as I let him into our apartment. "Here, at Peizheng?"

He nods.

"You speak better English than the English teachers!"

He lets out a humble chuckle as we take seats at the table and un-case our guitars. We take turns playing, listening, playing more. He finger-plucks a meandering, exquisite classical melody; I play an REM song, attacking my steel-string with a heavy pick. We praise each other's unfamiliar style. I get a sense that we could perform together. I show him some sheet music I brought—U2, Dave Matthews, Eric Clapton— and we attempt to play some tunes together. I strum the chords of U2's "Running to Stand Still" while he plucks the vocal melody, and it sounds fantastic and bizarre, familiar yet almost atonal, since he can read music but doesn't know the tune.

Halfway through listening to an Eric Clapton song on CD, he suddenly bolts up. "Time to go, I prepare for class."

I hurriedly lend him *Joshua Tree* and *Eric Clapton Unplugged*—the CDs and the sheet music. "Thank you," he says with a grin, respectfully accepting the materials with both hands. He stands with me for a moment, silently expressing appreciation, or perhaps its an apology for leaving so suddenly, and then he's gone.

❀

SIX DAYS later, Li Song returns. His new favorite song is "Tears in Heaven," and he and I play it together. He hums a bit of the melody, and I ask him to sing it now that he knows it. Without further ado he breaks into song, crooning with a rich voice that fills our little concrete home. He has a thick accent of course. "*Would it be the same, if I saw you in heaven?*" I pluck the strings, enjoying again the blending of our styles.

We invite him to stay for dinner and insist three times before he accedes. Instead of our customary wok full of vegetables, Byron prepares

Western cuisine for our guest: He browns potatoes, sautés onions, and fries actual omelets from a cache of eighty eggs we received as a gift from the school administration. When we all sit down, Li Song cranes to look under the omelet on his plate, forking it onto its side. "Are you vegetarians?" he asks.

"No, we're just nervous about cooking meat at home." Byron makes broad hand gestures as he often does when speaking with Chinese people. "I don't want to poison us."

"Do you eat meat with most meals?" I ask Li Song as we all dig in.

"Often, yes," he replies. "I usually like to eat meat."

"What kinds of meat?"

"My wife and I eat pig and cow sometimes, and some other things."

"What else?" I press him. "Do you eat dog?"

"Hmm?" he says, and I can't tell if it's his permanent wink or genuine confusion.

"Dog," I say louder. "*Gǒu*. Do you eat *gǒu*?"

"Oh, yes," he says thoughtfully. "Sometimes. It's not our favorite."

"Any other kinds of meat?" Byron asks. "Cat? Rabbit? Raccoon?"

"Yes. I don't know 'ladoon'?"

"Rac-coon," Byron enunciates, holding his hands a couple feet apart. "A little guy about this big, with black rings around his eyes." He encircles his eyes with his thumbs and forefingers. "They're stealthy, like big dogs."

"It lives in the forest," I add.

"Oh yes, I know it, it's very smart." Li Song smiles. "I don't think I've eaten it before."

"It's tasty," Byron says.

"Have you eaten snake?" Li Song asks. "It's delicious and healthy."

"Yes, we had snake," I sigh. "And turtle. With the Peizheng teachers and Principal Wu."

"Yes, snake is good, healthy," Li Song says. "I also like ass."

"Ass?" Byron chokes on his toast.

"Yes," Li Song says. "Ass is a good taste. Very good."

"How good?" I ask. "I mean, how often do you eat it?"

"Maybe once a month I eat the ass."

"I've never had it," I admit, stifling a laugh with difficulty. "How do you eat the ass?"

"Many ways, you can try it. Ass is popular in China."

Byron eyes Li Song seriously. "In America it's hard to get good ass."

"Very delicious," Li Song nods.

Byron asks, "Does your wife like ass too?"

"My wife really likes the ass," he nods calmly. "Maybe her favorite. It's a treat."

"A treat?" I manage.

"Well," Byron grins. "All we have left here is toast and potatoes."

A TORRID AFTERNOON sun blazes through the windows of my classroom. I strum my guitar, and the teenagers scream out: "West Virginia! Mountain momma! Take me home! Country roads!" We belt out the chorus three extra times. Looking at them, I try to ignore the fact that most of them are just mouthing the syllables, imitating others, probably missing where one word ends and the next begins. After the song, I quiz them on the words, and sure enough, they haven't learned a thing. But they do want to keep singing.

"Take me home," bellows Sandoh, interrupting me. "Take me home!"

Fat chance, I'm thinking. The bell rings, sparking their customary chaotic exodus. Mrs. Yuan stops all four of us *gwailo lǎoshī* on the ground floor. "Peizheng is very proud!" she gushes. "You are our best foreign teachers. Ever!" She returns the passports we surrendered to her the day we arrived, and at long last there are actual visas stamped inside. We're now legally here, big noses in the Middle Kingdom. But there's something else on her mind, and she doesn't waste time. "Maybe you would like to sing. At a wedding?"

"Sing?" Paige's eyes widen.

"Yes, maybe you can sing a Chinese song of love?" She turns a sidelong glance at me. "I hear Tony is very talented."

"All of us?" Paige asks.

"OK?" Mrs. Yuan nods. "Maybe you will do very well." The word *maybe*, we've realized, is how she signifies an order. "It is an important wedding in Guangzhou," she continues. "Principal Wu and I will attend. You will represent Peizheng! You will be famous! Peizheng is very proud." She hurries off, leaving the four of us staring at each other.

"A wedding?" laughs Byron. "Tony, did you get us into this?"

"I… don't think so…"

"Last week was the clothing factory," Paige shakes her head. "Now this? Singing at a wedding?"

Lauren smiles. "Who knows. Hey, do you two manly *gwailo* want to cook dinner at our place tonight? We have the ingredients for 'Guangzhou Spaghetti.'"

Up for a break from eggs and stir-fries, Byron and I leave campus with them and turn down an alley towards their apartment.

"Sometimes we're allowed to say *no*, right?" I shake my head. "I mean, '*No!* I'm not doing that!' Sing at a wedding? *No!*"

"Why don't you just have us all sing 'This Land is Your Land'?" Paige jabs.

I spot a Jianlibao soda can on the street and kick it. "Maybe I *should* bring my guitar."

"Seriously, why does it have to be us?" Lauren asks.

"'*Maybe you will represent Peizheng*,'" Paige parrots Mrs. Yuan.

"Peizheng is our *dānwei*," Byron explains. "Our work unit. We got the gift over the holday—all the eggs—because we're now loyal members of our *dānwei*. Remember? Now it's our duty to do our part. 'To uplift the nation.'"

Lauren ponders this a moment. "It might be fun," she says. I catch her eye, and she smiles.

"No, it's going to be 'look and laugh at the foreigners,'" Paige rolls her eyes. "We make fools of ourselves, everyone laughs, and then we're done. It's lame, but you just suck it up and deal."

We reach a quiet residential alley, climb a flight of stairs to their place, and enter. Inside, we melt. Their air conditioning feels impossibly luxurious, and the coolness sifts through my pores, awakening visceral memories of comfort and pleasure. My eyes pass languorously over their wooden sofa and linoleum floor. "How did you guys get the palace when we got the prison cell?"

"The boys were naughty last year, remember?" says Lauren. "Zach got the Asian Cravin."

There's a knock on the door, and Mr. Guo, the wiry teacher who sat beside me at the snake banquet, pays a visit. He must have heard us come in. "I am writing an English textbook," he utters in his nasally voice. "Maybe you can help with the translating?" He uses the killer *maybe* too. We agree, and we work with him for fifteen minutes, fixing countless awkward sentences and erroneous, often hilarious, vocabulary choices.

"Translating?" Lauren cries when he finally leaves. "How about *writing*? That's the third day in a row!"

Paige mocks Mr. Guo's snorting tone: "Maybe you will write my book for me. Maybe you will do my bidding—forever!" Then she inserts her own voice: "Maybe I will never see you again."

"*Maybe* we should hang a sign on our door," Lauren sighs. "'Foreigners Available.'"

❁

A FEW SHORT days later, available again, the four of us climb to the third floor of Classroom Tower B, where we are to begin training to sing a Chinese song of love. A lively melody dances down the outdoor hallway toward us. We step into a dusty room where a man is playing a dilapidated upright piano. He turns and greets us. "Herro!"

It's Li Song! He grins, welcoming us, his left eye doing its permanent wink.

Paige and Lauren introduce themselves.

"Your song is *Aobao Xianghui*," Li Song says. "A famous Chinese love song, very traditional. Everyone at the wedding will already know it. But it is one of the most difficult to sing." He explains its composition: First is a woman's part, where a lover beseeches her beloved to return; next the man sings, pining for the woman; finally, the lovers are united and sing together in harmony.

Li Song's hands return to the piano and he coaxes an attractive minor-key ballad from the faux ebony and ivory. I watch his fingers as Paige and Lauren jump right in and learn the woman's part; soon they have the melody down and are practicing their pronunciation.

Li Song turns to us and plays the man's part. Byron and I fumble through the lower register like cows in a crowded pasture.

Li Song stops. "Are you going to sing the notes?"

"We weren't?" Byron asks, as we glance at each other. Paige translates the lyrics for us, bit by bit: "*Return, my love, even if it never rains again, even if the flowers no longer open.*" She smiles. "Don't worry guys. Everyone will already know the song—they'll love it when you look like asses."

Li Song looks at us, and I swear he's winking at us. But perhaps I'm imagining it. He plays the tune again.

A WEEK LATER, despite two more practice sessions, Byron and I still cannot credibly sing *Aobao Xianghui*. On the morning of the big day, during a final practice, Li Song brings out his guitar. He plucks the melody while we *gwailo* sing it, and for a few moments it sounds slightly better than fingernails on a chalkboard. I try flattering him the way I do when we play together. "You play and sing so beautifully," I say. "Why don't you sing with us?"

He laughs a curt laugh. "Seriously?"

"Yes, you're our teacher. Why can't you go on stage with us?"

"Because I am Chinese."

At twilight, the four of us, the wedding singers, don what we individually deem to be appropriate attire, and we ride to the city's finest hotel, the China Hotel. We sashay through the main lobby, up a grand staircase, and into a cavernous banquet hall where chandeliers hang from forty-foot ceilings and illuminate a stage and two hundred white-clothed tables. Microphone squawks and the tinkle of silverware and porcelain echo off embroidered pink wallpaper. Lauren, who's wearing a sleek Western-style black dress, stands beside me. "I love the tie," she whispers, touching the navy and burgundy on my chest. "Such flair for fashion."

"I never thought I'd actually wear this," I say.

"At least we're not as nervous as the bride and groom. For us, this is just another stupid *gwailo* trick. They're getting married!"

"It's going to be me," I reply. "I'm going to break them up. I can hear the story now. 'She loved him…until she heard the bearded foreigner sing…she didn't know a man could sound so bad…'"

"You're not that bad. Well, yeah, I'll watch her during your solo."

"Solo?" I look at her.

Byron steps up beside us. He's in a white tunic and dark slacks, and he too is wearing the tie we got at the opening ceremony. "We're 'representing Peizheng,' right? The least we can do is pin the blame where it belongs."

Paige is decked out in a gorgeous, hand-tailored red qípáo. She chats with Principal Wu, then strolls over to us with two pieces of bad news.

First, our piano tape is lost. Wu-cat has dispatched his daughter Xiaofen on her bicycle to their apartment to fetch their own private karaoke tape of *Aobao Xianghui*. So we'll be entertaining the crowd with karaoke. Perhaps they lost the tape intentionally.

The other news is more troubling: This is Guangzhou's biggest wedding of the year. Not just one couple will be married tonight.

"Fifty couples?" cries Lauren.

"It finally makes sense," Byron sighs. "Li Song wasn't joking when he said this wedding was going to be on TV."

"This is ridiculous," says Lauren.

"Indeed it is," nods Paige sardonically.

Glasses of wine and beer appear in rows on long tables. Beside them stands an enormous upright greeting card, etched with a single red Chinese character. I don't recognize the word, so I look for it in my dictionary, but I can't find it there either. "It's a special character," Paige tells me, "made by pushing two of the same characters for 'happiness' next to each other. It means 'double happiness.' It's used to describe a happiness that comes from a union of different things, or a connection, or..." she chuckles, "marital bliss. Tonight there's going to be a lot of that."

Well-dressed older folks begin to trickle in and mingle by the drinks. I stare at this new character, thinking that we're that connection, and we're a part of that bliss: the foreign, the strange, the exotic—joined together with what here is normal and mundane to create union amid contrasts. *Why don't we feel honored?* We provide something else here too—the comic and the famous. We are white faces imported to make this event more impressive and prestigious.

"If we're going to bomb..." Byron steps away from us, towards the drinks. "We might as well get bombed."

I follow him and take a glass of beer. "We're singing a cappella in front of an entire nation." I laugh. "'Step right up! Enter the big top! Watch the crazy, big-nosed Americans sing our most treasured folk song!'"

"Wu-cat must owe someone a huge favor," Byron tosses his beer back and goes for a second. "He's pimping out his *gwailo.*"

Mrs. Yuan approaches us, giggling. "You are nervous? Maybe you will do very well."

I look at her coldly. "*Maybe* you know the song better than we do."

"I'm too old." She shakes her head, smoothing her dress.

Classical Western music swells overhead, and brides and grooms march in, two-by-two, in a parade of black tuxedos and red gowns. Television cameras pan the crowd. Byron and I find our assigned table, Lauren and Paige find theirs, and Mrs. Yuan sits with Wu-cat at a third. In a mixture of English and Mandarin, Byron and I introduce ourselves to the eight Chinese adults at our table. I explain what we'll be performing, and they look impressed and honored. They ask how old we are, and where we're from, but I'm soon too anxious to practice Mandarin for long. Byron and I partake liberally of the brandy presented to the table, and soon the polite conversation and clinking glass dissolve into a soft din in my ears. The first delicacy that arrives is chicken feet. I find myself eating boldly, pulling the taut, orange skin off with my teeth, as the Chinese do, and spitting the knuckles onto a white saucer. The dark brown cubes of congealed pig's blood arrive next, and I delve in, flavoring the slippery and silky texture liberally with hot red pepper paste, pushing morsels with my tongue into the roof of my mouth. Byron follows suit, and we toast and shoot more brandy.

Paige appears at my shoulder. "Xiaofen is back," she tells us. "She has *their* tape, a different tape from what we practiced with. But whatever. We come on at 8:30, as dinner is ending. We have to be waiting at 8:15 beside the stage. Lauren and I are over there." She points to a distant table. She glances at our shot glasses. "Hey, how much are you guys drinking?"

Dancing women in white feathers, then prancing green dragons, then screeching singers in leather frolic and spin on stage. My brain buzzes. 8:15 arrives, and our table sends us off with encouragement. We weave through the tables: brides, grooms, families, friends, and the sounds of celebration. "Time to shatter marriages," Lauren whispers, grabbing my arm as we climb the staircase to the stage. I stumble, and she looks at me and asks if I'm drunk. She glances over at Byron, who shrugs sheepishly. Actually my mind is focused like a laser, and a nervous pit in my stomach grows beneath the buzz. *Now.* A few yards in front of us the crescendo explodes: Shirtless men bang on drums, bird-like dancers pirouette to the booming rhythm, and fairies in white dresses twirl flaming batons. They all stop dead. Silence. Deafening applause.

Cameras flash and a million eyes are upon us. "Remember the *g* after the *d* at the chorus," Paige whispers. The music sounds strange. The girls start singing, and they sound great. Then it's our turn, but I don't know if I'm really singing, because the karaoke voice is loud. I throw my whole voice into it, just to hear myself. The lover runs away but then pines for his beloved, and Byron and I are alone, serenading the crowd: "*Nǐ naìxīn de děng dai wǒ!*" (Wait for me patiently!) We sing, and a ruddy face at the first table starts laughing, and I smile back for a moment, and it's just long enough for me to lose the melody, to beach us on some low note, posing as "*nǐ xīnshàngde rén*," (the one in your heart), promising to "*huílaí*" (return). Finally we stumble, stagger, re-unite, and Paige and Lauren sing with us, for us, and an ecstasy sweeps through my heart as we hold the long last note.

The room is applauding, and we bow. We stumble down the stairs, laughing and laughing—from the thrill and the panic and the release. "That," Lauren gasps, "was awesome!"

"We were awful!" I blurt.

"No—we pulled it off!" she cries.

"Very good!" exclaims Mrs. Yuan, approaching the foot of the stairs. "You're great singers! Hee-hee! I told you so!"

Thousands of eyes follow us back to our seats. This time I am the snake, the turtle soup, the exotic animal on display, the oddity served up for consumption.

CHAPTER 15

A Journey to Centuries Past

During the first days of his wandering life, in the first greedy whirl of regained freedom, Goldmund had to learn the homeless, timeless life of travelers. Obedient to no man, dependent only on weather and season, without a goal before them or a roof above them, owning nothing, open to every whim of fate, the homeless wanderers lead their childlike, brave, shabby existence. They are the sons of Adam, who was driven out of paradise.

—HERMAN HESSE, NARCISSUS & GOLDMUND

"YOU SAW them!" exclaims Wujia, shirtless, watching us pack. "The horses! My mother won't let us—ride them—so I watch them run—"

We tell him the story of our visit to the Great Wall, but his eyes glaze over, and the conversation feels like a one-way street. When we're finished packing, we bid him and Fujin a warm goodbye, grateful for their friendly, if tense, hospitality. I shoulder my backpack, and we step out a final time through the metal door, into the *hútòng*.

The Underground Dragon ferries us east, and we emerge under an ominous, gray sky that hangs over the train station like a hood. Colt has a train to catch, a journey to begin, and he's in a hurry. We embrace. We bless each other's next adventures. And then he's gone. Back to Guangzhou, back to California, back to a different kaleidoscope of skies, streets, and hurries. He's gone, and I feel the way I felt when I first arrived in Tiananmen Square, a wild delight and terror mingling in the bottom of my belly.

My feet carry me slowly away from the station, through the descending mist, on a path back to Tiananmen, past Mao and the five arches, up to Tiananmen Gate itself. At the walls of the Forbidden City, China's largest complex of classical palaces, I stop. Many nations have had royal palaces; China had a royal *city*, of which only emperors and their councilors and concubines were allowed to become citizens, and they formed a ruling class that lived for centuries and died in a perfect, proprietary world. Before me is the closed inner gate, where only once, in 1901, after mercilessly smashing the Boxer Rebellion, did *dà bízi* enter freely. I mercilessly ask first for a locals' ticket, but the rumpled old female half-hidden behind a dusty pane of glass and a collage of brochures shakes her head. When I call more Mandarin into the grate she straightens up a bit in her brown coat and orders me into the foreigners' line.

"No," I tell her. "I live in China. I teach English in Guangzhou."

"Sorry. You must purchase a *lǎowài* ticket," she uses the Mandarin version of *gwailo*. "It's 90元."

She plows on through my hesitation, shooting rapid-fire sentences I cannot follow. She finally glares at me. "The *other* line."

I see Colt climbing the scaffolding to take his glorious victorious photos; I see Lauren and Paige singing at the wedding; I see myself playing guitar at Peizheng. The trick was to be foreign. But now perhaps I can personify the other half of my current, hybrid existence, and be Chinese. "Look," I explain to her, enunciating the Mandarin slowly, correctly. "I have a work license. I am a teacher. I live in Guangzhou." I hand her my flimsy, rubber-backed, yes-you're-right-it-looks-fake work license, with its stapled-on passport photo.

She examines it. "A Foreign Friend. You purchase a *lǎowài* ticket."

"How can you charge me the Foreign Friends' price?" I ask. "I'm a poor teacher." I wouldn't fit any international definition of poor, but for my small stockpile of yuan savings to take me to Tiger Leaping Gorge or any distance into the hinterlands, I'll have to avoid the costly plight of Foreign Friends. "I'm very poor. I teach English at a high school. I am helping China to become great and proud. I'm uplifting the nation."

"I'm sorry. You must have a *residence permit*," she utters the magic words.

"Yes, of course. I do. Yes, here," I hand her the slip of paper.

"No," she shakes her head. "Sorry."

"But I work in China! Don't you wonder why I speak Mandarin so well? Here's a letter from my school. I must be charged normal Chinese prices."

She eyes a note I asked Mrs. Yuan to write for me. She flips it over, examines the immense red seal, and glares my way. In that moment I realize something about China: The more documents one has, the more insignias, stamps, seals, and official government imprimaturs, the more powerful you are. "Mm. OK," she eyes me coldly. "30元. Do you want the tape tour?"

I push the money to her, accept the ticket, and turn down the tape tour. With an outrageously sweet sense of triumph, I step across the threshold.

The forbidden world is colorless. Low, damp, pale heavens sag over courtyards of naked granite. I cross a broad courtyard, and the pallor is broken by the first of a dozen widely-spaced, red-walled palaces. The roofs are angled tiers of gold. Black metal lions glare at me as I pass into Longevity and Happiness Hall, where I examine museum-style display cases of ancient leather shoes, delicately-etched porcelain bowls, and jade statuettes of horses. My eyes linger on the curved handle of an ebony comb, and as I gaze at it, my mind wanders backward, into centuries past, to the luxurious estates of Cao Xueqin's classic of Chinese literature, *The Story of the Stone*, where courtesans and courtiers flirted at lavish feasts, hatched petty conspiracies, and led romantic lives without leaving their palaces. The year is 1420, and as I wander through a lush garden, Emperor Yongle stands before me; I watch the intelligent brutal emperor command a few of his million slaves to build, to his precise design, this endless complex of pleasure domes. A century later, when the slaves finish, Yongle's descendants in the Ming dynasty rule from here. Then it's 1664, and I watch Manchu marauders ride in and burn the palaces to the ground. The Manchus start the Qing dynasty and rebuild the royal city, and history cycles on. In 1911, Sun Yatsen brings down the Qing Dynasty, and then comes Mao Tse-tung, then Deng Xiaoping.

Snapping out of my reverie, I find myself perched on a large stone next to a pool, staring at a glistening leaf on a sapling tree. Two young women are giggling on the other side of the pool. "You said you liked lemon, so I did too—I was nervous!" One laughs and looks at me as I eavesdrop. Our eyes connect. She glances away, but then a minute later, she glances my way again. They soon leave. *I'm not a courtier right now.* I think back to my Peizheng companions and try to remember why I pushed them away, why I wondered around alone, why I ended up so solitary. The thought of Lu Lan brings a sweet tingle and a sudden knife of sadness.

I pull out the book, *Narcissus & Goldmund,* and fly away to young Goldmund's side in the cloister. He recovers physically, but the stirrings in his heart only deepen. Confused and disappointed with himself, longing to remain on the monastic path to holy perfection, he gives himself completely to Latin and Greek. Nevertheless, the artist's streak in his soul drives him elsewhere. In the older, colder Narcissus he finds an intellectual, a friend, a teacher, and a man who speaks of destiny and the difference between love of the good and real love of all that comprises God—good *and* bad, sin *and* perfection. Goldmund is captivated.

The ashen sky falls in fat drops, and I leave the forbidden world. Tiananmen Square is vast beneath the rain, crawling with pedal-powered tricycle taxis. I wave them off and continue on foot, threading through streams of people, relishing the scents: roasting plum sauce from a row of restaurants, floral perfumes cold from the air conditioning of fancy boutiques, aromas of pan-fried wheat and oil from street vendors operating big black ovens.

❀

IN THE afternoon, the sun finally blasts through the rain clouds vengefully, and I return to the train station, ready to leave. A different surly woman behind a different pane of glass says a variety of incomprehensible things before accepting my rainbow of *rénmínbì* and handing me a "hard sleeper" ticket to Xi'an. Minuscule printed characters confirm that I leave tomorrow, at 10 am.

A bus slaloms through seemingly every nook of the city, carelessly banging around sharp turns, and delivers me with a newly bruised elbow at another palace for emperors. The Summer Palace. It's a leafy paradise where, for centuries, royalty fled the city's estival heat. I'm just in time to see the brass poles of its gate swing shut. A woman locks it up. "Closed," she says, in English. I mumble protestations: that I rode all this way to see this place, that I leave tomorrow, that my guidebook obviously listed incorrect hours. To my utter surprise, she furtively waves me closer. "You can discover Small Gate." She points down the street.

I nod, partly understanding, partly trusting her gesture, and partly just following the silent intuition of my feet. The street plunges into a labyrinth of *hútòng*. After winding left and right, at a dead-end, through the branches of a prodigious willow tree, I spy the charcoal gray walls—and a small stone gate standing ajar! A man in a stationery shop spies on me. I smile at him, turn, and push through the branches.

Like Alice in Wonderland, I emerge into a vast dreamscape of hills, trees, brick paths, stone bridges, and a gorgeous lake. The sun, now slung low in the sky, blazes a brilliant trail of orange gold across the water. A giddy gratitude lifts me as I alight onto a path and follow it to a bridge that arches as steep as a semicircle over a finger of the lake. Gazing across the lake, I count seventeen silhouetted arches on a longer, classical bridge. The path takes me into a covered sidewalk whose wooden walls are emblazoned with paintings of battles and banquets. At the end of the walk, I come upon a tall man in a burgundy shirt who's selling postcards.

"No thanks," I shake my head.

"You speak Mandarin!" comes his response.

"A little. How's business?"

"Not too good," he says, glancing about. His postcards depict the lake and the graceful seventeen-arched bridge. He laughs at himself. "The place is closed. How do you like the Long Corridor?"

"The paintings are beautiful." I take in the battle scene on my left. "Are they old?"

"The Summer Palace is hundreds of years old—emperors built it and rebuilt it and visited often." He has a handsome face and an unusually straight jaw line; his Mandarin is crisp. "But the Long Corridor was whitewashed during the Cultural Revolution, and then the Red Guards destroyed it." He closes his eyes, as if he watched the destruction himself. "It was repainted just a few years ago. How long have you been in Beijing?" he asks, resuming a tour guide's tone of voice.

"Five days. I came to see the *huíguī*."

"Yes, everyone's happy," he nods.

"Are you happy?" I ask.

He pauses. "I don't really care. What does it do for anyone, for me and my family? Chinese people are poorer now—the government spent so much on huge gifts for the people of Hong Kong."

"Wow, most people say, 'It cleanses our dishonor white as snow,' and things like that."

"I don't always read the newspapers. They lie."

"Are there many people like you?"

"Of course. The newspaper lies, the government lies. There are so many corrupt officials and *huàidàn* (bad eggs). For China to be strong again, we must have an open government and the rule of law." His name is Pei, and he follows me around the lake, telling me stories about the places we pass. He points out the moored Boat of Purity and Ease, and tells me it's made of stone but, miraculously, floats like any other boat. The Qing empress decreed its construction in 1888, hosted banquets on it, and went on to redesign all the islands and courtyards to fit her own favorite fantasies. Pei turns back to politics and war, and runs me through the horrors China endured when carved up by the "Eight Colonizing Powers" during the Qing Dynasty. He recounts the misdeeds of the "merciless capitalists," seeming at times to expect an apology for America's part. I just listen, watching the hot pink sun die splendidly on the water.

I click my camera, letting it chop up and flatten the world around me. Pei tells me about the China Democratic Party, and I mention the party that the dissidents in Guangzhou told me about—the New Light Party—but he hasn't heard of it. "China needs more parties, more movements, more ideas," he nods. "More lawyers." He looks at me thoughtfully. "Hong Kong now needs more lawyers too."

We climb through scraggly bushes and trees to the park's highest point, and from there we take in all of Beijing—its monstrous, living, sprawling, smoking expansiveness; its glassy downtown buildings sprouting construction cranes; its countless, identical apartment buildings standing at attention like pink stone soldiers. The place *feels* political. Guangzhou can hardly be bothered as it hurtles full-speed-ahead toward economic miracles, but here ideas and ideologies are the coin of the realm, constantly changing hands and being rebranded, reborn, reformulated, reorganized. Communism's demise is ignored, finessed, or vigorously disproved while the rare, glorious victorious moments at which Pei scoffs dominate the news pages and television screens.

I buy three postcards and bid Pei goodbye.

"*Yī lù shūn fēng,*" he says. I recognize the phrase as the one Lu Lan taught me when she was in my arms. "May your road be smooth and your journey safe."

CHAPTER 16

The Scent of the Winter Plum Blossom

為學日益為道日損

Learning consists in daily accumulating,
The practice of the Tao consists in daily diminishing.
—*Tao Te Ching*, 48

I AWAKEN TO Morning Exercises. *"Yī, èr, sān, sì, wǔ..."* (One, two, three, four, five...). The loudspeaker counts off the numbers, and a thousand children on the athletic field shout them out as they do calisthenics. *It must be a weekday.* Sighing, I part the mosquito netting and place my feet in my flip-flops on the concrete floor. *Monday.* For breakfast I peel an Asian pear with a vegetable peeler, throwing shards of blotchy brown rind into our blue wastebasket. I devour the fruit's grainy white flesh. I have a pastry too, or a bite—until my tongue wanders into a dollop of the pungent red bean paste. It tastes like apple butter and refried pinto beans, and I can't stomach it yet.

A rare crystal-clear sky domes campus. Students smack ping-pong balls on the dozen concrete tables. CLICK-CLOCK! CLICK—they all stop to smile and wave at me. I wave back as I walk by on the concrete paving stones, passing through the palm trees. The five-story classroom towers stare down at me, and I can now read the propaganda emblazoned on Tower A. *Turn towards modernization, turn towards the world, turn towards tomorrow.* Li Song told me that in 1963

Peizheng assumed the politically correct name High School #57 and switched to training local government and military children. That was during the mania of the Cultural Revolution, and it probably helped the school escape the pillage endured by many "bourgeois" institutions. Today, the school is again called Peizheng, and it's again one of Guangzhou's more prestigious. The scattered ping-pong tables, bald basketball courts, unsanitary swimming pool, and hard dusty athletic field wouldn't amaze anyone in suburban America, but here amidst this cheek-by-jowl closeness and roaring construction, they're an oasis. In addition to the miracle of their existence is the miracle of their constant use: The school's 2,200 students continuously rotate in and out for athletics—and for the Morning Exercises that rouse me every day.

I stop for a moment beside the basketball courts, under one of three enormous grandfather banyan trees. Children are playing basketball with exuberance—running, jumping, and diving—and their gleeful cries and the sounds of bouncing balls echo off the high tile walls of the buildings. I close my eyes and just listen, savoring the noise and their energy. The bell rings, and there are shrieks and laughter coming from every direction. The students flee to class, taking their sounds with them. I hear footsteps dashing up the outdoor stairways, followed finally by silence. Monotonous recitation then spills down from above: Mandarin, in cadence, call and response, call and response. Words, silence, words. My mind wanders to somewhere I've never been: I'm on a grassy riverbank, and I'm walking and walking, searching for something, climbing a steep hillside behind a building, a sacred building, and I'm scrambling upwards, all for something I yearn to find at the top.

The clap of a tennis shoe on concrete yanks me back to Peizheng. My eyes open as a boy races past me, papers clutched in a fist, his footsteps pounding up the stairs.

I ascend the five flights of Classroom Tower C. Unlocking my room, I find my lectern still covered with the morning's delivery of dust. Sweeping my hand across it, I spot something I've somehow never noticed before: a small Chinese flag mounted above the chalk-board. It hangs there quietly in a glass frame, five yellow stars standing on a red field. Gazing at it, I imagine for a moment that I'm working as a government propagandist. I'd have a plan and a clear notion of what to teach, but probably no idea whether I were actually getting through. *It would be about the same!* I chuckle. An idea dawns on me, a feeling more than a thought. *I don't have to follow an agenda or push propaganda. I'm actually free.*

Awaiting my students' arrival, I open a letter that Mr. Chen handed to me as I left the dormitory. "Tony: Hello," it begins. The stationery is lemon yellow with cute pink frogs.

> I'm a student of yours in Tenth Grade. You have taught us for five weeks. In these days, I feel your way of teaching is not very outstanding. I'm sorry, just in my opinion. At the beginning of class, you usually poses a topic first. I think the knowledges you gave us were very useful, but most of those, we had learnt it before. And then you let us practise one by one. I think this part has spent too much time. After I had answered your questions, I have to wait and wait until the bell rang. I feel very depressed. So I have a propose. Can you please have a look at our English book we're learning first? And then combine our lessons to give us knowledges. Then you can take a sample for examination with some of us (not all of us). This way will make all of us become more interested in English. All above are just my opinion. I think you won't mind my view. If you don't approve of me, up to you!

Not very outstanding. I fold up the letter, which is clearly from one of my best students, maybe Iceboy. Suddenly I'm overcome with frustration, dumbfounded as to why Mrs. Yuan hasn't given us copies of their textbooks. I'm already struggling to maintain discipline and prevent the rowdy kids from running roughshod over my hopes for orderly classes. With order, I could get them all to speak, I could create captivating classes, and then, just maybe, I could stimulate their innate urge to learn. *Not very outstanding.* I stare out the window, contemplating the dilapidated skyline. The guitar was an idiotic idea. I was trying to shut them up by making them sing.

An idea drops into my brain like a basketball through a hoop. I let my prepared propaganda fall by the wayside, and I step to the board and chalk up a map of a traditional American town—city blocks, stoplights, a bank, a school, a supermarket.

"Hellloooo Toooo-ny!" cries Sandoh, streaking in a second early from the sweet crystalline morning. His classmates clatter into the rest of the seats, and those who have brought their tiny notebooks copy down the words I've scrawled on the board: *map, street, bank, post office, supermarket, intersection, directions.* I explain a new word—*skit*—and they listen attentively. I divide them into small groups and then point to the board. "OK, this is a map. You are in this town, by the bank, and one of you is lost. So the others help and give directions." I look quietly from face to face. "This is how you make a skit."

Pacing the room, eavesdropping to the best of my ability on each group's whispers, I let them get to it. Ten minutes pass. I call a group of five girls to go first, and they step to the front of the room.

"You are lost?" Jenny turns softly to Sucky.

Sucky stands beside her on the stage, and she nods, reticent.

Jenny continues: "For the supermarket, you go right. Take your left on the Oak Street, and then go on the right."

Alice adds: "Remember to walk... on the sidewalk."

"Thank you," says Sucky. Each girl speaks at least a few words.

Delighted, I motion them back to their seats, and I give them a score on the chalkboard: 9.0.

I point next to Sandoh, and he and four buddies, including the irrepressible David Beckham, rush on stage and act out their own version of a Hollywood action movie. The lost person, Beckham, happens to be packing an Uzi, and he holds up the bank and loudly guns down everyone else onstage. The boys hurl each other into desks for, perhaps, cinematic realism. I jump in to halt the violence, righting the desks, sending them back to their seats, sighing, realizing this was all a stupid idea. *I haven't gotten anywhere.*

"OK, yes, pretty similar to an American city," I finally say, writing 8.2 on the board. The boys protest in noisy unison; they're shocked. I explain that one boy never spoke. They nod with a silent and piercing recognition. *Maybe I have gotten somewhere.*

The other groups go, and they get it immediately. Suspense hangs in the air when I go to score each skit. I teach the lesson again in the afternoon and again the following day, and I find myself often just watching. They stand before their classmates and perform, improvise, and aim for a perfect ten. Many clearly adore performing, and competing and winning seem to capture everyone's attention.

O N W EDNESDAY afternoon, a time we don't have any classes, I describe the skits to Byron. He says I'm not really teaching them anything, but he congratulates me on finding something I like, and we just laugh together about our lives, the pace of this life, the rhythm of working a mere twelve hours a week. He's using his extra time to hone his skills authoring short stories. I'm playing enough guitar to hopefully be a rock star when I get home. We sit there on our golden plastic stools and sweat comfortably in the afternoon, discussing our dreams and savoring the slowness of the day. Our conversations are punctuated with whole minutes of silence, but we're soon on one of his favorite topics, philosophy.

"We all want to change the world in some way," he says. "The 'will to power' is strong. This is what Nietzsche talks about—an inherent drive to assert oneself, to resist oblivion, to achieve something, to change the world. This imperative is behind everything, driving everything, even when it's repressed."

I've begun reading an English translation of the *Tao Te Ching*, and I've been absorbing the way it encourages something else, letting our guidance come from nature's primal course rather than from our personal desire.

"That would be religion," says Byron.

"The opiate of the masses?" I smile.

"The opiate of the *people*," he corrects me. "The *masses*—that's American propaganda dehumanizing communism, dehumanizing

Marx." He pauses. "Think what you think, of course, you need to. We all need to. Go where your brain goes, and watch when you have the appetite for more. Our future is dictated by our past thoughts and experiences, and we have to follow it. What's truly rare is something new—those moments of clarity—since it's what we're most deeply scared of, what we avoid at all costs. As Dostoevsky, such a brilliant writer, said, 'Taking a new step, using a new word, is what people fear most.'"

"I don't want to be scared of anything," I counter slowly. "Not of what I don't know, not of these new, weird Chinese ideas. But I don't know if it's possible. I want to 'know thyself, know the other,' as Sun Tzu says. I want to learn about China, this place, without imitating anyone who's come before. I want to experience everything as directly as I can." I glance at him again, but he's looking out the window now, and he seems gone. Silence retakes the concrete room. The conversation is over. *We're both loners, introverts. We're people who can live together without ever really getting close.*

Some time later he speaks up. "Hey, are you interested in a barbecue?"

I look up from the *Tao Te Ching.*

"Yeah, a barbecue. Wang Yin invited me. She told me to invite you."

"Quiet? With glasses?"

"Shy," he nods. "She starts talking when you get to know her."

"She's in my Teacher Training." I teach a woman named Wang Yin in a weekly session Mrs. Yuan arranged to help the English teachers. Wang Yin is an attractive young teacher who never speaks, whose story is familiar to us both: Princeton-in-Asia sent interns here for the first time last year, and one of them dated her, led her to believe he would marry her, and then at the end of the year left—for good. It doesn't seem like a coincidence that this year we men live on campus, under lock and key. "So, now *you're* getting to know her?" I ask. "Like Zach 'got to know her' last year?"

"I know, I know," Byron chuckles. "We're not that close. She speaks enough English, I'm just asking her to teach me Mandarin."

"Right," I smile. "Not imitating anyone. Taking a new step is what we fear most."

"I'm—"

Our baby blue phone cries out from its perch on our TV. Most Chinese families didn't own phones until ten years ago; this is the first ring from ours. I pick up the receiver, and a stream of Cantonese flows into my ear.

"*Zhè shì shéi?*" I ask (Who is this?).

The voice gets louder. *How can you teach my child American songs? America wants to rule the world and turn our children into prostitutes and murderers.* Or perhaps he's saying: *This is the police—we heard what you said about forks being better than chopsticks. You will undergo twelve years of re-education in Qinghai province.* Or maybe it's: *How can you live in Canton and not understand Cantonese? You should leave our contry!*

"*Wǒ tīngbudǒng*" I say. (I don't understand).

"*Wei?*" And then a click.

I teach Byron a few statements to use if it rings again.

"When do I learn how to swear?" he asks.

"Ask Wang Yin to teach you," I smile.

"Shut up with that!" he laughs.

"Seriously, whenever I do, I guess. 'Dog farts' means bullshit."

"When do you use that?"

"In the market sometimes."

I do tag along, and we meet Wang Yin at the school gate. Quiet as ever, she leads us through residential streets and quiet alleys. We walk by four seated women who are laughing and loudly clacking red mahjong tiles on a table. We pass an old man cobbling shoes at a street-side "shop" that consists of him, a table, a chair, tools, leather, and a half dozen rubber soles. Two students bicycle by us, ringing their bells continuously. I realize something: I have yet to find a Guangzhou street that feels unsafe.

We knock on a metal door, and a young woman lets us into a sparsely furnished flat. The air pulses softly with Cantonese pop music, and the aroma is thick with the wafting aroma of green tea. Young adults stare at us, a few of whom I recognize as Peizheng teachers. Wang Yin leads us out back, into a courtyard where guests stand around circular grills, smoking, laughing, and turning iron skewers spiked through gray balls. The scents of charcoal, oyster sauce, and roasting meat lace the air. She introduces me to a Peizheng biology teacher named Lu Lan who is soon leading me off to a buffet table laden with smooth pink and gray golf-ball-sized meatballs, ears of corn, and piles of the alarmingly red sausages from the market. The way her long hair falls loosely past her shoulders makes her stand out in a way very few girls or women at Peizheng do—long hair has been out of fashion since the 1949 revolution. And for decades standing out hasn't been a good idea. I notice that a few others around us wear clothes in bright hues that are also only now becoming cool. Lu Lan hands me an ear of corn and two pinkish gray meatballs which she names "fish," showing me how to dip the spongy balls into a sour-smelling black sauce and impale them on a heavy iron skewer. She goes off to get drinks. Doubting I'll have the guts to eat them, I nevertheless take the skewered balls over to a spot at a grill and hold them over the flames. Thick smoke eagerly stings my eyes, and I'm squinting painfully when she brings back two glasses of steaming tea.

She wanders off again, and through tears I watch my fishball melt, stretch, yawn in half, and drool onto the hot coals, transmogrifying into a black belch of smoke. I leave it for dead and pierce a pinker ball, probably pork. The people at the next grill effortlessly cook multiple balls at once; they jabber in Cantonese, idly watching me, pointing at me. I feel like I'm deaf and dumb, onstage again, and I accept it this time.

"Put it further in," Lu Lan says in English, surprising me. "Over the fire." My eyeballs are raw and my knuckles singed, but I hold the ball lower and further over the grill. *Why is this so difficult?* Smiling, Lu Lan takes the skewer and shows me how to slip it into a groove on the lip of the grill, and then the weight is much easier to handle. She looks at me, and I meet her eye, and there's a pretty smoothness and angularity in her cheeks. The cooking pork smells sweet and we try out my halting Mandarin. She asks me whether I'm "*xíguàn* China," and this time I know what it means. "Yes," I reply flatly, "I am accustomed to life in China." I char several more items before finally sitting down on the concrete stairs beside her. The pork ball is tough and tastes awful. I was scared of undercooking it, so I seared the sauce off and the skin to leather. The yellow corn is only slightly burnt.

"Would you like to teach me English?" she enunciates, as I somehow swallow an entire crunchy fishball. She regards me with a shocked smile as I choke it down. Her slender neck reminds me of a swan. "If you'll teach me Mandarin," I finally reply, coughing.

"Ok." She points at my mouth and I pick a piece of corn from my teeth.

✿

THE NEXT day Lu Lan shows me into the Peizheng Biology Department office. "Mrs. Shen, Mrs. Jiang," she introduces me demurely to her colleagues. She takes me into an empty classroom, seats us at a black laboratory table, and avoids my eyes for several moments.

"Do you know about Moon Festival?" she finally asks in English.

"No, what happens? Does the moon change?"

"Yes, it becomes orange," she says. She laughs. "No. But watch out. It starts tomorrow night." And in a mix of Mandarin and English she tells me about the coming festivities. "In the daytime," she says, with my help, "families offer fruit and chicken and rice wine to the ancestors, and burn the incense. Mm, in the night," she continues, slightly giggling but apparently frustrated, "children are carrying around red *dēnglŏng*—" We pause to look it up. "—lanterns—people eat treats and mooncakes. My friends and I are making paper boats and float them on the lake. With candles." She pauses, and as she shifts our knees collide under the table. Her vocabulary in English is clearly larger than mine in Mandarin, but she speaks even more hesitantly than I do. "We used to write our desires on the little slips of paper and watch them float away."

"Did they come true—your desires?"

"Mm, I don't remember." She starts a lot of phrases with this 'mm.' "I don't think so," she laughs but continues more seriously. "Everyone likes to watch the moon. I guess that's the thing. Sometimes sweethearts, mm, exchange flowers." We move from topic to topic—my family, movies, whether girls should live at home before they're married, as she does—because every time the pesky language barrier blocks our path. That's the point, I remind myself, why I'm in this laboratory. The language barrier.

"*Xiàge xīngqīsì jiàn*" (See you next Thursday), I say at the end of the lesson, watching her smile in approval at one of my few correct phrases. We wish each other happy Moon Festival weekends and fold up our lists of new words, written mostly in her pretty handwriting. "*Zàijiàn*," she says goodbye curtly, like a teacher.

✿

T HE NEXT night it begins, Moon Festival, and I stroll through endless narrow streets. Giant red paper lanterns dangle from overburdened telephone poles, vendors hawk sweet poppy-seed mooncakes, and an aura of enchantment and magic permeates the air. Four of my students rush up to me, and with hands and mouths full of candied taro, juicy pomelo, and sweetened sticky rice, they wish me a happy festival. Down by the river, I discover a small park where families are placing miniature boats in a pond, and I imagine slips of paper inside carrying away their desires.

My three colleagues are in Hong Kong for the holiday weekend, and I am alone.

October 8

I've always longed for more space and time away from people. I've always assumed I'd finally figure my life out when I could be alone. But now, today, I felt loneliness, a weird, unusual sadness, an emptiness, a grayness at the edges of things. I don't miss my gwailo colleagues—I don't feel that close to them yet for some reason. And I love the expansiveness here, the time and space to just be in the present, to be simply alive. But this Guangzhou solitude, this anonymity in a crowded city, is strange and wildly complete. No one cares for 10,000 miles. This is the fear I felt as I fell ill—not just that I would die, but that no one would give a damn.

Maybe loneliness has been in me all along, and I've just never gone deep enough to feel it. I know I'm sensing things deeper here. There's something terrifying inside me that I don't yet understand and can't yet touch.

❁

L U L A N folds her legs under the chair beside me. Our noses are in an orange Chinese textbook. We're dissecting a passage on foreign students who complain about their housing, and she asks about my apartment, wondering if I want to move to a different one.

"*Bú shì lǐxiǎngde,*" (It's not perfect), I reply slowly. "But it's OK. I guess…." I switch to English. "I don't really care?"

"*Wǒ bú zài hu*" (I don't care), she instructs.

"*Wǒ bú zài hu,*" I repeat.

"Mm," she approves. "This phrase is common in Cantonese, too."

"*Wǒ bú zài hu,*" I say again.

"*Wú suǒ wèi,*" she adds, a wisp of hair falling from her ponytail. "Mm, this also means 'I don't care.'"

I repeat after her, and I ask in Mandarin whether either of the two is like "*méi guānxì,*" which I hear all the time. I enjoy forming the question and enunciating the falling and rising tones, and then watching her understand. She smiles and answers, and for the first time the language sounds beautiful, this Mandarin. It's an exquisite language, with delicate musical melodies in its tones and a strikingly raw simplicity to its grammar.

"'*Méi guānxì,*' means 'it doesn't matter,'" she explains. Looking at her, as my ears open to discern her words, I feel my eyes open to discern more too. She tells me why some Chinese call foreigners '*dà bízi,*' though I already know. "Is mine big?" I ask her, touching my nose, turning, laughing self-consciously. Hers is small, unobtrusive. Sitting there on her hands, quiet, thoughtful, briefly laughing at me, she seems too young to be a teacher.

We finish with the textbook, and she asks again about my complaints, as if there must be something that makes me unhappy. I talk about Mr. Chen, locked gates, concrete floors, and the poisonous, capricious water that shuns our house for days at a time.

"So everything is perfect!" she says.

"Yes," I smile. "*Lǐxiǎngde,*" I pronounce the word carefully. "Right?"

She nods. "You say it well. You want to get it just right, don't you?"

"When I hear other foreigners, I don't like their accent." I've been called a perfectionist, but, honestly, things can be *lǐxiǎngde*. It just takes time.

"Your accent is…" she pauses for effect, "getting better." She peppers me with questions about her new favorite topic—my singing performance at the wedding—since she didn't manage to see it on TV. She looks up a word in her dictionary "I was deprived. Can you sing it now?"

"No way!"

"Please?"

"I don't think I could sing it then. Do you know *Aobao Xianghui*?"

"Of course. It's a classic. It's about a Mongolian warrior waiting for his princess." She's disappointed when I still shake my head. She takes out packets of newspaper and unwraps what turn out to be traditional Dumpling Festival treats called *zòngzi*. Dank seaweed-smelling green corn leaves envelop a lump of hot sweet sticky rice that contains boiled hunks of pork and dried dates. I watch her eat delicately with her fingers, and I do my best to mimic her. "These were going to be your prize for singing," she shakes her head at me. "They're my favorites." As we eat she asks again about our place and about our air conditioner, which doesn't work. *Does she want to come see the place? Does she want to go somewhere more private?* It would be wrong. Romance, attraction—whatever this is—is wrong, illegal, miscegenation, trouble for foreigners, trouble for Princeton in Asia. *Or maybe it's legal, and just improper.* I don't know, but I don't invite her over. When it's time to say *zàijiàn*, I can't resist asking her something else. Does she like bowling, the hip new rage sweeping Guangzhou? She regards me for a moment, and answers a question I didn't ask. She's busy this weekend, she says. I translate this mentally. *She just wants a tutor.*

✿

T HE NEXT day Mr. Chen hands me another letter from a student. It's on the same stationery with the pink frogs.

I'm pleased you have received my letter last time. And I feel your way of teaching became better. Really. At least you had made the class lively and interesting. Maybe now also introduce American culture for us. Everything for example. You can broadcast music for us. And if you sing to us I think it's better. We'll be very pleased to hear you sing again. Or you may play games with us. And I'm very sorry to say that I feel you often betray signs of impatience when we can't understand you. I think your explain is clear. And you even use body language. But after all we are Chinese. And not all the Chinese are good at English and comprehend ability is strong. OK! Tell you something you don't know. Last week there were fewer students to have class with you. They didn't hate your teaching. They're just naughty. Some boys shirked school. All of us will stand by you whatever happens. Forever.

Your student, Keroppi (my penname).

An anonymous stamped envelope has been included, so I write back to Keroppi. "I focus on your oral English," I tell him or her. "That is why I am here. It will be helpful for all of you to practice informal situations. I want to ensure that all of you speak in class." Folding up the letter quickly as my students rush in, I realize I should take attendance. It's discouraging that they're skipping class, but I can't reformulate my lessons again.

The first skit begins, and they board the airplane: passengers, pilots, flight attendants. The plane takes off. The pilot thanks everyone for flying Peizheng Airlines. Suddenly two passengers, Sandoh and David Beckham, stand up, shout, and hijack the flight—and my lesson plan. I glare at them, wondering what is so irresistible about imitating Hollywood. I force them to redo their skit, but it's like pulling teeth, and when they finally do it, they take so long it robs other groups of time for theirs. At the bell, I dismiss everyone, and Sandoh darts out first, as always.

Ralph, a thin serious boy with a disheveled mess of black hair, stays behind. His classmates have clearly discovered grooming and the opposite sex, but he's a late bloomer. He stands rigidly before me, and he formally invites "the four American teachers" to his home for dinner.

❀

TWILIGHT DESCENDS, and three of us *dà bízi* meet Ralph on
a street near campus. He still wears his navy blue uniform as he
leads us along an avenue shaded by tall, anonymous apartment towers. Each tower holds a vertical grid of metal-cage balconies. Ralph
unlocks the metal front door of one of the towers and lets us into a
dingy lobby. A shaky elevator yanks us up to the tenth floor. His apartment is a small concrete place, slightly smaller than ours, but with a
magnificently decorated living room. Ralph introduces his mother
and father, pours tea from an elegant pot into six small glasses, then
sits attentively. To our astonishment, his father is Master Liang Feng, a
painter of some renown who has displayed work all over China, in the
U.S., and elsewhere.

Master Liang has a serene, intelligent face with small eyes and scant
rough hair. He leads us on a tour of the paintings on the walls, and
Byron admires them while Paige translates for us. His modern Chinese
scenes are harsh, remote landscapes in muted colors with rare microscopic human figures lost amid gigantic mountains, towering clouds,
and roaring rivers. In one painting, towering ash grey mountains command the entire canvas, and a few trees and a lonesome temple clinging to one ridge look like an imperious God's afterthought. In another,
a minuscule fisherman watches a colossal river gush down through the
rock walls of a canyon.

Master Liang seats us on an austere mahogany sofa, and thanks us
for coming. We apologize that Lauren had to stay home with a cold.
Byron asks whether his artistic freedom is ever affected by politics, and
Master Liang shakes his head. "Art is actually flourishing freely today.
There are so many excellent painters that many cannot display their
work, but today it's not because of the Communists." He pauses, then
smiles bitterly. "Chairman Mao was no supporter of the arts, but it was
he who spoke about conflicting styles of art and said, 'Let a hundred
flowers blossom.' This is finally happening. We are progressing... in
so many ways." In another of Master Liang's paintings I see a different

declaration. It depicts a distant train zipping over a high bridge in an immense mountain range, and it seems to urge China to hold onto her traditions, her heritage, her natural beauty, but also to strive for strength and modernization.

We kneel around a low black table for a Cantonese feast. Ralph's mother, who has been smiling in obvious pleasure during her husband's remarks, brings in steaming platters of seafood and fresh stir-fried greens. Her hair is cropped closely at her ears in a politically correct bob, and there is a slight stoop to her shoulders. Her days are spent at a restaurant on Shamian Island, we learn. She sits to eat last.

"How is Ralph doing in school?" Master Liang asks, turning to me. I glance over at Ralph, who sits with an impassive face beside his mother. He's an only child, I realize. The Liangs are a good, modern family.

"*Hěn hǎo,*" I reply directly to Master Liang, who smiles in surprise and appreciation, and glances at his wife. I go on in Mandarin. "Really well. Ralph is smart and he gets English quickly." This is gentle flattery: Ralph is well-behaved but often appears confused, as he did during today's airplane skits.

Master Liang speaks directly to me. "He has a marvelous opportunity with you here. Thank you." He says something else about kindness and travel, and I finally have to turn to Paige. Byron has been awaiting her translations all night, but I've been trying to understand on my own and cultivate a notion that my Mandarin is beyond flailing and perhaps nearly mediocre. In the market I construct simple questions, but I rarely understand the answers, and no one seems to grasp the notion of speaking slowly—it's either *on* or *off*, rapid-fire or stony silence. Saleswomen and taxi drivers hear my inquiries and unleash torrents of incomprehensible syllables. I understand Lu Lan's delightful, lucid enunciations, and to me she is unique.

Brushstroke. Original. Characteristic. I memorize the new words flying through the air. *Calligraphy* hangs on my tongue, and I repeat the word quietly to myself as Master Liang shows us some of his. Calligraphy is at least as revered an art form as painting, and his is stunning. His characters flow in a wild, cursive freehand known as the grass style, and as with his paintings, there's a vital boldness, a seem-ingly unassailable freedom in his hand. He insists on giving us gifts from his portfolio of poetry, and he offers me a poem on the wondrous winter plum blossom. Carefree yet sharp, the untamed, black tails of his strokes fly through the ancient, stoic lines.

> Without enduring bone-chilling cold,
> Could its delicate sweetness so assail the nose?

I accept the gift gratefully, reading the words over and over. *Only dedication brings sweet success. Only solitude brings strength. Only true suffering brings true happiness.* In a flash, I see a world far away, a blur, hurtling down a mountainside, something gargantuan and out of con-trol, rain and suffering and death. Fear and yet peace. I'm there, terri-fied, yet safe. I'm there, and I'm here, repeating the words of the poem, looking around the neat room, mystified and grateful. Master Liang is shaking our hands warmly, giving gifts to Byron and Paige, and bid-ding us goodbye.

His eyes meet mine and hold me there a moment as I thank him.

CHAPTER 17

Into the Belly

*The free man is he who does not fear
to go to the end of his thought.*
—LÉON BLUM

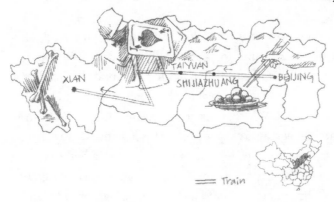

T HE TRAIN stretches along the platform like a twenty-jointed finger. Car 14 has a narrow aisle, windows on one side, and bunks full
of people on the other. I sidle down the aisle to Berth 8. I shrug off my
pack, stow it on the rack overhead, kick my shoes under the bottom
bunk, and without setting foot on the sticky floor, climb the ladder
into the cozy top bunk. I rotate in place, so that the overhead rack is
a foot from my nose, and I watch passengers board and pile luggage
onto the rack. My right shoulder is touching a wall, and on my left is
nothing: I could easily fall through the two-foot gap between the three
bunks of Berth 8 and the three bunks of Berth 7, and plummet eight
feet to the floor. Above me, a speaker crackles to life and drones news
and weather in Mandarin. The glorious *huíguī* remains the lead story.

One by one, five passengers—all men—stow their duffel bags and
sit below me on the bottom bunks. Together, the six bunks of Berths

7 and 8 become a small home, and I watch the men get to know each other by complaining about the heat, describing their destinations, and sharing cigarettes. They puff enough smoke to utterly engulf my two-foot space below the ceiling. Just as I start to cough, an air conditioner breathes its first. I paid extra for air conditioning because there were no bunks left in regular "hard sleeper." That's what this is: *hard sleeper.* Colt could only afford the rows of crowded benches in "hard seat" for what must have been 34 grueling hours of hell to Guangzhou. *Soft seat* is assigned seating, like on an airplane. *Soft sleeper* offers private rooms for the ruling class.

A jolt, and everything moves. Steel cries out against steel, and I hang my head off the bunk to peer out the window. The depots of Beijing roll slowly by, and a thrill catches in my throat. *I'm heading for the hinterlands of this empire. No going back now.* A man climbs onto the top bunk of Berth 7 and stares at me. A cigarette hangs from his lips, and a large pink scar is chiseled out of his left cheek. I say "*nǐ hǎo*" (hello), to snap his gaze. "*Nǐ hǎo,*" he nods, and after a hefty, thought-ful puff of smoke, he asks my nationality and age. He's a photographer with the China International Travel Service, he reveals proudly, and he explains to me the various parts of this vast country. "The coast is the face of China," he says. "It's rich, prosperous, and smiling." He carves a smile in the air with his finger. "Now you," he jabs his finger at me, "you're going into the countryside—the belly of China."

He says no more, and I peer again out the window. *The belly.* A cloy-ing chicken odor wafts up through the cigarette fumes. I climb down, slip my socked feet back into my shoes, and sit beside the four men on the bottom bunk. One of them, a baby-faced man in a blue polo shirt, is dealing cards onto the sticky red table. The other three men smile at me while shelling peanuts, stacking chicken bones, and organizing cards in their hands. "He speaks Mandarin!" calls the photographer from his top bunk. They all look at me expectantly.

"*Wǒ huì shuō yì diǎn,*" I say. I can speak a little.

"Not bad!" shoots the baby-faced dealer. "Are you accustomed to life in China?" He has deep dimples and an enormous forehead.

"Yes," I say, as always. "Well, a bit," I add. "It's very interesting." They ask about America, and I say it's also a big country, like China— "difficult to describe in a few words."

"Everyone has a car, right?" asks an older man, gray-haired at the ears.

"Most people." I nod. "Not everyone."

"The crime rate in America is very high," explains the dealer, picking a card from his hand. "Lots of—" he uses a word I don't know. He slaps the card down, and with that they take turns hurling cards violently onto the table, laughing with such genuine friendliness it's hard to believe they met barely thirty minutes ago. I watch but can't make sense of the game. The older man asks whether I like cards, and I nod but admit I don't know their game.

"It's easy," says a man in a garish plaid shirt and dotted tie, slamming the Nine of Diamonds onto the table. "You just match the suits." He shows me his cards to clarify, pointing at the Queen of Diamonds.

The fourth player, my sixth roommate, has hair that sticks up like a carrot and a nose reddened from embarrassment or a cold. He appears to win, and he tells me to play in his place. I refuse, but everyone insists—it's apparently inevitable. "Sit down," orders the dealer with a smile. "Take your cards."

It's my turn. I emphatically slap down the Jack of Spades, but the older man puts his hand on the card with a laugh. "Don't cheat like a Japanese!"

I get away with the Eight of Spades but make so many mistakes they lose interest in the game and focus on me. Where did I live at Peizheng? How much money did I make? Did I graduate from college? Do I have loans? Where's my wife? Do I believe Jesus will save me? The older man pours me tea, and I answer the questions. When I describe my recent stay in Beijing and complain about being barred from Tiananmen, they consider it strange that I even attempted to enter the square. "You're a foreigner," nods the dealer, as if to explain everything. I mention that since China now has a new ruler, it will hope to snatch Taiwan next. They agree that that's what all Chinese hope for. The older man shakes his head. "America wants to be the policeman of the world, but you shouldn't intrude in China's affairs. The world is beginning to listen to a new voice—the Chinese voice."

They offer me some sour dried fruit and vinegary green peppers, and I amaze them by successfully using chopsticks with my left hand. They gape at me eagerly, as if they've always heard Caucasians were freaks and now finally have an excuse to simply stare. I look down and explain that yes, indeed, I am left-handed. After I manage to pincer a dried lychee and pop it into my mouth, I reconfigure the chopsticks slightly for a stronger grip, and that's the opportunity the older man needs to jump in and teach me the right way: one stick must be stationary, and I must be able to click the ends together and make a sound. They all instruct me, out of both pity and, it seems, a desire to indoctrinate me with correct thought and action, as if something horrible might happen were someone needlessly different. All Chinese are right-handed, as if it were law, but after a bit of tinkering they seem satisfied with me, a lifetime leftie.

"You must be very intelligent," the mustached man finally nods.

"Well," I disagree. "I can't figure out this game."

"No, most Americans are left-handed," the dealer says.

The man with the garish tie eyes me. "In China, we have no gays or left-handed people because we have self-discipline." He speaks matter-of-factly, and I just let it go.

I get up to search for the bathroom, letting the sickly guy back to the table. As I walk down the aisle, I pass people similarly comfortable in each little six-bunk home: Every bottom bed now appears to be a communal couch, each small table between them a place for ashtrays, jars of yellow tea, playing cards, newspapers, spare socks, bananas, packets of pork jerky. Shoes are off, games are on, and the mood is mellow for the two-day haul to Xi'an. A red-uniformed stewardess is rolling a cart down the aisle, refilling each home's hot water thermos. The water's free, but she's asking a few yuan for soft drinks, shrimp crackers, and red plastic souvenirs. I shimmy around her cart and reach the end of the car, where I wrinkle my nose at the piercing stench of urine as I locate the bathroom. The metal room is alarmingly wet, and the toilet is a hole through which, from the right angle, the tracks can be seen speeding by. The floor sways, the wheels beneath me clatter. I hang my toilet paper on a nail, balance carefully, and squat.

Back in my bunk, the speaker, inches from my ear, blares about etiquette. "Railway guests must use proper trash receptacles..." Before the noise can drive me insane or the cigarette smoke asphyxiate me, I climb back down and claim one of two fold-out vinyl seats under the luggage rack. My companions apparently have no qualms about wantonly tossing their chicken bones, cigarette butts, and used tea leaves onto the floor. My eyes are drawn out the window. Miles of beautiful, green farmland sweep by, stretching endlessly. The lush farmland gives way gradually to a countryside painted with lighter greens and rawer beiges, then to still paler swaths of terrain that look taut and tired as if worked too hard. Civilization has picked and plowed this land continuously for over four millennia—the longest continuous civilization anywhere on earth. A small village rushes by in a blur of men squatting on a concrete platform; they're there, then gone. They squat, at every station, every park, every hospital, every event; there always seem to be more people than can be accommodated. It's as if China doesn't have enough chairs. Only here aboard this hard sleeper is there room. Here are the folks at the front of the line, China's new middle class, the ones who love Deng Xiaoping's reforms, the ones who are turning some meager profit, the ones who no longer need to farm the tired earth.

The farmland vanishes as we roll into the expansive metropolis of Shijiazhuang, the capital of Hebei Province. "Special fast" trains like this one stop only in the largest cities. The train slows, slows, and lurches to a halt. The dealer hops out, and I watch him wander across the spacious platform, beneath hammer-and-sickle banners, towards capitalist *gètǐhu* with their wagons of orange soda, noodle soup, and roasted chicken haunches. Meanwhile, beside me, the guy with the tie pushes up the window and buys a bowl of pork dumplings from a vendor. The torrid afternoon rushes in, smelling of sewage, and I marvel at how quickly I grow used to things—like air-conditioning, like the curt music of Mandarin, like solitude. I step down into the heat, to let it make me uncomfortable for a moment.

Six different people remind me to reboard, and I smile. *How could I feel alone when I have a billion parents?* I sit again on the foldout chair, and the sniffling, spiky-haired guy, who could use some parenting himself, takes the other chair as the train resumes its roll. We gaze together out the window, watching pinches of mountains slowly approach from the horizon. China is a geological staircase from the Pacific to the Himalaya, and we're ascending the first step, entering the province of Shanxi. We're climbing into the belly. Lumpy hills sprout up around us, and I feel my solitude again—this state defined by what it lacks. I feel the expansion of nothingness inside me, the expansion of new and unseen spaces to explore. Solitude is *now*. Through the window, the sun detonates on the ragged horizon, shooting rays of pink and orange through spiraling strands of cloud.

The stewardess comes by with a meal cart, and the ill man hands her 10元. She scoops food onto a paper plate: a mound of white rice, a dollop of fatty beef, a spoonful of chopped green stalks, a sprinkling of chili peppers, a bright red sausage and, right on top, a rubbery fried egg. It seems expensive, but I opt for the same. I've been getting by on bananas and crackers, and it's time for a real meal. As we chopstick the sustenance into our mouths, he asks in his rural accent about jobs in America. He's on his way out to Gansu province to do construction. Buildings, he explains, are built differently here in China. He goes on and on, and I soon grow tired of trying to understand his stream of words. My eyes, my ears, my brain—my whole being—suddenly feels exhausted. I make a final comment, trying not to be rude, and then I stop listening. I spit out a bone from the last bit of beef, choke down the undercooked rice, and toss the plate into the hanging garbage bag. At least the droning voice in the speaker will be happy with me.

Medieval Germany rises up before my mind's eye. I climb into my bunk and relax with *Narcissus & Goldmund*. The monk Narcissus teaches Goldmund about astrology, a forbidden subject in the cloister. He also teaches him science, which he calls "the determination to find differences." He explains who they are, as people, these two devout yet opposite men: Goldmund, who's still a boy, is ruled by the passionate senses, while Narcissus is ruled by arid reason; Goldmund is an artist, Narcissus a thinker. Shaking his head, Goldmund disagrees, denying all the differences. He wants to be strong, to be certain, to be holy, to be a monk.

I visit the bathroom to floss and brush, taking care to spit every drop back into the sink. My roommates bid me good-night, and I climb up top with my journal. I write about the *huíguī* and politics and war, about solitude and fatigue and friendliness, about trying to follow the conversations around me, and about the Chinese viewpoints that seem increasingly trite and shallow. On the stroke of ten, the car goes black. Mandatory bedtime. I unfold my cube of blankets, check my pouch and possessions, and stretch out. Like a lullaby, the bump-bump-clack-clack of the tracks rocks me to sleep.

CHAPTER 18

The New Light Party

治大國若烹小鮮

Ruling a large country is like cooking a small fish.

TAO TE CHING, 60

A CARROT SALESMAN in the market tells me the news. "Deng Xiaoping is dead." I continue haggling with him and tell him I don't believe him. He nods insistently. He finally packs up his produce, as others are doing around him. I move on to the scarred man selling incense. He confirms the impossible. The Paramount Leader, the emperor, the successor to Mao Tse-tung, is gone, whisked away by winter winds and some type of lung infection.

In China, emperors' deaths are traditionally accompanied by small events, like earthquakes, floods, and revolutions. Mao died in 1976, when a heaven-shaking earthquake near Beijing leveled entire cities, killing a quarter million people. Deng followed Mao and held the reins for twenty years. Until today. I rush home, tell Byron, and dial the American Consulate. A man answers with a calm voice and a mild Georgia twang. "It's true. Deng is dead. Things look OK now," he says. "Stay in touch. If there's trouble, it'll start in Beijing, and there'll be time to evacuate." Every television channel carries retrospectives on Deng's life: He was born in this quaint town in Sichuan Province; here he is as a young revolutionary worker in a French car factory; here he is with Mao, who called him "that little fellow." *Weren't Deng's market reforms great?* He reformed our socialist economy; he initiated free markets in

Shenzhen, Zhuhai, and Guangzhou; he said, "It doesn't matter if the cat is black or white, so long as it catches mice."

I wander back out onto the streets, my curiosity getting the better of me. Traffic is nonexistent. The market is now closed, as are government buildings. Many shops are already decorated with fresh flowers and portraits of Deng. I explore the alleys of the market all the way down to the river, wondering whether the displays of sympathy are genuine or simply politically correct.

The day goes by without an earthquake or a revolution, and then another day, and another, and suddenly it's Chinese New Year, the Year of the Ox. Firecrackers ring and roar in the reopened market, and a huge ox made of cardboard and dressed in confetti charges down the alley. A new era and a new year, all in a single week.

People are out everywhere again, and from various conversations I surmise that the displays are genuine: People really believe Deng brought prosperity to Guangzhou. Vendors repeatedly mention small bottles, and then I spot them—displayed on windowsills or arranged with photographs on staircases. Deng's given name, *Xiaoping*, sounds like the Mandarin for "little bottle," and so throughout his tumultuous political career people have displayed bottles to show support for him.

On TV, Communist Party Secretary Jiang Zemin dominates the screen with emotionless grimaces. Prime Minister Li Peng strides about as well. The banished but popular Zhao Ziyang is mentioned, and then the screen goes white. *Could the banished leaders who have been living in Hong Kong since the 1989 Tiananmen Square massacre try a power play? Could this powder keg blow?* We're left to speculate. Deng followed Mao, but not based on any imperial dynasty's coronation, let alone a popular election. There are new uncensored TV specials too. One declares China to be "the most Internet-ready country in the world"—without mentioning that almost no one owns a computer. Another declares that the people of Hong Kong are now, as strange as it sounds, even more "eager to be reunited with the Motherland"— despite the fact that political chaos is exactly what Hong Kongers fear when the British colony returns to China this coming summer.

Another program explores America's desire to rule the world and to subjugate China. "The U.S. has achieved its position through slavery and environmental pillage, and Chinese people must become strong and smart and protect the world from American hegemony," says one analyst. The evening news repeatedly plays footage—as if to scare people—of American military exercises and American tanks, fighter jets, and aircraft carriers arriving in Taiwan. Byron decides it's propaganda designed both to obscure political uncertainty among the leadership of the Communist Party and simultaneously to foment fear in order to rally the masses around the Party. For once I agree with him.

Second semester begins, and I tell my students about American culture, in the hope that at least these teenagers won't succumb to jingoism or hatred. With the leadership vacuum in Beijing and with the American military massing in the Taiwan Straits, war between this country and my own suddenly seems possible.

Or perhaps it is all just propaganda.

Heeding the unfamiliar call of duty, I lecture my first class. "In America, most high school students spend about one hour on homework each night. Some—"

"One hour?" Sandoh interrupts immediately, glancing around the classroom. "Americans are lazy." He grins into his desk. "And fat!"

"They are not lazy," I counter, trying to remember how much time my classmates at Milton High School really spent on schoolwork. "The children, not the teachers, move from room to room—like you do for my class. Think about it, they're like you. They're also in school and taking tests on math and English and science and—"

"Do they study Chinese?" Money asks.

"No, not too many. A lot of students study French and Spanish." I describe my high school classes and courses, but they're either not following me or they're just bored. I ask if they have any questions. They leap to life. It's the first instant I've truly thrown class open. They ask about everything they associate with America: The NBA, New York, Michael Jackson, superhero movies, Kobe Bryant. We move on to my hobbies, my hometown, my distant family, my nonexistent girlfriends.

Watching their appreciative smiles and searching eyes, their eagerness to ask and understand, I realize that they're not interested in the propaganda—they never were—and that I would never be able to control what they think anyway. My mind jumps back with them, to my own ninth grade days, and I devise a plan.

Using some Mandarin, I explain that they are to come up with a *huàtí* (topic)—something of their own choosing—and that they will work on it for two weeks and then make an oral presentation to the class. I watch them ponder for a few minutes. Walking from child to child, pad of paper in hand, I take down each student's *huàtí*. Hong Kong, the Eiffel Tower, a nearby village named Huadu, Tom Cruise, grandparents, the food of Sichuan Province, Julia Roberts, Star Wars, Australian wildlife, Italian soccer.

Alice, who started the year as Sally, looks up at me when I reach her desk. "*Rénquán.*"

My eyes widen. "Human rights?"

She nods. I write it down and move to the next student.

March 4

Jiang Zemin, humorless and conservative, tapped by Deng in 1989 to a top post, is apparently the new ruler of China. Things are returning to their rhythm. "Growth must continue. Modernization and industrialization must go forward." These are the government's priorities, according to the local news, which also praises the peaceful transition as evidence of China's political maturity.

In the brief upheaval, I saw some unexpected beauties in this Chinese way of life. It's striking that people aren't afraid of each other as much as Americans are. There's plenty of poverty, but there isn't the abject homeless misery that one finds in American cities, and so while the poor and rich live as next-door neighbors, people here have enough in common that internal justification for malevolence is needed, and it's rare. There's more materialism here than I expected, but still far less than back home. People seem content with little: A man with a street-side tool shop who sells a few screwdrivers a day seems perfectly at ease. People also seem more innocent, less jaded than Americans, and it's refreshing. But perhaps this is because they have less knowledge about the workings of their system, their government. It evokes Biblical questions about knowledge of good and evil—as if they who know become cynical, and ignorance is bliss. Americans make their own decisions about things, and at a significant level, they know. Chinese, on the other hand, are making only small decisions while the big ones come down from above, with the government playing the role of parent, or god. Many Chinese people seem to see their government the way Western fundamentalists see God: omnipotent, mysterious, never far from hand, and ready to dole out justice with wrath and impunity.

Standing under the Chinese flag, Raymond is the first to present his *huàtí*. He looks at me and then reads aloud from a piece of paper. His topic is wombats and kangaroos. "The diversity of Australia's wildlife is unpara-paralleled," he stumbles, probably plagiarizing an encyclopedia or tourist brochure. I give him a 'C' and tell everyone why. "You have to write and read only your own work."

Money goes next, describing two world cuisines. "Everyone knows, Chinese food is the most nutritious in the world, and American food is unhealthy and makes you fat. But I like hamburgers. And I like ice cream too, and ice cream was invented in China. But chocolate is American…" She goes on, and it's quite long, but to me not quite original enough for an A. B+.

Sandoh is at the lectern next, and he presents a fluent report on the history of basketball, chronicling in terse but surprisingly correct and numerous sentences the impact of Wilt Chamberlain, George Gervin, Michael Jordan, and Kobe Bryant. I give him an A, his first.

Alice reports on human rights, but her words sound like plagiarism, like she's reading blurbs straight from some party-line newspaper. "The illogical stance of those countries championing human rights is rooted in hypocrisy." She looks at me, and I realize that she's trying to please me, perhaps for an easy A. I sigh and give her a B-. George steps to the lectern, and he quietly asks to change his topic to Tibet. Sensitive to the enormous controversy around the "Two T's"—Tibet and Taiwan—I cautiously nod. He begins. "People of the Tibetan Autonomous Region are very happy today. They have modern things, like refrigerators and hospitals. They are free to progress with development and they are liberated from rule by religious people and superstitions..." Again, the party line. Still, his English is raw and sounds original. B+.

On Thursday, as Donkey is beginning his oration, there's a knock on the classroom door. Two young men in white polo shirts enter, eyeing me, toting a camera and a tape recorder. "Would you like to be in newspaper?" one asks. Unsure what to say, I welcome them in English and smile for the camera, quietly terrified. Donkey stumbles through a description of FC Barcelona, the Catalonian soccer club. I call on Adam next, and his presentation on computers is dull and short. The good students, the ones who are usually energetic, are energized, preening and performing with the reporters in the room; everyone else has fallen silent. The crop of *huàtí* is disappointing—most reports are mostly dull and too short—but Jrace's talk about New York City earns an A for her interesting coverage of the five boroughs. Iceboy earns the other A as he enthralls the classroom with a *huàtí* that's on everyone's mind: Hong Kong's imminent return to China. The big event is just three months away, and his monologue is optimistic but nuanced with rhetorical questions.

The reporters seem unable to comprehend anything being said, and they're already packing away their notepads and gear. They leave just as Iceboy finishes.

Jrace raises her hand, and she asks me what I think about Hong Kong.

I pause. "Chinese people should be proud to welcome Hong Kong back," I say. "It will be a reunion for so many people and families. It will be a time to celebrate."

Another hand goes up. A girl in glasses named Angle. "But what do you think will happen for the people of Hong Kong?"

"It's a mixed blessing," I acknowledge. "I don't know. But I think 'One Country, Two Systems' can work."

She isn't satisfied. "Will they have the same freedom in their newspapers?"

"Hopefully. That will depend on the journalists. You should buy a newspaper now and another in a year and compare them."

"You're going to be in the newspaper—you should buy one!" Donkey crows. "You're going to be famous!"

Everyone laughs and applauds, but I can't bring myself to smile.

❀

THE NEXT day, on my way out of our apartment, Mr. Chen hands me another anonymous missive. I stop in the park and take a seat on a bench by the river. The letter is on plainer stationery and the handwriting is different.

> About Hong Kong return to China, I remember that you said it was good for China, and you were happy. As a Chinese, I've the same feeling like you, because China will become stronger. But if I'm Hong Kong people, I won't feel especially happy and I will even feel worried. Today, HK's rich and strong can be seen by the whole world. It's initiated by English Government and HK people. But once China takes over, will it be still rich and strong? Maybe or may be not. In the future, I really want other foreign countries to try to take over Guangzhou to see if it will become rich and strong like HK under their jurisdiction. But I still hope China will become stronger and stronger year by year.

The boldness is impressive, and I save the note. Deng's death, along with the censored news from Hong Kong, which airs here but nowhere further into mainland China, has the local people thinking. Still, urging a foreign country to take over your city seems like a big step!

I slip the note in with my bookmark in *The Search for Modern China*, a scholarly tome that Byron lent to me. Opening the book, I read for several hours about this great country's horrendous, marvelous, revolutionary history. Sun Yatsen, the well-traveled scholar from Guangzhou, led a rebel army and brought down the Qing Dynasty in 1911, but the new government, founded and guided by a group called the *Kuómíntăng* (Nationalist Party), failed to satisfy the millions of peasants, laborers, merchants, and scholars. The *Gòngchăndăng* (Communist Party) grew rapidly, inspired by socialist and communist idealism sweeping the globe. These two rivals secured power in various parts of China's vast territory, and ideological differences between them led to overt power struggles and finally to civil war in the 1930s. A truce was called in 1937 when Japan invaded, but at the end of World War II in 1945, the civil war resumed. The Communists were led by Mao Tse-tung, and they finally won, capturing Beijing and declaring the People's Republic of China on October 1, 1949. Chiang Kai-shek's Nationalists fled to the island of Taiwan, and they set up a nation of their own there. Here on the mainland, Mao and the Communists set to work. They methodically conquered and unified virtually every land that had ever been called China, from Tibet to Manchuria. Then they went about redistributing land and modernizing the nation's agriculture and industry. Enthusiastic implementation of communism increased productivity and ignited an exhilarating sense of self-reliance among the people. Mao ordered still more aggressive steps to organize all of China into giant communes, but this plan largely failed, and horrendous famines swept the land.

Convinced of the inherent benefit of revolution, Mao launched something new: the Great Proletariat Cultural Revolution. It was 1966, and to cleanse people's minds of old traditions, false hopes and fears, and capitalist greed, he unleashed a fervent era that saw children dressed as "Red Guards" chastising and beating their own teachers, friends, and parents on account of perceived "bourgeois" or "capitalist" ideas found in, perhaps, a poem or an uncle's foreign acquaintances. Families were forcibly split up. Urban youth were dispatched en masse to rural work camps. The government pursued this puritanical path well into the 1970s, even as exchange with the West resumed and American President Richard Nixon visited.

Meanwhile, the island of Taiwan had grown into a capitalist powerhouse, partly because of American military and financial support. Most people on Taiwan viewed their island as a separate and independent nation, while Beijing continually referred to it as a renegade province and threatened to invade at any official use of the word "independence." Mao died in 1976, and the government immediately went in new directions with policy. Political freedoms were granted fitfully to the populace, and this led to mass movements to reform government, fight corruption, and deepen democracy. The largest of these movements were protests in the Spring of 1989 that brought millions of students and workers into city streets all across China, including at Beijing's Tiananmen Square. Deng Xiaoping, who had maneuvered into political preeminence, responded cruelly to the demonstrations in Tiananmen, calling in the army's most obedient regiments at dawn on June 4 to gun down all protestors who had not left the square.

I put the excellent book down for a moment, and I notice propaganda banners that weren't there last week. They make use of a special word—*huígui*—to refer to the handover of Hong Kong. I can decipher the phrases: "Celebrate the Glorious Victorious Return of Hong Kong!" "Long Live *One Country, Two Systems*!" After the international ignominy surrounding the 1989 Tiananmen Square protests, Beijing hailed as a major triumph its negotiations to win back the colony of Hong Kong from Great Britain.

My eyes drift to the far side of the river, where dozens of enormous billboards scream their advertisements, and it looks like capitalist propaganda facing off from one side of the water against communist propaganda on the other: China here, America there. One of the billboards features a gigantic replica of the unusual character I saw at the wedding—"double happiness"—and alongside the character, two people, one Chinese and one *gwailo*, are happily playing ping-pong. It's an ad for a sports equipment company, one of China's new large corporations, but the scene it depicts warms me. Looking at the image of harmony fills me with gratitude—to be here, to be strange and scared and lonely and lost, and yet to be learning constantly. My students and this country are learning from me and teaching me. The beauty of this almost overcomes me, and I feel a lump in my throat and a tear in my eye.

A middle-aged man in sunglasses is staring at me from another bench. He notices me notice him. "May I sit down?" he enunciates precisely. I nod, and he rises and sits beside me. He wants to know where I'm from, how old I am, how I got here, how long I've been in China.

He finally points to a grove of trees. "Will you come to our English Corner? We want to learn a little bit by a little bit."

I follow him and sit with his group of English enthusiasts. They're young and old, male and female, shy and assertive. One man wants to know how to phrase past tense questions in English. An intelligent-looking woman with glasses and mittens asks me about Wang Dan, the imprisoned leader of the 1989 protests who has appeared a lot lately on Pearl TV, a Hong Kong channel.

A blade of chilly evening slices through the afternoon as I ask her first what she thinks.

"He's a troublemaker," an earnest young man cuts in. "You can tell that he hates China." This is the official opinion.

"That may be true," I say.

"He was trying to do good, but he was selfish," the woman says.

Glancing furtively at passersby, like a teenager sharing a *Playboy* magazine, I hand them my book and open it to a page recounting Wang's role as a leader in the days the people took over Tiananmen Square. They puzzle through a few sentences, then flip a few pages further, to a spread of photographs—the masses of students in the square, the statue of the Goddess of Democracy, the tanks, the hundreds of slain bodies. Everyone knows about the widespread protests that year, but none of them knew about the military onslaught and machine gun massacres that rocked Beijing. I tell them what I know as they turn the pages. The young man urges skepticism. "American books are full of propaganda."

We discuss AIDS, which another man explains was created by the U.S. as a biological weapon, and terrorism, which occurs frequently because of "splittists" in China's western provinces. The woman informs me that the American media often lies to the world, and I look from eager face to eager face, wondering how we might ever agree on anything.

Lᴜ Lᴀɴ and I do agree on something. We both want to climb all seventeen tiers of the ancient pagoda at the Temple of the Six Banyan Trees. It's Guangzhou's most famous religious site, but few visitors attempt to climb the pagoda since the red floors and stone archways grow successively smaller as you ascend. Crisp, cool, sunny air—what passes for winter in Guangzhou—inspires us as we duck so low we're practically crawling. We emerge triumphantly on the top balcony. Catching our breath, we gaze out at the city, a sea of low metal roofs spreading in all directions, washing against tall, glassy towers in the distance.

This morning, noting the divine weather, she suggested we abandon the laboratory and pilgrimage here. The pagoda was constructed in 1097, during the Song Dynasty, she explains, but the temple itself was consecrated earlier, in the year 674, by Huineng, China's most famous Zen Buddhist. Her English suddenly amazes me—she seems almost fluent when she's relaxed. She looks comfortable and happy communicating with me. Her hair is in a ponytail and she's managed to keep a fashionable orange vest and white scarf clean.

"Are there many Buddhists in Guangzhou?" I ask.

"No, this is the only temple in the city. Are you Buddhist?"

"Yes," I say, and pause. "I'm Christian too."

"Mm, Americans *are* free!" She laughs.

"Or weird."

The wind chills the sweat on our necks as the city traffic below us honks, screeches, halts, and hurries. Standing on the millennium-old stones, we witness it all, enjoying the sensation of hovering in midair. Our eyes meet. "Yes, you are strange," she says. Her smile bends like lightning, and my mind races.

The monks far below us begin to chant. Igniting giant hanging coils of yellow incense, they're soon enshrouded and obscured by smoke. Tranquility emanates upward and outward from the tiny oasis. We sit on the rail, and Lu Lan tells me that several thousand years ago, five gods rode giant rams into a small fishing village. It's our myth, she tells me. The gods, disguised as homeless vagabonds, asked strangers for lodging in the village. They were taken in, fed, and treated well, so the gods proclaimed that the village would never know famine; it would become a great city, they said, a place of abundance and prosperity. In the millennia since, Guangzhou has known weal, woe, and revolution, but never the brutal famines so frequent across most of China. The City of Five Rams, as Guangzhou is thus called, is indeed a great city today, a place of plenty, a burgeoning economic powerhouse, a fabulous hub of trade. But the fact that this temple, while remarkable, is essentially Guangzhou's only one, seems to reveal how completely modernization is shredding the city's history and landmarks. Today's *Guǎngzhoūrén* clearly esteem economic improvement over their own cultural history. Marx denounced religion as the "opiate of the people," but Mao went considerably further and ordered the destruction of all religious establishments. Deng permitted a rebirth of Taoism, Buddhism, and Islam, but at a glacial pace, and adherents are still barred from joining the omnipotent Communist Party. We'll all soon see what Jiang Zemin has in mind, but whatever happens, today's *Guǎngzhoūrén* certainly seem more interested in taking advantage of Deng's market reforms to improve their lot financially than in reclaiming any of the city's annihilated spiritual traditions.

On the way out of the temple, Lu Lan shows me how to burn incense for good luck, to touch it to my head, to bow. We each burn two sticks. Outside the temple gates, we stop at a nearby jade market, and she helps me shop for a birthday gift for my sister. We pick a bracelet of fine, pale, smooth, pure jade, and she helps me bargain, first in Mandarin, then in Cantonese, cutting forty percent off the price.

She guides us next to one of Guangzhou's excellent seafood restaurants. With delight she orders two of her favorite local delicacies: prawns in scallions and a whole, steamed, black-scaled yellow croaker. While we await the food, she produces a copy of yesterday's *Ram City Evening Journal*. Splashed on page two is a picture of me, looking confused, and an article exploring in some detail my unfortunate inability to understand my students' Chinese. No one spoke a word of Chinese while the reporters were around, I tell Lu Lan in confusion.

The dishes arrive, lavishing our noses with sweet aromas. Before we dig in, as my mouth is literally watering, my tutor reveals a Chinese custom: A man, before eating a whole fish like this, should offer his girlfriend or fiancée the best bites from the fish's belly; otherwise he will prove selfish and a bad provider, and the girl's father, particularly, will look poorly upon him. She looks at the fish a moment, pointing with her chopsticks and eyeing me expectantly, teasing me to take the choicest bits of the salty white flesh. I laugh, refuse, insist she eat first, but finally I'm the one savoring the way the succulent belly flakes off the bones. She finally takes a bite too, closing her eyes, smiling at the delectable and buttery fish.

"I think they're criticizing your tutor," she says, gesturing to the newspaper, again wearing her teacher's smile. "They don't think you're learning to speak Chinese."

"Yes, it was poor reporting!"

"Why don't you pick a topic for us?"

"I don't know. Thank you? I want to thank you. For helping me." My sentences come short as we switch to Mandarin. "Today at the market. Buy that jade—how do you say it?—for my sister."

"*Shǒuzhuó*," she says. "Bracelet. *Shǒuzhuó*. You're welcome."

"You're very kind. To me. Of the one billion Chinese, you're my favorite so far."

"You don't have to thank me." Seeming embarrassed, she switches to English. "Would you like some tea?"

"I'm OK."

She knits her brow. "Does that mean you want some?"

"No."

"The word 'OK' is difficult."

"It usually means 'yes.' But 'I'm OK' means 'I want no changes.' So it means, 'no.'"

"OK." She laughs.

"You don't want any changes?" I ask in Mandarin. "Everything is perfect?"

"Nothing is ever completely perfect, right?" She looks at me.

Double Happiness

❁

WHAT PASSED for winter vanishes one morning, and spring embraces Guangzhou with fiery zeal. The sun rips through the haze, the half-built concrete buildings feel taller, and the odoriferous bodies in the streets seem to press in closer. I sweat just going a few blocks. Stepping into a shop in a row of bright yellow camera shops, I hold out my broken Chinon, explaining its malfunction in my best Mandarin. A curly-haired man unscrews the back and fiddles with it. "Can't fix it," he apologizes.

Deng is dead. China is about to reconquer Hong Kong. It's no time for a broken camera.

"You should buy a new one," he says. He obviously assumes I can buy whatever my heart desires. He tells me to go to Electronics City. I say I've never heard of Electronics City, and he offers to take me, but I know he's just being polite. He tells me his name, Yang Youwen, and, feeling confident, I introduce myself with my Chinese name, the name my Amherst professor gave me: "Bao Tongning." It's a phoneticized version of Tony Brasunas, flip-flopped so my last name is first. He nods appreciatively, and he insists a third time that I let him help me.

A few hours later, at twilight, Yang meets me at the front gate of the school. He's standing beside a small motorcycle and wearing a red helmet reminiscent of the thin plastic baseball helmets sold in the U.S. as souvenirs. "Just to be safe," he says, in crystalline Mandarin, opening the side-trunk and extracting a battered white helmet for me. It's even thinner than his, I notice, pinching the thing between my thumb and forefinger before I strap it on with a flimsy snap.

"Hold me here," he says, and indicates his waist. I climb on and instantly the bike darts from the curb, whipping my head back, and I lunge for a tight hold of him as we roar down a narrow alley in the warm evening. We barely miss a slowly turning bicycle-wagon carrying bundles of spinach. I'm slammed into his back as we screech to a stop at a red light. Back at full speed a moment later, we cruise beneath an underpass and turn onto a highway, ignoring all painted lines. We zip like a dragonfly in front of an onrushing truck and then back into an open lane, but there's another motorcycle merging into the lane too. We swerve back out, into the glare of the truck's headlights, then we swerve back in. My right knee grazes the other motorcyclist's left knee. My heart skips a beat, but we share the lane until we swerve onto a dark quiet alley and park outside a place called The Source of Three Treasures.

Inside, it's a restaurant and bar that resembles in an eerie way a spot back home in St. Louis—blond wood paneling, dim lighting, Budweiser ads on the walls. A waitress in a red and white checkered apron seats us, and Yang asks for Budweisers. He compliments me on my Mandarin before offering a few tips. "The word for *man* is made up of two characters: *field* and *strength*," he shows me, scribbling characters on his napkin. "See? See how you can remember that? *Peace* is a woman under a roof. See? It's simple," he continues, sipping a beer when they arrive. "*Good* is a woman holding a child."

"It's easier than in English," I nod at Yang's scrawlings. "But in English we have letters, and it's easy to know how a word sounds."

He disagrees and tells me about phonetic radicals, and while I miss bits of his rapid-fire dissertation, following for stretches feels almost as exhilarating as the motorcycle ride.

He turns next to politics, and speaks with passion. "Jiang Zemin can never be an emperor like Mao and Deng were," he explains. "He has no personality. Only Zhao Ziyang, who will return soon, hopefully, believes in something. He truly believes in democracy. He's the only honest leader we've had since Zhou Enlai. But it's always so difficult, even though the Communists are now scared and have to—"

"What are the Communists scared of?" I cut in, to slow him down.

"There are already nine political parties in China, not just one, and we are just waiting for free elections. My party, the New Light Party, has thousands of members in every province, but we have to wait a few more years. Then we will win. The people, the *lǎobǎixìng*, will support us and elect us." As the waitress brings another round, Yang neither hesitates nor lowers his voice. "There are so many people in the countryside who have nothing. Communism is nothing anymore. It's betraying the people it promises to support. No one believes in it."

"Guangzhou doesn't seem very communist."

"The Communists are so *fŭbài*" he wrinkles his nose in contempt. I reach for my dictionary: corrupt. "There isn't a single law that the politicians must obey," he goes on. "They just make laws for us. I had some faith in the government until there was a fire in my neighborhood. Everyone knew the man who started it, but his brother is high up in the Party, so the newspapers said it happened at a different time. They said that someone else—my neighbor's friend—started it because he wasn't as wealthy as the rest of us. And now he's in jail. Everyone knows it's a lie."

"Do most people believe the newspapers?"

"No," he says bitterly.

"In America we have more knowledge about how our government works, and the press is free of government control, so we trust our newspapers more."

"Yes," he says. "In the U.S., people have individual power, free opinion. You are young and quick and optimistic. There can be quick change. Here," he smiles ruefully, "we know change happens not in months but over centuries."

"We have problems with corruption too," I say. "People seem to buy power. I think people with wealth and power always want more wealth and power." I pause as he pops his second can of the expensive import. "What do you—what does the New Light Party say?"

"We need more democracy and less corruption," he declares, an abolitionist's conviction returning to his voice. "Real elections. And a free press. But corruption is the biggest problem. Once the people can vote, the corrupt leaders will have to clean up, or leave."

"So what do you do—protests? Rallies?"

"Yes, that's where you come in." He laughs good-naturedly as I watch the waitress watching us. "We have a meeting next Wednesday night, and I want you to come and talk to us about democracy."

"Me? What could I do?"

"Just tell us what you think. Or what Americans think...of China. Or even just listen. You don't have to do anything. It's safe. We meet at my friend's house and cook Mongolian hot pot."

"Are you scared that the police will find you?"

"There are good police and bad police," he says. "But anyone can live in fear. I don't. We didn't fight the Japanese and the civil war and the revolution for this!"

I contemplate his request as we chat, but eventually I suppress my curiosity and choose not to help organize an alternative Chinese political party. Getting caught could easily end my time in China—or worse. "I'm with you in spirit," I say, noticing Yang's disappointment. "I'll be educating people in the park."

We finally zip over to Electronics City. A gargantuan hybrid of glass-walled shopping malls and scruffy factory warehouses is rammed full of TVs, stereos, cellular phones, pagers, ovens, cameras, computers, and much more. Nighttime shoppers throng and haggle over the contraptions—brand-name factory extras, according to Yang—and communism seems like another lie, like a truly ancient myth. I pick out a very basic model, disappointing Yang once again. He recommends a few others, one of which has a nice red strap, a decent zoom lens, and a price tag that says 675元. He exchanges rapid-fire Cantonese with the salesman, bringing the price down, before turning to me with a smile. "*You* should be doing this." And with that, he winks at me and leaves, stepping next door to examine computer monitors.

"It's very nice," I tell the man in Mandarin. "But... actually it's too expensive." *Lu Lan pretended she didn't want that bracelet.* I turn to go. He calls after me, touching my shoulder, holding out his calculator. "480," reads the LED.

I shake my head. "250元," I offer.

"480元," he insists.

I shake my head.

The man nods angrily, repeating, "480元."

I take a deep breath but go no higher.

He looks me in the eye. "We're a family, we have to buy our rice."

They mention food when they bargain. Lu Lan kept talking about dinner. "We haven't even eaten yet," I try. "We're hungry. I can't spend all our money."

He comes down, bit by bit, to 400, I come up to 280, and we settle on 325. His anger evaporates into camaraderie, and he shows me how the camera's buttons work, how to load film, how to change batteries. He combs his hair with his hand happily. "Your Mandarin is good."

"No, you're flattering me!"

He smiles. "Flattering? You know about that? You're becoming Chinese!"

I laugh with him and then leave to find Yang.

The motorcycle whisks us back home, and I thank Yang warmly. In the fresh, warm night, I stay up late, reading the final chapters of *The Search for Modern China*, and feeling strange, disconcerted, almost dishonest that I ever tried to understand this country and its people without knowing their history. This society has wrought amazing transformations in barely a century. Yang and millions more like him must feel proud and bold, as if only their imaginations limit what they accomplish.

CHAPTER 19

The Faces of the Emperor's Soldier

*Interpretations of this vast and elusive country
will always change according to the angle of one's vision
and the flash of time of one's observation.*

—JONATHAN SPENCE, AUTHOR OF
THE SEARCH FOR MODERN CHINA

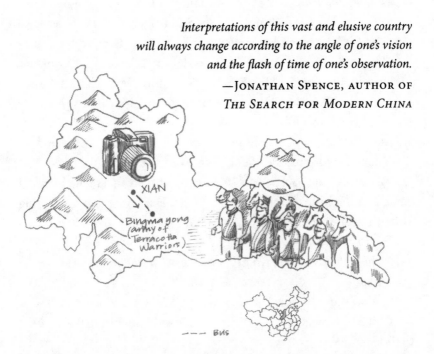

RAYS OF sunshine glint on the puddles that pockmark the train station's enormous plaza. The place is mobbed with the eternally chairless, and innumerable wretched families simply flop beside their suitcases. I navigate between the puddles. Two men approach me. "*Bīngmǎyǒng?*" they ask aggressively. "*Bīngmǎyǒng?*"

Qin Shihuang, China's first emperor, unified the Chinese states and constructed the nation's first capital here in 221 BC. The region had already been the cradle of Chinese civilization, but it was then, when the city sprouted glorious palaces, theaters, and parks, that it became the world's grandest city, with an unrivaled population of two million. Marco Polo had seen nothing like Xi'an in Europe.

Today, I can't figure out what these pushy and unglamorously-dressed men are saying until I read a cardboard placard that one is holding. There's a single phrase in a dozen languages: *Terracotta Soldiers*. I follow one of them into a maze of parked white minibuses, realizing *Bīngmǎyǒng* is the Chinese name for the world-famous earthen warriors that guard Emperor Qin Shihuang's tomb. "We leave in ten minutes," the man says, glancing at his watch. He indicates a rusty minibus, and I step over to it, look inside, and ask the driver whether his bus actually arrives at the *Bīngmǎyǒng*. The driver nods and the bus is numbered 39, as the *LP* suggests it might be. I break my vow, pay him, and climb inside.

I take an empty seat behind a schoolgirl in a pink blouse and an older man, apparently her father, who wears a charcoal blazer. As I wedge my big blue backpack beside me, the girl steals a glance at me. I smile, but she whips her head back around. Her father says something to her, and she turns back to me. "Hello?" she asks.

"Hello," I reply.

"Where do you come from?" she asks, with the uninflected ring of recitation.

I follow the textbook: "I am from the USA." I introduce myself with my Chinese name, Bao Tongning, and say in Mandarin that I'm going to the Bīngmǎyǒng.

"You speak Chinese!" exclaims the girl. Her name is Wen, and her pleasant and patient father is Mr. Zhu, who tells me they're from the capital of Shanxi province, Taiyuan, a city that must be huge and that I surely passed through on the train. I feel stupid since I've never heard of it.

The bus rumbles out of the lot, down several streets, and onto a rural highway. We wend our way through the Wei River valley, a fertile summer countryside of tall yellow grasses and bushy persimmon trees. Xi'an marked the start of the ancient Silk Road, which went all the way to Constantinople, and while political power has moved eastward over the millennia, this city continues to serve today as China's gateway to its wild west.

A farmer leads goats along a path between wheat fields; a boy in a straw hat pushes a wooden wheelbarrow alongside the highway. We stop where a woman sells persimmons in piles. Two farmers climb aboard with four cages of chickens, cramming all the clucking poultry into the aisle. One cage rattles against my knee, and I hold my bag beside the wire so the chickens don't peck my leg.

Gazing at the rolling hills, my mind journeys away, backward, replowing and reharvesting my entire year in Guangzhou: the skits, the mass wedding, the hospital. Lu Lan's clever smile warms my heart, and I remember for a moment so much more: the snake restaurant, the market, the duties of the "*gwailo* available," and then the quickness of the others' departure. Paige took off the day after school ended without intention for further time in China; Lauren departed a few days later to spend her summer at home before returning to Asia to work in Vietnam with Save the Children; Byron is probably still trying to line up another year in China, but he too went home for the summer. It's just me here now, sliding alone into the belly, insatiably curious or incurably foolish or chosen by fate perhaps never to leave.

A pink concrete promenade of hotels, restaurants, and gift shops—the customary welcome mat to China's biggest tourist draws—rolls into view. Hordes of Chinese tourists wear the same gray pants, white shirts, and plastic yellow tourist visors, and they photograph everything; behind them, tour buses armed with loudspeakers blare different identifying songs so the masses can find the right bus home. When we park, Little Wen approaches, and she personally requests my company. I remember that I was worried about being bored amid mass tourism at the Great Wall, and that that place far exceeded my expectations. I nod to her, and we stroll through the crowds, under the sun. The Zhus ask me whether American students respect their teachers as much as Chinese students do. I regale them with tales of my rambunctious teenagers—the misbehavior of the bad ones, the diligent attention of the few good ones, the joyful way so many sang folk songs. Wen laughs at my story about skits as her father buys us piping-hot baked yams from a metal cart.

I manage to be Chinese enough for a Chinese ticket, and the three of us pass through a fortress of turnstiles and enter an enormous building. Grand twin doors usher us into a small lobby where a television proclaims the *Bīngmǎyǒng* the eighth wonder of the world. We push through another pair of double doors and finally enter the cavernous vault itself. Cool, musty-tasting air floods our faces. The tomb could hold a 747. Instead, thousands of pottery warriors stand in rigid regiments, separated by low walls of packed earth. In the silent rows of muscular infantry, stern cavalry, ready crossbowmen, and stately charioteers, each face is unique; all are poised to attack and await only the eternal emperor's word. This amazing necropolis was discovered just twenty-five years ago, when two peasants digging a well struck the archaeological find of the century. Today, it remains an ongoing excavation: The soil has not been completely removed from the statues, and we have to walk on bridges suspended ten feet above the helmeted heads. Mr. Zhu and Wen walk ahead of me, and I let myself fall back. I am standing before the massive imperial army, fighting for my life, conquering my fear, going on adrenaline, stabbing, being stabbed, slaying, being slain. Death by the sword.

Or would I again side with the imperial army?

Placards report that the generals' bronze swords, which have been treated against rust, remain sharp after two thousand years. A lead alloy in the archers' arrowheads remains lethal today. Nonetheless these heroes haven't been able to fend off the relentless looting by archeologists or thieves, and unfortunately the hangar is *so* gigantic that from up here on the walkways everything seems miniature: the drawn swords, the linked limestone armor, the loose-hanging bootstraps, the fierce eyebrows. Warlike tension creases every face, but their supposedly unique expressions are inscrutable, and it's frustrating—to be so close and yet so far.

"*Bāo Lǎoshī,*" I hear Wen's soft voice calling me. It's the first time

I've ever been honorably addressed, and it melts me. "We're going to another tomb now. Do you want to come?" she asks.

"I think I'll stay in this tomb a little longer," I finally say. She nods, and we wave goodbye.

Suddenly I sense my aloneness acutely. Lu Lan's face appears before me again and cuts a hollowness somewhere in the middle of my chest. I tour the tomb, stopping, leaning over the rail at one spot and locking eyes with a terracotta swashbuckler in the front row of infantry. He smirks at me, or it's my imagination. Not far from the soldier's drawn sword, a live security guard, who actually is smiling at me, mimics a camera with his fingers. Photography is prohibited—the *LP* even reports film confiscation and fines—so he may be bored and trying to tempt me into a confrontation. He'll have to do better, I decide. As a representative of the modern repressive regime, with thousands of his ancestors arrayed behind him, he's not going to goad me easily. The gawky young man persists, following me, nodding at me. "*Lǎowài*," he whispers. I take out my camera and point to it. He nods.

"Take a picture?" I whisper. "You'll take my film?"

He shakes his head, and then walks off.

I gaze at the faces of the soldiers for guidance, but what I see is myself. I've already chosen this path. I've already given in. By stepping onto that plane to Hong Kong, then that train into China, I let go long ago. And now that I've moistened my lips, I sense it is a cup from which I am to drink deeply, whether its taste turns sweet or bitter.

I snap forbidden photos of the stone-cold regiments: the faces, the carefully carved swords, the arrowheads. I frame a close-up of the smirking soldier whose face now looks determined, confident, and loyal. *I'll take him with me.*

I can't ignore how this artificial eyesight, this cutting the world into squares, captures just the outline of the experience. Yet it locks something in and ties something to me, a personal conquest and a personal surrender. I return the camera to its bag and step out of the dark vault, into the unfolding yellow sunlight.

CHAPTER 20

Yī Lù Shūn Fēng

花有重開日人無再少年

Flowers bloom many times,
Man is young but once.
—CHINESE PROVERB

A NARROW FLIGHT of stairs takes us up into a cool, dark room. There are rows of sofas instead of the bucket seats I expected. We sit beside each other just as the screen comes to life. I whisper to her that this is my first Chinese movie. She promises that the next one will actually be Chinese, and she smiles at me. Suddenly before us is an exotic world: Los Angeles, highways, explosions, car chases, and white men scowling and shooting up the city while chasing a scantily-clad blonde. Jackie Chan leaps and runs and darts, serendipitously saving her again and again. Behind me, the young Chinese faces are illuminated by screen flicker, and to them this is America: licentious, free-wheeling, violent, sexy, criminal. I feel strange and embarrassed, taking it all in, and I find myself sliding away from Lu Lan. I watch her jaw clench mildly as a car explodes. She glances at me, then back at the screen.

Jackie flashes his grin a final time, roars off in a red convertible, and the credits roll.

Lu Lan and I emerge into sweltering heat and a sea of people on Beijing Street. Beijing Street. After the Communists "liberated" cities around China in the 1940s, many important avenues were renamed.

Central streets became People's Road or Liberation Avenue, while cities' best boulevards often became Beijing Street. Guangzhou's most fashionable shopping avenue is indeed called Beijing Street, and this is probably why Lu Lan brought me here. She gazes at the high heels and jade jewelry displayed behind panes of glass. I marvel at the boutiques' foreign-sounding, yet domestic brand names: Bossini, Harbour Type, Calf Land.

There are no white men shooting the place up. In fact I don't see any other white men at all, even thought it's a Saturday and the boulevard is overrun with people and movement is difficult. We spot rural folks here and there, and almost step on a group from an ethnic minority wearing hand-woven robes and ornate silver necklaces who have formed a permanent encampment on a corner; they're seated on a blanket, and all generations are represented—from an infant girl to a toothless grandma. They are selling jewelry and giant machetes and large desiccated red things.

"Those are dried animal parts," Lu Lan informs me. "Including the genitalia."

"Really?" I ask. "You're so smart," I smile. "You should be a teacher."

"My classes are boring these days," she sighs, as we move on. "Biology is just the same thing over and over."

"Stop by English class sometime," I suggest. "We're doing oral reports. Everyone talks about something different. You know—basketball, ice cream, New York."

"Mm, I'll sneak in one day as a student." She smiles slyly. "Ice cream sounds good." She stops at a stand and buys two vanilla ice cream sundaes, handing one to me. I thank her and switch to Mandarin to please her, asking what she thinks about Jiang Zemin.

"I'm not really into politics. But Americans are, aren't they?" she replies in English.

The sundae is full of odd gelatin balls that taste like saccharine and tofu and are hard to swallow. As I contemplate what to do with them, she leads us into a sparkling new building, all black trim and mirrors, a shopping mall nearly as tight, crowded, and chaotic as Electronics City.

"Wang Yin and I bought a radio there together," she points out a store. "Mm, you have to strike deals in Cantonese, like at the Jade Market. You get bad deals if you speak Mandarin."

"If we had more time," I try Mandarin again. "You could teach me. Cantonese."

She nods and looks away, eying some skirts in a boutique. I stop in a bookstore for a road atlas of China, but they're out of atlases, or don't carry them—I can never tell. I can't decide whether to celebrate the coming Hong Kong handover in Beijing, which will surely be a huge bash, or in Hong Kong itself, where things might be more, well, circumspect. Lu Lan recommends Beijing, since I've already been to Hong Kong. She hasn't been to either place. We pass the first guitar shop I've seen in the city, and she points at the shop and asks whether I like guitar music. I strum the air with my fingers. "I like to play."

"So my students tell me," she smiles at me.

I nod. "I play in class. I'm no good, but at least they laugh!"

"No," she looks at me wickedly. "You play at night. The girls on the second floor of your dormitory told me. They can't sleep."

I stop. "I've kept them awake all year, and they're too polite to tell me?"

She laughs, swallowing a lump of ice cream, glancing at me with a sort of chastising indulgence, as if to say: *What can we expect from you, foreigner?* She asks in Mandarin about the mass wedding again, saying that it's finally, definitely, absolutely time right now to sing the song for her. I'm still embarrassed. "You can hum it," she suggests.

"What?"

"*Hēnghēng.*" She pulls her hair into a ponytail and teaches me the word by purring through her lips. I hum a few notes, and she claps her hands and hums along with me. "That's it!" We stand there in the mall and hum the whole song, all the way to the finale where the lovers reunite.

"Let's go to the park," she says. "It's a better day to be outside." So we hail a cab and swerve through the downtown streets. Over his shoulder, the cabby asks me questions—where am I from, am I married, why am I in China—and I feel nervous answering in front of Lu Lan, but I perform well enough for her to touch my shoulder and say, "Good." A swarm of children invade the road, and the driver has to zigzag across two lanes and veer around a parked car. But wheelbarrows of melons are there, and we barely miss hitting an old woman. A policeman atop a red platform shows us a white-gloved palm, and the cabby slams the brakes. It's a human stoplight. "So, how do you like Jiang Zemin?" I ask.

"What do I care?" the cabby shrugs, as the white glove waves us through. "At least he's better than Li Peng," he refers to the aging Premier.

"Do you like Zhao Ziyang?" I ask about Yang Youwen's favorite.

"You foreigners are funny!" He emits a laugh that indicates we don't need to talk anymore.

We get out at Culture Park, an expanse of dust and trampled grass that features a skating rink, an amphitheater, and the hulking Guangdong Provincial Aquarium. Lu Lan and I spot two teenagers making out in a knoll between landscaped bushes. "That's the problem," I say, pointing to them, "if you live with your parents until you're married!"

She laughs, but in fact it's the first kiss I've seen anywhere in China. Even husbands and wives rarely seem to touch in public. "Mm, let's take that ride," Lu Lan points to a bright red merry-go-round bristling with shrieking children.

I point past it, to an enormous wriggling black box. "What's that?"

She shrugs and starts walking towards it. "Let's see." I follow, and we're soon poised before a ticket window. "You buy the tickets," she says, pushing me forward. "It's your assignment."

I step up to the window and ask for *liǎng zhāng piào* (two tickets), but it's the wrong window—or the wrong ride—and I get flustered and lose my place in line. Lu Lan laughs at me, sweetly and genuinely, and I realize everyone here laughs at me, but with her I feel like I get the joke. I can laugh too. She translates the bigger words and sends me back to the window until I succeed. Gently sweating under the hazy sky, we stand in line, watching the dark box swallow twenty of the bodies ahead of us, close its mouth, and toss to and fro. She falls quiet as I look at her, then past her, past the big black box, and into the sky. I can see a vast green meadow with a river, and I'm talking through a tornado of emotions—love and confusion and joy and a strange, heavy regret.

Darkness engulfs us. We sit in the front row of what seems to be an extra-wide bus. I'm beside her, and the doors close like jaws, snapping away every tendril of light. A giant screen flashes where the windshield would be, and suddenly we're on the moon, surrounded by starry outer space. The wheels start to roll, and we bounce along, over moon boulders. There's a giant hole on the surface of the moon, and we drive up to it and plunge down into it, and our bus transforms into a spaceship and we fly, darting and banking hard to avoid asteroids. We bump into the walls of the moon shaft, and everyone is truly thrown about. There are no seatbelts of any kind, and I hold on to protect myself, but Lu Lan and I are beside each other, our shoulders colliding. A jolt throws us as we enter Earth's atmosphere, and her left arm smacks into my chest. We're both giddy from the fitful massage of the bumps and jolts and moments of smooth flight, and then we swoop low and dive into the ocean.

Under the sun again, we're laughing together, and I tell myself that even make-believe is better in China. My arm is around her shoulder for a moment as we stumble away from the box and find our balance.

May 27

Time is short if I'm going to fall in love! I think it feels the same to her. Beneath all the fun and butterflies and flickering delights, she knows it can't happen—falling in love across these boundaries of blood and oceans and skin and origins. I can't let myself feel otherwise anymore, it just seems wrong. I'm drawn to her, but she would get in the way of everything, my journeys, my adventures. I'd have to leave her and hurt her. It's better for us to control our feelings.

When I'm not with her, I'm strolling through this insanely busy city, through parks and markets and alleys and department stores, and everything is fascinating, bristling with the familiar and the weird, and the more I learn, the less I seem to know—about China, about myself, about anything. I don't remember how the old me answered any of these questions. I'm lonely, too, but I know some part of me craved from the beginning to experience all of this alone. Solitude itself may be the only immutable, existential, international truth.

Double Happiness

Right now I am on my outdoor hallway. The hot morning air seeps into my pores, and life ambles by comfortably. It's another day without power or water, another now, unchanging, and as I read and write and play guitar, I realize this time could be as good as any I'll ever have. With a few weeks remaining in this semester, Mrs. Yuan just now asked for my grades for last semester. So maybe my job matters in some small way. Not that I'm here to give out grades. I'm here to teach what I can and learn what I can, to be curious and to be useful.

✿

Lu Lan and I navigate a maze of booths selling video games, toy musical instruments, high-heeled shoes, portable music players, sweaters decorated with fashionable foreign flags. There's a banner for Tiger Beer, and pretty young women in white gowns are giving away cups of it to help young people acquire the taste. The practice is distasteful, but the flavor of the beer is fine. Lu Lan grimaces and disagrees, so we pour out the yellow frothiness right there on the street and stroll on. We haven't seen each other in over a week, and now she's about to leave to visit her grandparents. I'll be gone when she returns. But this street fair is exciting to her—something new—and she insisted we come. She guides me into shop after tiny shop jammed floor-to-ceiling with outlandish women's apparel: vinyl vests, purple corduroy, knee-high white boots. She holds up a glossy orange blouse over her T-shirt and spins in place. I nod and ask her to spin again, and she smiles and indulges my desire. The words "Panda brte fiendip" are inexplicably emblazoned on it. In fact, all the merchandise seems to feature Roman script—not advertising, or even coherent phrases, just letters or misspelled words in random strings. Letters are hip here these days, much as Americans seem to get tattoos of Chinese characters they don't understand.

I can't find an atlas, but I spot a black belt pouch for securing my valuables while on the road. The words "Dry Ice" are stenciled on it. Lu Lan makes fun of it, trying the zipper and the Velcro pocket, evaluating my fashion acumen. "You're going to hold your money in *this*?" She looks incredulous. I tell her I'll wear it on my belt, and she decides that at least my braided leather belt is cool. A thrill runs through me as she touches my hip.

Outside, a drizzle begins to fall, and we stop into a restaurant called Do Me Fried Chicken, which makes me laugh, and I have to explain to her why. "It's a way in English to say 'make love to me.'" She gives me an embarrassed smile as a clerk in a referee-like, green-striped uniform brings our order. I work on a plate of flavorless spaghetti, and she munches on her favorite, fried chicken, which colors her lips bright orange.

She frowns at my chest. "You're not buttoned." A middle button in my plaid shirt has come undone. "Do I have to teach you everything?" she gnaws on her chicken. "At least your Chinese is improving."

"Really?" I ask, fixing the button.

"Slowly." She smiles.

"Your English is improving rapidly," I observe. "I must be the better teacher."

"Or you have the better student."

She tells me about her family and her grandparents, explaining they would never come to a restaurant like this, and I finally learn that she's twenty-three, a year older than I am. She has an older sister who works as a nurse, but Lu Lan is the smart one, she explains happily, the one who aced the *dàkǎo*, China's gigantic test that dwarfs the SAT in both length and life significance. These days many of my students are locked away studying for the feared *dàkǎo*. Lu Lan says she's proud of being a teacher, and I know it's half true—she's already bored of biology—but what I'm thinking is that her Mandarin is the most beautiful I ever hear, that I'll miss it, and that I'll miss not only that.

Outside, the rain falls harder, and we hide under an awning. I can't bring myself to say anything. *Do you feel the same thrill I do when we accidentally touch? Do you know this is both perfect and impossible?* But I have to hope that she hears what I don't say, and before I can fail at speaking, she pulls a gift out of her bag. It's a small blue travel atlas of China. "Mm, time for your final lesson," she says, meeting my eye, then looking away. She teaches me the words, "*Yī lù shūn fēng*." It's a phrase that literally means "one road favorable winds," and that is used, she explains, to wish someone happy travels, luck, and safety. She pronounces it for me several times.

"*Yī lù shūn fēng,*" I say.

She smiles, pleased. "*Yī lù shūn fēng.*"

"*Yī lù shūn fēng,*" I whisper, and I lean over, by her ear, and kiss her on the cheek, and her smile bends and freezes. I take her into my arms.

"*Yī lù shūn fēng,*" she says, hugging me back for an instant.

And then she's gone.

CHAPTER 21

A Victory in the Cradle of Civilization

莊周夢蝶

I dreamt I was a butterfly.

—TAOIST PHILOSOPHER CHUANG TZU

MIST SWEEPS in over the hills of the Wei River valley, devouring the yellow sunlight. A harsh rain begins to pelt the highway. As the bus returns to Xi'an, the rain strengthens and lightens repeatedly, like a whimsical emperor. A downpour punishes the stone flatness of the train station plaza. I push off the bus and elbow through the crowds, hurrying around the puddles. "*Dìtú, dìtú!*" An old woman pushes right up to me, waving shiny pink maps of this city. I pull out a 5元 note and trade her for one. Night is coming, and I need to find somewhere to sleep, to eat, to rest. A long queue of red taxicabs flip on headlights. The driving rain forces me beneath an awning where a dozen others stare through the downpour. Construction workers on the far side of the street labor on, digging trenches, throwing shovelfuls of mud onto the sidewalk; past them, beyond their mounds of mud, chic clothing boutiques radiate bright light and glamour through the grayness.

I open the *LP* to the Xi'an page, and I find the Victory Hotel, which it labels "cheap and basic." The rain softens, and I pull my tan cap low, hoist my pack, and head into the city, guided by my new map. The fancy boutiques smell sweet but are smaller and less splendid than Beijing's. Past them, a row of small groceries offer fresh mangos, oranges, pears, and kiwis scrupulously arranged on tables and under protective sheets of plastic. I press on, passing a crowded KFC with its imposing red and white splendor and big-nosed logo. A twilight sun emerges tentatively, chasing the gray into alleys, and I slow down a bit, relaxing, taking in this new city. A group of young women approach, and pass me. "Hello!" one says boldly, turning to face me just after they pass. They all giggle and shove each other forward. "Wait a minute," I say in Mandarin, and that freezes them in their tracks. I step towards them, and I ask about the Victory Hotel. The girl who said hello, who wears the latest fashions—blue jeans and a pink Bossini T-shirt—tells me which bus to catch and where, and we lock eyes for a second. I only understand part of her words, but her body draws me like a magnet, suddenly, startling me. Something about the smoothness of her skin. She smiles. I thank her. They all wave and dash off.

The bus shows up just where she said it would. I push aboard, and the mass of passengers squeeze me against a window. I watch the city pass, thinking of the girl, counting the months it's been since I've had even a kiss. A real kiss. Before my eyes fly rows of computer stores, restaurants, bookshops, laundries, apothecaries—all a bit shabbier than those in Guangzhou and Beijing, a bit dustier, a bit emptier, a bit dirtier. Everything, that is, except for the gleaming red *huíguī* banners everywhere that "Celebrate the Glorious Victorious…"

The monstrous city walls rise before us, in good repair, as if expecting a Mongol invasion. We cruise through a tall stone arch, and on the other side lies an identical city. I alight soon at the Victory. The word lingers on my lips. *Victory.* I pay for a dingy, threadbare chamber, drop my backpack, and close the door to the world. *Victory!* Joy charges through my veins. *I'm here, alone, in the middle of China. I did it.* My eyes close as I clench my fists and celebrate.

Some time later—minutes or hours—I awake without remembering falling asleep. I'm on a bed. It's night. I see a face, a man, staring at me from the other bed. I bolt upright. "Who are you?" I ask.

He just smiles.

I ask again, in Mandarin. He lunges forward, reaching for a filthy rucksack on the floor. His long hair swings behind his ears as he pulls out a bottle, pries it open, and pours brown liquid into a small glass. He comes closer, holding the shot glass out to me so close that I can smell the pungent liquor. I shake my head. He grins, gives a full-chested cackle, and throws it down himself. Refocusing his eyes on me, he pours another shot. I refuse again, but manage, "*Gānbēi.*" He nods in appreciation. The writing on the bottle looks Korean—there are more circles than in Chinese script. I realize the room was cheap because I only paid for one bed.

Ravenous, I hurry out for food. Raindrops glisten on neon signs and on the leaves of the trees that line the narrow street. There's a row of open-front diners, and a woman stir-fries green peppers, garlic, rice, and red bits of pork in a huge black wok over an open fire. The aroma is heady, almost titillating, and I follow my nose past her and sit at one of her six round tables. A different young woman brings me a hot glass of tea and giggles awkwardly, kniting her brow, looking at me the way a patient teacher does a student. I stammer about a chicken dish with exotic ingredients. Other diners simply stare. I finally give up and point at the wok, and she laughs and offers an English word: "OK."

I flip open my red dictionary. *Cashews, bones, discount, directions.* I write and pronounce the characters, over and over. The fried rice arrives, its garlicky steaminess rising into my face and cleansing my pores like an herbal exorcism. I hold my chopsticks strongly in my left hand. And just like my journey, the delicious greasy concoction slides "into the belly."

Contented, walking home slowly, I get the feeling the city is just as anxious as Guangzhou, albeit less ready, to advance, to bring Westernization, to rush industrialization, to "realize the Four Modernizations." *The Four Modernizations* was a propaganda phrase during the Revolution that referred to four enormous nation-transforming projects in science, industry, agriculture, and the military. More recently, in 1978, political dissident Wei Jingsheng suggested a fifth modernization was necessary: democracy. He received fifteen years in prison for his insight.

The wild-eyed Korean pours hot water from our room's red thermos into his tea mug. He mixes liquor and tea as I slip under my bed's musty blanket. I open *Narcissus & Goldmund,* and in the cloister Narcissus's pronouncements prove correct: Goldmund's inner battle between his heart and mind reaches a torturous climax when he hikes deep into the woods and comes upon a beautiful woman. They make love for hours, and the teenage Goldmund awakens to a world of senses. He leaves the cloister that very night to join her in a moon-drenched meadow, and days later, when she leaves him, he strikes off into the wondrous countryside alone.

CHAPTER 22

A Bottle that Pours
Any Beverage You Imagine

學如逆水行舟 不進則退

Learning is like rowing upstream:
Not to advance is to drop back.

—CHINESE PROVERB

"CHOCOLATE MILK!" Adam holds up an imaginary bottle of the exotic dairy product. He pours from the bottle into an imaginary glass, smiles, turns in profile, and chugs it down.

He pretends to hand the bottle to the boy next to him, Arky, who mimes pouring from the bottle into another glass. "Jianlibao!" he grins. "I *love* Jianlibao!" He simulates quaffing gulp after gulp of the popular lemon soft drink.

I can barely believe how quiet and focused the two boys are today.

Arky hands the bottle to Iceboy, who stands at the center of the stage. Iceboy pours himself a tall beverage. "Champagne," he announces, with a debonair glance, sipping at a tall slender glass. He holds his imaginary bottle up to the crowd. "This bottle, my friends, can pour any beverage you imagine. It's amazing. It's incredible. And it can be yours if you send me…" he thinks a moment. "Thirty million dollars!"

The whole class laughs in appreciation. They get it, completely. I step to the board and chalk *10.0.*

The next group performs a commercial for a camera that captures smells. They improvise, learning from the students who took the stage before them, obviously absorbing new words and new ideas. It's happening too fast for me to direct, too fast for me to fear—*they're learning!* I just nod and take it all in.

✿

THE NEXT week, I place my students "In an Amusement Park." The first two groups offer dull performances, and after one boy mumbles—and even *I* am bored—I add something to the theme. "Looking for a Lost Friend at an Amusement Park." It's better, it engages the next group, and the hour is immediately more fun, more fertile. I glance happily at my beloved ceiling fans in the middle of a skit. *I can make it all up as I go along.* Sandoh runs out the door gleefully to make the point that he's lost, and I watch the fear of chaos and of pitched battle rise in me—there it is—and it passes. *Now.* He runs back in, full of mock delight, embracing the others in his group and letting out a grateful sigh.

That afternoon, with only two weeks remaining in the school year, I receive a third letter from Keroppi.

> After I read your letter, I knowed your purpose of teaching. And I thought over all of your lessons again. I think from the beginning to now, every lesson is useful. Some of my advices in the past were wrong! I felt very sorry and I beg your pardon. You not only give us knowledges but also make all of us happy. Really. We believe you. You're a good teacher. I gave you so many childish ideas and you don't mind. I think you have room in your heart to consider kindly even your enemies. I thank you and beg your pardon again. Why I didn't come to talk to you? I'm not afraid. Just I'm good at writing. This may be the last letter I write to you. At last, I wish you happy every day, every hour, every minute, every second!

With a tickle of pride, I fold up the letter and place it in my wallet alongside my *rénmínbì*.

✿

THE FOLLOWING week brings the year near its close. I give exams. I sit on the breezy hallway outside my classroom and call my students out one by one. Jenny, the nervous-looking girl who was the first waitress in our tiny café all those months ago, is first again, and she sits opposite me. I speak very slowly. "What...is... spaghetti?"

Her eyes shift blankly.

"Remember...?" I ask. "Food?"

"Um, yeah." She blinks again.

"Spaghetti?" I repeat. She shakes her head. I try "Airport?" Nothing. "We spent one class on skits about an airport?" Nothing. "Skit?" She giggles the giggle that signifies embarrassment. I sigh and mark down a C-.

I duck my head back into the classroom to call the next student. Sandoh crouches on one leg on his chair, clapping his hands, and Leon and David Beckham are goading him on in Cantonese. I remind myself that I don't need to control everything, that it's just a few of them, the "naughty" ones Keroppi wrote about. The grades I'm giving might count, or maybe my students know that they won't. "These are your final exams!" I remind them anyway. "You should study now while you wait."

I call Money next. She's one of my best ninth graders. "What is spaghetti?" I ask.

"Spaghetti is a type of noodle," she answers. She knows *skit, directions, commercial,* and a dozen other words. Money. I get to mark an *A* next to a name.

Sandoh is next. "It's a food from France," he says, about spaghetti. He knows *roller coaster* and *kiss,* but not *dessert.* Far smarter than he looks, he was probably bored all year. I mark down a *B.*

There are a few other pleasant surprises, too, but I give only two more A's in this class, fewer than I did for the oral reports. Most of them have learned little, but a few actually *have* taken something in, and for a moment this blows my mind—that I helped someone, that

I got through somewhere, that I played a part in increasing human knowledge. Perhaps I could have done more. I could have learned earlier to trust my intuition, to follow my instincts, to make it all up as I go along. May I become—I pray to the ceiling fans—one of the students who has learned.

June 24

It's my birthday, and everything is over, everyone is gone. I'm 23. Three days of steady rain have washed the city clean. Yes, it's raining on my birthday, the day I bought my train ticket to embark on this unscheduled dream into the heart of China. Maybe rain bodes ill, maybe I'll meet my maker on the road, maybe this birthday will be my last. Maybe Chinese superstitions are rubbing off on me.

For now, the end. I recall like it was yesterday strolling through this campus, thinking, "46 weeks to go." Yes, they have gone, and now they end, rushing to a close as I knew they would—yes, the way childhood did and college did. I knew it, I expected it, yet still it's amazing—nothing ever happens in the future or the past, only now. It's a mystery I can't solve.

And so I leave. To trek across this "Middle Kingdom." I don't know how many months it will be; I don't have a ticket home; the only certainty I have is Beijing, the huíguī, and Colt, who left two months ago for Inner Mongolia. I don't have a way to leave behind my fears of being abandoned, confused, killed. But I recognize them now. They are the same fears that paralyzed me when I arrived here last August. For this new journey nothing is set up in advance. No one is waiting for me. I'm blind, solitary, ignorant, free.

CHAPTER 23

The Sun Is Redder in the West

Taking a new step,
uttering a new word,
is what people fear most.
—FYODOR DOSTOEVSKY

I ARISE LATE, feeling dirty. The Korean is still sleeping, so I leave quietly, taking my pants, shorts, T-shirts, and socks—everything I'm not wearing—down the street to a laundry shop.

No washing machines await me inside. A large, round-shouldered man looks up as I enter. I start with the obvious. "Do you wash clothes?" He points to a counter, and I unload my items. A smaller man emerges, takes my pile to a hanging scale, and grins at me. His frayed, white work shirt is rolled up his thin arms and he asks the usual questions; to make it interesting I have him guess.

"Oh, are you American?"

"Right," I reply, surprised. "How did you know?"

"I can usually tell Americans," he says. "But actually, you're not acting so American. You're not telling me what to do."

"What do Americans tell you to do?"

"America thinks it's in charge of the world. Americans all think they're so important," he tosses a yellow ticket on the counter. "You think you're always right."

"American and Chinese people should learn from each other," I reply carefully. "We can help each other."

"When America talks about something, about a problem in the world," he pushes my clothes into a garbage bag, "you expect to be the only voice, but more and more there is another voice in the world: the Chinese voice."

This is now the third time I've heard about the Chinese voice. Perhaps there was a national news story about it. "Chinese people should always be able to say whatever they want." I struggle with the grammar. "You know what I'm scared of?"

"Hm?"

"I'm scared that China feels that its recent past has been difficult, that it hasn't looked like a strong country. Your culture has five thousand years of history, and so Chinese people are proud. Soon you might feel that China should—"

"War?"

I nod, surprised again. "War is often how a country shows its—"

"Are you afraid of war?" he interrupts. "I'm not afraid of war. I'm not afraid to die!"

"Well, I—"

"China is ready to stand up. We're not afraid of America. Don't tell us what to do!"

"Are you a peaceful man?"

"Peace?" He slams his fist down on the counter. "Has America given China peace? Has Japan? I'm not afraid to die!" he booms. "Are you?"

"Many, many people will die in a war," I fire back, but I mispronounce the word *die*.

"There's no fear in here!" he gestures to his chest.

I glance around for the other man, but he's gone. I edge towards the door. "China and America should help each—"

"America better not forget!" He comes around the counter after me. He swings an arm at me—and pats my shoulder. "Don't forget what I said," he laughs. "Don't forget."

"OK," I stammer. "Thank you." I stumble outside. "And don't you forget this," the bigger man finally reappears. "*Bàoxiào*," he says, but I don't know what that means—*America should respect China?* He repeats himself, but I just nod as he grabs my arm and pushes a piece of paper into my palm. *"Zhè shì gěi nǐ ná qù bàoxiāo de."*

I hike off down the sidewalk, shaking my head. *I better get out of here—preferably before the war.* I glance at the piece of paper and look up *bàoxiāo.* The man didn't want me to forget my receipt.

MOST OF China's mosques were demolished during the militant frenzy of the Cultural Revolution, but the Great Mosque of Xi'an remains. Feeling its draw, I set out across the city. Great South Boulevard has eight busy lanes of asphalt, including two for bicycles, and I have to sidle and dodge through thick crowds. The sun scorches creation, and young women carry parasols. I turn down an alley, out of the sun, and enter another world. The pavement is replaced by uneven cobblestones and the din by silence. The scents of sesame oil and baking wheat rise to my nose as I pass a tiny café where three men with thin beards wear the white skullcaps of the Hui, China's largest Muslim minority. They gnaw on lamb kebabs and tear off chunks of flatbread. One man in a tight collar scowls at me. Unsure what to do, I smile back at him, but he keeps scowling. I look away and continue on. The alley narrows, and I duck beneath wet green bed sheets that hang from clotheslines. Three teenage boys sitting on stools and leaning back against the mud-brick walls stare at me, and one who's cleaning his teeth with a metal tooth-pick calls out to me. He asks me my age, where I'm from, whether I'm Christian. I answer, and get directions from there to the Great Mosque.

In another alley, two saleswomen stand behind a long table covered with carved stones. One asks me my sign. "Tiger," I reply. She smiles and touts the benefits of an orange stone *zhāng* (name-stamp) with a tiger carved on one end. "You carve your name on the other end," she explains, turning it over to show me. She asks me my name. She has a gorgeous smile, and there's a sudden magnetism between us, a silent communication—relaxation, attraction. She asks why on earth I'm in this alley, and we laugh about the idea that I've come from farther away than her stones. I ask her about the Great Mosque, but her directions are different from the boys', and I want to ask her to take me there, but I just wander off, alone, confused, down another alley, past dark wooden doors and smoky cafés and fly-infested butchers' shops. I finally realize that I'm lost.

In a construction site, amid a cluster of filthy lean-to dormitories, workers are hammering away on the foundation of some new building. China has a great tradition of this *kŭlì,* which is usually translated as hard labor, but literally means "bitter force" and specifically denotes back-breaking work undertaken by thousands. *Kŭlì* built Great Walls, great emperors' mausoleums, and the cities of great military empires. The English word *coolie* derives from this term. Pushing on through the clamor, laboring through the heat and dust, I grow frustrated. *What am I doing here?* I stop, look around in irritation, and as usual someone is staring at me. It's a man who looks ethnically Han—the majority in China, but the minority around here. He smiles and says I just missed the turn. "You're so close. You speak Chinese—that's great!"

His directions are short and sweet, and soon I'm walking amid souvenir stands of goods that remind me of Qingping Market in Guangzhou: curved daggers, bits of turquoise, electric fans, porcelain bowls, cured hides. Two blond tourists step off a bus, snap photos, and speak what sounds like Dutch. The Great Mosque stands on the corner, and I sigh in relief as I pass through the ornate stone arches of its gate.

It's a spacious green oasis with birds flitting about overhead and singing contented songs. A little girl in a blue dress prances around inside a wooden gazebo, and she lifts a toddler boy onto a railing to watch me. They both stare silently as I draw near. "*Nĭmen hăo,*" I smile, greeting them. They giggle, and the girl asks me the same questions adults always do: What country am I from? How old am I? Their father is in the Prayer Hall, she explains, which lies on the other side of more arches, gazebos, and stone walkways. The pudgy boy beams at me, and I photograph him. "Again!" he demands.

I find a seat in a nearby grove of trees, beside a babbling creek. I open my journal, and thoughts pour out onto the page—thoughts about solitude in this fascinating sea of people, thoughts about trust and strangers, thoughts about loneliness and irritation and attraction. *A striking difference between this culture and my American one seems to be the focus in the U.S. on the individual. The Enlightenment, the consciousness revolution that guided the founding of the U.S., discovered and championed the individual at every level. That revolution never happened here—they gave up or didn't try. The focus here remains on society as a whole, on stability, on continuity, and this seems only more true with Deng dead. If this government stays in power, the one "modernization" they'll likely achieve is the military, which conveniently is the one usually used to show off. I'd have to bet on war within 50 years. I hope I'm wrong. But if this empire stays together—if the wealthy eastern third doesn't pull itself away from these hinterlands in another massive revolution—it will become unbelievably powerful. And world history doesn't have a lot of examples of major empires rising to preeminence peacefully.*

As for right now, there's no conflict between China and the U.S., between myself, the traveler, and the folks here who see me as a "big nose." In fact, there seems to be a harmony between me, whatever I am, and here, whatever this place is. I think I love it. I feel a delightful, new attraction to the beautiful women all around me, and I don't know if this is from the long separation from "my people," or if the "Asian cravin'" that I feared with Lu Lan is real. Am I actually more attracted to Chinese women? Or is it simply that I've gone longer without a kiss, without even a caress, than at any time since I was 15? It doesn't matter. This is freedom—I can do or be anything here.

Removing my tan cap in the heat, I find a flat spot on the bank and do something I haven't done in many months: sit and simply watch my breaths. I gaze at the water and let my thoughts come and go, and let the air come and go. *Now.*

I rise some time later and step through the trees to the Prayer Hall. Large red pillars etched with Chinese and Arabic script in black and gold frame the Hall's door. Men in white robes and skullcaps slip out of their shoes and pad inside. The sounds of afternoon prayer spill out into my ears, and I remember the Temple of the Six Banyan Trees, and Lu Lan, and the pleasure I felt finding China's spiritual and religious life. Something is needed to balance the politics and the business and the rush for modernization.

✿

SOUTH OF the Muslim District lies an old-fashioned neighborhood of winding cobblestone streets and signs written in flamboyant characters. Passing a teashop, I inhale a bouquet of fragrances: raw grasses, flowers, dried fruit. A row of art galleries exhibit paintings of bamboo, mountaintops, tigers, people—even portraits, which are unusual in Chinese painting. I wander into a woodcarver's shop where the walls are covered with scowling, rainbow-hued masks, then into a calligrapher's shop proffering black ink stones and elegant scrolls of poetry.

Back on the sidewalk, I stop to watch two men crouched over a game of Go. They sip tea and take turns placing white and black stones, slowly filling a wooden board until the stones seem to form white and black dragons that eat each other.

I found no neighborhoods like this in Guangzhou.

My steps carry me all the way to the city's towering walls, where a steep stone staircase leads up. I ascend the stairs to find an utterly deserted plateau atop the broad barrier, a vantage that would make Qin Shihuang proud. The sun is setting directly before me as I stroll over the flat stones. *Westward, into that pink and crimson swirl, I continue tomorrow.*

I walk further, and first a speck, then a recognizable figure, and finally a man on a bicycle pedals up to me and asks a few friendly questions. He offers me his bike. I refuse, but he insists, so then I'm riding atop the wall, the cool evening breeze in my mouth, smiling, wondering.

Why did this man appear and loan me his bike? Why did the man at the Bīngmǎyǒng insist I take a photograph? And the woman at the Summer Palace? And the PLA soldiers at Tiananmen Square? Somehow, whenever I let go, whenever I let myself be lost, I find myself anew, and some anxiety drops away; some new force takes over and the world opens up, spreads out naturally, and embraces me.

CHAPTER 24

Friends in Poetry

學而不厭誨人不倦

Never cease to study further and to teach others.

—CONFUCIUS

IT'S THEIR final class, and I witness things I've never seen in my students before. As they file in, they are silent and seem sad. Some of them hand me greeting cards that utilize familiar, broken English: "Don't forget me, I hope our friendship will be lasted as long as PRC's and USA's. It won't be broken, will it?"

I write my home address on the board, and they copy it down with unusual diligence. They pay close attention as I speak about the joys of communicating in a foreign language, about the possibilities if they forge onward with English.

Sandoh raises his hand. He asks about my plans. "Where are you going in China? What will you do when you get home to America?"

"Study Chinese," I joke, not sharing the truth—that I have no idea, that I'm here looking for ideas, that I'm here seeking my fortune.

Alice, née Sally, who didn't want to sit next to boys and who reported on human rights, raises her hand. "We'll miss you," she says, brushing her hair from her face. "Already… we really miss you."

Raymond, the competent boy who plagiarized about wombats and kangaroos, stands and smiles. "Teacher Tony, we have a gift for you." He produces an oblong green box containing a Chinese scroll. "It's from everyone." He gestures solemnly to the whole room. He steps forward and hands it to me.

Opening and unfurling the scroll, I find Chinese calligraphy along-side a painting of a bull and a stork. The calligraphy is a poem about friendship. The bull and the stork "like true friends, feel each other's pleasure and feel each other's pain." On the scroll's reverse side are the signatures of all of the class's twenty-nine students, hand-written in a rainbow of hues. I read the poem aloud in Mandarin, and my students applaud for several moments, and there, again and perhaps for the last time, I'm a celebrity teacher, the *gwailo lǎoshī*.

I dismiss my students, and they leave quite slowly.

"Don't get into trouble," says Sandoh, with a grin, on his final way out the door.

CHAPTER 25

The Silk Road

人往高處走水往低處流

Water inherently seeks low places,
Man inherently seeks the heights.

—CHINESE PROVERB

A COUGH WRACKS my body, throwing my head upward, into a nasty collision with the bunk above me. Smoke and chatter rise from the bunks below. A dull beige landscape slides by my dirty window. I feel trapped on a moving prison, on the edge of illness, on the edge of the Gobi Desert. I've never been one to rest well in crowded quarters. Rubbing my head, I make a sandwich of weird weightless peanut butter, white bread, and canned strawberry goo that I bought in the Xi'an train station.

The afternoon passes, taking us across a sea of dusty, undulating hills that on maps is called the Muus, an arm of the Gobi. Thankfully, by nightfall, the men have inhaled all their cigarettes, and I drift off. Several times in the darkness my bowels cry out, and I shuffle to the toilet, wondering what will become of me if illness snaps its jaws around me.

At dawn, I gaze out the window, and the beige expanse is unchanged, but there's something new about the light, a harshness, a splendor that dazzles my eyes and floods the parched monotony. Gashes, crevasses, and then small canyons riddle the landscape. The Yellow River appears, meandering through this no man's land, and then finally, jammed into the valley alongside the river, rises a metropolis: Lanzhou.

We roll to a halt, and I depart the train and station quickly. Longing to avoid nightfall in another urban grid, I look at a map of this province, Gansu. I decide on a Hui Muslim village called Linxia. "Muslim"—the word conjures visions of exotic lands, places I've never been, places my father taught me about in his geography classes. I think of my parents and realize that no one back home has heard from me in weeks. A woman at a phone kiosk eyes me warily as I draw near. "No long distance calls," she snaps, shooing me away, yelling other things I don't understand. I take a stab at sarcastic Mandarin and say "thank you," and watch for her response. Something punches me in the arm, a computer monitor strapped onto a moving motorcycle. Cursing, cradling my arm, I sigh and move on. The place resembles Xi'an and Guangzhou: broken sidewalks, no trees, grimy restaurants, air like tea water, and a sun that is a mere suggestion, a memory invisible through viscous overhead haze. Everything seems to stink of sweat or fish sauce.

The legendary Silk Road once left from this very outpost, crossed the upper reaches of the Yellow River, and forged off into the desert towards Europe. But today not even the hot smog leaves the valley. *We're all trapped.* I cross the street and enter a gigantic square named The East Is Red Plaza, an expanse of pavement bordered by manicured bushes and festooned with red *huíguī* banners. Obviously it's another locus fashioned by the authorities to awe any and all dimwitted citizens.

"The Telephone and Telegram Office is a good place to make international collect calls," advises the *LP*. I walk several blocks and find the building. The metal door scrapes the floor loudly as I enter. "Sorry, no collect calls," apologizes a woman behind a counter. She speaks softly.

"You may buy one of the bank cards." Back out in the heat, I find the bank, but it's still closed at 11:40 on this Wednesday morning. Or maybe it's already closed for *xiūxī*, the Chinese lunchtime siesta. I walk on and buy a bottle labeled "Liángxuě Mineral Water" that is probably just bottled tap water. I take a deep pull. Dehydration is a greater risk than water poisoning.

A yellow pickup-truck taxicab approaches, and I decide it's my best option. I hail it and climb aboard. The cabby greets me with a glare, and we wade onto a broad road, a slow mess of dust and honking vehicles. Exhaust laces the air like microscopic bubbles of some exotic plague. In a neighborhood of squat adobe homes, we roll so slowly that two women, clothed head to toe in white, walk past us.

The cabby tells me he's Buddhist, which surprises me. "Buddhism is finally legal again," he adds.

"Deng was permitting that, right?" I ask. "A slow rebirth of the three big faiths, Taoism, Buddhism, and Islam? But adherents can't join the Party?"

"It's much better today than it was ten years ago," he says. What he's not saying is that ten years ago was far better than during the Cultural Revolution, when teenagers pulverized shrines, mosques, and temples to show patriotism. "Lanzhou is 70% Buddhist," he declares proudly. I ask if he means Muslim, since it's towards central Asia that we're so very slowly crawling. "70% Buddhist," he insists. "Most Chinese are Buddhist at heart." Perhaps the cabby's faith impresses more than just me, because a higher power of some creed intervenes, traffic parts, and we're suddenly at the station. "Find a bus out here on the street," he advises. "Don't go into the station. The prices are higher for *lǎowài*."

I decide to trust him, and I soon spot a bus with a hand-painted sign with the characters "Linxia." I step aboard. The driver is busy with another passenger, and I quietly ask an elderly man in the first row how much he paid for his ticket.

"11元," he frowns, stroking the long hairs on his chin. He wears the white skullcap of the Hui.

"You," the driver cuts in. "Where are you going?"

"Linxia," I reply.

"50元."

"What? Locals only pay 11元."

"Insurance," he replies. "Mandatory for foreigners. Go inside, you have to buy insurance."

"Insurance for what?"

"An accident."

"Are you going to have an accident?"

"No."

"So why do I need insurance?"

"It costs 50元."

"I'll give you 35元," I hold out the cash. "That's triple."

He nods and takes it. I push down the aisle and manage to squeeze into a spot on one of the six benches. My backpack slips down in front of my knees like a stuffed fish. There are three women on board. The two dozen other passengers puff on cigarettes as we roll away from the station.

Up we climb, out of the city, higher and higher, winding into China's highlands. The Silk Road, this ageless link to the exotic goods and ideas of the West, hoists us up onto its first harrowing cliffs, and as our wheels near the edge, I gaze out, back over a valley of farmers' fields that look like brown and olive shoeboxes. The air thins and cools, and as if from an eternal slumber, my senses awaken and drink with relish the textures and hues around me. My backpack is blue jay blue, the large cloth covering a man's basket is carrot orange, the seats are all dry grass green, the lacy hats on the men's heads are eggshell white, and the landscape expanding to the horizon is mottled peanut beige.

"Hello," a young man smiles at me from across the aisle. "You are traveling?" He too wears the white skullcap of the Hui, and he asks the standard questions, but in English, so I answer in English. He was born in Linxia to a farming family, he tells me, but he managed to get abroad on a rare scholarship and graduate from a university in Pakistan. He dreams of studying at a European or American university. Amazingly, he already speaks Tibetan, Urdu, Arabic, English, Mandarin, and the

Lanzhou dialect of Chinese. Yet a hint of desperation strains his voice. The local government has an iron grip on the farmers out here, he says. "They tell us what to do—what to plant and when to harvest. We're left with the shell of communism—the bad parts—and the only way out is through the Party, or by joining the army."

"Can't you go to Lanzhou or another city?"

"Some can, but we're still in the *dānwèi* system—we lose everything if we move. The government is so *fŭbài*. How do you say *fŭbài* in English?"

"Corrupt," I reply.

He smiles. "It's better that we talk about these things in English."

"How about the *huíguī*?" I ask.

"Hong Kong?" He chuckles. "It's nothing. They take our food and money and build beautiful 'friendship monuments' in Beijing and Hong Kong." He sighs. "Government officials often demand bribes— for everything—they too have to eat—but there's nothing left here for us. All the food and money goes back to the coast. And then Beijing just forgets about us."

We bounce through a poor village of white plaster and red brick. Scarlet, hand-painted characters on a white wall declare, "Having a daughter is as good as having a son." The traditional preference for boys persists, apparently, as does the government's inclination to shape attitudes through signs. "If you have a second child, maybe to try to have a boy, and don't pay off the official," this farmer's son explains, "you lose your job. In some other places I think farmers are allowed more children for farming. Not here. We still have what they call one-child-policy."

He falls silent, and I gaze at the passing farmland. Eventually I open *Narcissus* and fly mentally to the German countryside, where Goldmund hoofs it, village to village, living on impulse and generosity. He stays in farmers' barns and playfully tempts young wives out into the night. One night in a forest, a fellow traveler takes Goldmund by the throat in order to steal his one gold coin, but Goldmund's will to live takes over, and he betters the other man, killing the robber with his pocket knife, feeling the man's blood run through his own fingers.

My eyes jerk up as the bus veers sharply. My seat catapults me into the aisle as we swing around a hairpin turn. A jeep is there, coming at us, and we brake, swerve, brake, and pass the jeep, driving on the edge. My seat catches me again when we cut back into our lane. Exhaling, I notice that no one else looks perturbed, that the driver is handling the wheel as calmly as before.

We pass through another village and then reach Linxia, which looks more like a small city after the villages we've passed. The broad central boulevard is paved. Crescent moons grace numerous tall spires against a clear, cobalt afternoon sky. The bus pulls into a gravel parking lot, and passengers grab together their sacks, baskets, cans, boxes, and crates. I step down just ahead of my new friend and offer him my water.

He declines. "Are you looking for a hotel?"

I nod, taking a swig of water. "Nothing too expensive."

He leads me down a dusty dirt lane between shops and squat cinder block hovels. We stop at a building that is encased in bamboo scaffolding, reminding me of Guangzhou. He points inside, where I see men with hammers pounding on the walls. He bids me farewell. I pay 38元 ($4) for a full room, and it turns out to be far nicer than the ghetto I called home in Xi'an. The room has two beds, a desk, a television, and even a private bathroom, and it resembles an American hotel room—until I discover that a dozen bathroom tiles are missing, the open plumbing is rusted through, the wooden chairs wobble over, the blinds don't work, the threadbare carpet is riddled with stains, and the sheets are too small to cover the beds.

But I feel like a king, because it's all mine. Delighted, I leave my pack and head back onto the street to explore. Flanking the hotel are rows of open-front shops that are jammed with merchandise: chopsticks and dinner bowls, spark plugs and hubcaps, leather slippers and flowery prayer mats. Strolling slowly, I exchange nods and smiles with vendors and pedestrians. Several old bearded men glare at me, but this time when I smile they don't scowl. They nod with a trace of pleasure. They're sitting around a pot of tea in an open-front café, and they wave me over, so I sit with them, exchanging greetings, answering their basic questions. One man, the owner of the café, his clay-orange cheeks splotched with brown, launches into local history with a mix of pride and disgust. He and many of his friends were imprisoned during World War II, the Japanese occupation, and the ensuing communist civil war, their Muslim faith making them secondary citizens and often *a priori* suspects of crimes and sedition. Many were jailed, others hid or escaped and banded together, and those who did started their own Hui political party in order to pursue an independent state. They failed, and after many years and many martyrs, finally, reluctantly, they settled for this, what Beijing calls an "Independent Autonomous Prefecture." This very town, Linxia, was made the prefecture's capital. He *needs* to tell me the story—I sense it—he *needs* to get off his chest what happened, and I do my best to follow his heavily accented Mandarin.

Another man cuts in, asking if I've eaten yet. I lie, mostly so they don't feel compelled to treat me to a lavish feast. They go on, telling me that just last year the PLA came into Linxia and brutally dispersed a Hui demonstration, killing two people and wounding dozens. The newspapers didn't report any of it. I listen as long as I can, but so many strange words fly by me I soon feel lost. I thank them for the tea and go.

At the center of town stands a mosque with a gorgeous emerald green dome. A wooden bench beside it welcomes me, and I sit, alone, studying my dictionary and taking in the passing scene. Women in black turbans with long attached capes pass by as if in mourning, but I think it's their customary dress; young men in white T-shirts grunt, lugging a baby-blue gas tank past me; two lovers stroll by, hand-in-hand, smiling, dressed in fashionable colors; an old man in a navy blue communist-era "Mao Suit" shuffles by. Beyond them all, at the distant horizon, the sun dips toward the purple peaks of Tibet. Lanzhou felt like the dreariest place on the planet—like some personal hell, like illness in exile. Here, I'm still alone, and I can't put my finger on why, but this place feels peaceful, open, and welcoming to me.

The rich aromas of lamb kebabs flood my nose and brain, and I'm lured off of my seat. The vendor's cart is across the street, and I'm nearly to it when a young man is at my arm, launching into breathless, broken English: "My name is Qiu, how are you? Nice to meet you and I'm very well, thank you. Like to talk? At my home." I look at him, absorbing his smile, and he turns and walks away, motioning insistently for me to follow.

I go along, and he leads me past a loud auto mechanic's, down an alley, through an ill-fitting wooden door, and into a small home. The concrete floors are scrupulously swept; the furniture is sparse and plain. Qiu barrages me with questions as his mother carries in noodles, chilled peppers, and tea on an elegant wooden tray. She smiles shyly at me and withdraws. I eat while he carries on in enthusiastic broken English, smiling at me oddly, as if we're plotting some conspiracy together. He takes down my name and address and then confides in me that he prefers speaking Arabic to speaking Chinese and often uses his Arabic name. He wants to go to Lanzhou Foreign Languages University to improve his English and then to travel to Australia. "Right now I need a pen pal," he smiles. I ask him whether he is Hui, though by his white cap I know he is.

Awkwardly, nodding, he whisks me back outside, leading me down street after street, crisscrossing the city, and we see six mosques in less than two hours. When the white moon reveals itself overhead, Qiu makes a promise. "Tomorrow," he points to a distant building. "We will see the tomb of Hamuzeli, the father of the Hui People. And we will burn incense at the famous Taoist temple." He smiles, and I feel wary and confused by his enthusiasm. Nevertheless I give my assent.

❁

THE CLAMOR of construction yanks me awake at six, but I feel exquisite. An unfamiliar bliss courses through my veins. I depart my hotel and hike to the edge of town. People on their way into town zip by me on bicycles, roar by on unmuffled motorcycles, or walk by pushing wheelbarrows of leafy produce. I continue on, toward rolling green hills that rise to mountains at the horizon, feeling exhilarated, as if touched by lightning, realizing I've finally left civilization behind. I am free to journey into the unknown.

The road leads over a swift stream, and at the bridge, I step off of the road and onto a grassy bank. Kneeling, leaving the rays of the rising sun to strike the bank behind me, I gaze into the stream, ingesting the morning air slowly. I release into meditation, letting my breaths slowly flow up and down, in and out. The rays soon strike my chest and then dance on the shimmering water itself. In the silence, gazing into the eddying mirrors, I panic. The cold currents jump up and grab me. *No one knows where I am! No one cares!* I see Lu Lan's face, and I can't fathom why I left her behind, why I pushed her away. The couch in the women's apartment in Guangzhou appears, and it's our Thanksgiving celebration, when everyone was there, ten *lǎowài* huddled together to celebrate, and to me they were all superficial and boring, cowardly animals, scared of really experiencing the world, this world. That world *is* this world. *I was pushing everything and everyone away.*

After some time, I return to town. Passing a woman with a wheelbarrow of fruit, I realize I'm famished. I buy a handful of fresh *lónggǎn* (dragon eyes). The tan rinds of the grape-sized fruits yield to the puncturing push of my fingernail, and I seize the juicy, white flesh with my teeth. The sweetness spreads down my tongue. A young Hui man sells me hot, freshly fried wheat bread. I find a comfortable perch on a flight of concrete stairs and bite off a semicircle of the golden dough. Eating the simple food, Goldmund's words jump to mind: "To a wanderer, a simple scrap tastes more delicious than a whole meal with the prosperous."

Below my vantage point, two children wash green onions with a hose. Beyond them, the street fills with wagons, pedicabs, bicycles, and cars. Shops open their doors one by one, revealing families eating breakfast. For a fleeting minute, my brain wraps around this entire experience—this land, this empire, this China—coalescing all of the beauties and ills into a single idea. A breeze sifts by me with more thoughts, and the singularity dissolves.

Rainbows lure me into a tailor's shop. Swatches of silk in scintillating yellows, emerald greens, citrus oranges, and blood reds feature wild gold and black embroidery. The threads dance into dragons, flowers, and abstract geometries. Carefully folded, the sheets of extravagant fabric stretch from floor to ceiling. The tailor, a round-faced Hui man in a plain white shirt, sits sipping tea and stroking his beard. *"Zǎo ān,"* he says, and I return the morning greeting. He shows me a shirt he's working on, motioning me so close that I can smell his mug of strong green tea. I praise the silk. He smiles, showing me the tiny stitches he makes. When I ask, he echoes the Lanzhou cabby's words about religion and freedom: It's getting better, and here in the Hui capital, every Muslim may even leave the country once for the sacred hajj pilgrimage to Mecca—provided that he leaves behind a 3000元 bond. He beams as he describes his own hajj, three years ago. "Thousands of us prayed together in Mecca. I was so happy. I cried."

A woman enters the store, and he greets her with "selia amu," which sounds oddly like *Salaam aleikum*, the Arabic Muslim greeting. Surely as the centuries cycled by Arabic influenced the Chinese spoken here and created a Hui dialect. The tailor rolls up his sleeves. He knows which silk she wants—purple with circling red and gold dragons— and he wields shears and a yellow yardstick. Several minutes later she leaves with the handsome material folded under her arm.

"She makes robes for government officials," he explains. Sitting down on a bolt of sky blue silk, he resumes describing his hajj, and he tells me he's been studying Arabic since his return. He teaches me a few words in Arabic, and I teach him a few in English, and we laugh together. I photograph him, capturing his smile, his spirit, his calmness. I thank him and turn to leave, but before I do, I turn back in order to thank him again for the photograph, as if I've used him for something. *I should leave this device behind and ditch this need to capture. Just be in the present moment.* He nods again, and I stumble out, unable to part with the camera.

I do however decide to leave Linxia. I'm quite close now to Xiahe— the place Colt extolled—and I feel it beckoning to me. Xiahe is a smaller town higher in the hills that's shared by Huis and Tibetans. I retrieve my pack from the hotel, but before leaving town I honor my promise to rendezvous with Qiu.

He's delighted to see me. His brother and father sit beside us in their concrete home and watch us speak English. Qiu can't go to the tomb of Hamuzeli today, he apologizes. He's wearing a mysterious smile again, and my mind races to detect his motives. He only grins, so I glance at my watch. There may only be a few buses to Xiahe, and it's always better to start a trip early in the day. I mention this, and Qiu promptly offers to accompany me to get a ticket. "You can leave your bag here," he suggests.

Leave my bag here? No way.

There isn't much of value in it. *Let's do an experiment.* I mentally mark its position, how it leans, and the way it's tied. I leave my pack.

Outside, the sun blazes its unapologetic inferno. Qiu offers to hire one of the motorized wagons that converge around me, but I wave them off and we walk. At the bus station, he goes right up to the counter and asks for a ticket "for the *lǎowài*," which even I know is not the best strategy for obtaining a decent ticket. "There are buses every hour until five," he reports back, grinning. "But they're 34元 for you—it's more expensive." I reply that I'll buy my ticket later, and this seems to please him. He insists on hiring a motorized wagon for the trip home, so we roar over the uneven concrete, whipping recklessly between farmers' tractors and pedestrians, and I feel once again that I'm a spectacle for the prestige of my companion, that I'm conferring honor on someone I barely know.

Back in his home, my eyes dart to my bag. It's untouched. I feel my chest constrict sharply. Shame overtakes me and tears rise to my eyes. Silently, I apologize to these simple people for my suspicions. I look at Qiu and feel an inch of my heart open. The face in which I saw deceit holds only curiosity. I tell him to write to me, and I promise to write him back. The whole family bids me farewell. I thank them for more than I can say.

Walking to the bus station, I gaze into the sky, feeling strange, uprooted, and afloat on some vast cloud. How much of this paranoia, this fog, this dark fear is inside me? It feels endless, bottomless, and deeper than anything else, as if it's all that I am underneath my happy facade. My eyes amble across the azure ceiling of the world, finding nothing.

Double Happiness

❁

T HE BUS pulls out, and the dirt streets of the town roll by me. Proud and placid, the Hui people relax in the heat, more at ease than China's mainstream Han, who always seem so anxious to *zhēngxiān* (push to be first), to strive for riches, to nab those rare chairs. It seems that these people up here in these desolate Tibetan highlands and Muslim lowlands—areas that together account for half of China's surface area—aren't really Chinese at all. They might all crave their independence. If it ever comes, it won't be peacefully.

About a mile out of town, we pull over. The scent of burning motor oil rises through the bus as passengers step out into the afternoon to frown or to offer mechanical advice. I remain in the bus with *Narcissus & Goldmund.* The sculpture of a woman on the wall of a church touches Goldmund's soul, and he temporarily halts his travels to apprentice with its sculptor. He settles in the village, learning slowly to immerse himself in art, to open himself to inspiration, to express his heart through his hands. He creates a superb statue of St. John with a grave face inspired by Goldmund's memories of Narcissus—and he wins both his master's praise and induction into the local sculptors' guild.

I put down the book as people reboard. The bus is fixed, and our trip turns into a brutal uphill climb on *dà bízi*-shaped slopes. But we do it—we summit these first foothills of the Himalaya—and we wind around switchback turns and swoop down into pine-forested valleys. We cross plateaus and traverse narrow riverine bridges. The paved road ends in a verdant mountain bowl that cradles a beautiful town, and instantly I know it's Xiahe. We roll right down a main street lined with ancient brick and wood buildings. Three monks in hot pink robes pass by amid crowds of pedestrians. The sun sinks behind the surrounding peaks, and we pull over. A man wearing a backward green baseball cap leans into the bus. "Labrang Hotel? Labrang Hotel?" he calls out.

A hotel? Why not? I take my pack, hop out, and climb onto the plywood bed of the man's motorized wagon. He guns the engine, and we roar down the alleys of Xiahe in the twilight, passing Huis, Tibetans, and Han Chinese. We zip to the other end of town and off into rolling pastures. Darkness gathers around us, and I spy just a few lights ahead of us in the distance. A cold wind whips at my ears and through my flimsy shirt. I cross my arms to keep warm, regretting packing so lightly, closing my eyes, just choosing blindly to trust this time, and suddenly seeing, instead of darkness, an entire fertile world on the edge of a precipice, and exhilaration wells in my heart, and beneath it is a sweet gratitude.

The breaks squeal and the driver calls to me. He points between two large fields. When I climb down, he spins the wagon around and returns to town, taking the roar of his engine with him. The road leads me alongside a river, and the few lights ahead turn into a gate enclosing an inn.

The lobby is a wooden place in a sweet state of decay. I rent a bed. Unlocking the door to my tiny room, I find a big white surprise. *Lǎowài!* A tall Caucasian man, another stone in this barrel of rice, the first I've seen since the Dutch couple by the mosque in Xi'an. He looks up from a book. I watch myself ask him, one by one, all the questions I find tiresome.

"I'm twenty-nine," Shaun says. "I was living in Indiana, near Purdue, teaching social studies. I was engaged and ready to settle down. Then I came to China to teach English for a year. What was I thinking?" He laughs, watching me collapse on the other bed. "I broke up with my fiancée that fall," he continues. "I've lived in Fuzhou, on the coast, ever since. I went back to the U.S. last Christmas, and I just couldn't relate. The only women who would talk to me were fat and smoked. I mean, how many women here are fat *or* smoke? This place is just what they say, 'Ugly White Man's Heaven.'"

I tell him I'm famished, and he recommends a Tibetan restaurant in the nearby woods. So I stroll back out through the hotel gate and cut left into a forest, the moon providing the only illumination. A path leads me through birch trees to a hut with chipped white walls. I knock on its heavy wooden door. A bronze-skinned man with black hair gathered in a ponytail appears.

"Hello," I say in polite Mandarin. "I'm so sorry to bother you. Is this a restaurant?"

"It is indeed a restaurant." He smiles, letting me into the single room. A woman gets up from a table and reaches into cabinets above a small white stove.

Hesitating, I ask for Tibetan food.

"Great!" the man laughs, pulling out a chair for me. "That's all we have." He hands me a blue bowl of thin white yogurt swirled with honey. I taste a spoonful, and it's fresh and sour and delightful. The woman sets a larger bowl of raw brown barley flour in front of me, and I stare at it a moment. *Tibetan cooking is light on preparation.* The man sits next to me and shows me how to mix water, yak butter, and milk powder into the barley. He does it with one hand. "This is *tsampa*," he says. "The most common Tibetan meal." He watches patiently as I try the cupping and grinding motion. "Tibetans eat many other foods too. Yak, lamb, dumplings."

I pop a bite-sized ball of the mixture into my mouth. It's hearty chewing—an honest, nutty flavor. "I thought Tibetans were Buddhists," I say between balls. "Vegetarians."

"Tibetans are Buddhists," he agrees. "Yes. But we live in the Himalaya. If we didn't eat meat, we'd all be dead!"

"Are there many Tibetans here in Xiahe?" I ask, scraping the bowl with my fingers to make a final orb of *tsampa*.

"Many," he nods. "Labrang Monastery is here, which is the sixth biggest Tibetan temple. We get many tourists too."

"Tourists—are they your main customers?"

"Tourists, construction workers, pilgrims to the monastery."

"Mostly Chinese?" I eye a golden brown classical guitar leaning against one of the plaster walls. I haven't touched a guitar in weeks, and just looking at it, my fingers curl for the frets. A fat-mouthed Buddha painting—all brilliant blues and greens—hangs above it on the wall.

"No, mostly Tibetans."

"Is that your guitar?" I finally ask.

"Yes."

"Do you play it often?"

"Not really." He looks at it sheepishly.

There's a hasty knock on the door, and he rises to finger open the latch. A crowd of white American teenagers—three girls and three boys—rush in and seize every vacant seat and all the air in the tiny place. I gape for a moment, but then I'm translating for them, placing their orders, and hoping the couple has enough food. The teenagers chat about their ten-day tour and how amazing it is and where this whirlwind summer between high school and college is taking them. They ask me questions, but I don't say much, partly since I'm shocked—and disappointed—by their presence. A guy with glasses in a plum-colored Land's End fleece plays the guitar. He runs through some expert jazz riffs. I stare at the traces of barley flour left in my bowl, watching myself psychically push these young people away. With a sigh, I answer one of the girls' questions. She sits closer to me, telling me that they have a twenty-hour bus ride to Chengdu in the morning. She smiles, calling herself crazy.

Chengdu is a huge city that I'll reach in weeks, if ever.

I wish them luck and thank the cooks. Outside, the moonlight glows white on the bark of the trees as I return to the inn alone.

CHAPTER 26

Walking to Heaven

The time came when the risk it took to remain in a tight bud
was greater than the risk it took to blossom.

—ANAÏS NIN

OUTSIDE MY door, mountain peaks rise on all sides to kiss a newborn sky. Crisp morning air rushes into my lungs, and I feel weightless as I step down the mosaic path that bisects the courtyard. Tiny orange, yellow, and white flowers dot ankle-high grass on either side of the path. The inn's walls are covered with murals of the Buddha and natural scenes. My senses feast on the art and vibrant colors as if to finally satiate themselves after all of the months and miles of concrete.

Outside the courtyard, the river that last night was just a whisper now speaks with a full voice to the morning light. The road crosses the river and runs off between two fields, but I leave the road and stay with the river, walking on its rocky bank. A stream splashes down from the mountains and joins the river, and I turn and follow the tributary uphill. At a narrow point, I vault over the stream, onto the higher bank. On a grassy knob where the bank is flatter, a woman is lying supine, completely still. I draw closer and see that her shirt is pulled up, exposing her brown stomach. Her head faces away from me, but I can see her fingers clutch and release a few blades of grass. I'm tempted to get closer and to talk to her, but I'd probably scare her.

The dirt path I'm on widens to a rocky road, and after several bends, weaves between three brown adobe homes. In a lush meadow, four monks in burgundy robes boot a soccer ball, and a man in a brown bowler hat leads a donkey down through the game, towards the river. Past the meadow, I crest a hill and the village of Xiahe spreads out below me. Enchanting and smaller than Linxia, it is more a large meeting of brown homes. Presiding over the community is Labrang Monastery, a majestic white palace stacked with green roofs.

A girl with dirt-streaked cheeks rushes up to me in the vegetable market at the edge of town. "Yoppee!" she shrieks. Two more children happily chime in behind her: "Yowpee!" I play with them for a moment, slapping hands with them, asking them what country *they're* from. They follow me halfway to the monastery.

Labrang is a stunning sight to behold. Its whiteness stands stark against the green mountains, the eight columns of its portico are vermilion red, its roofs are forest green, and its three shimmering, sky-piercing spires are radiant gold. Robed monks come and go through its doors, passing me where I stand in the large dusty square. A tour bus rolls up in front of me and disgorges Chinese tourists in predictable bland garb and yellow visors, yet this time the domestic Chinese tourism conjures a vision of Americans: us, visiting ersatz Native American teepee-and-wampum parks, marveling and laughing at the pitiful spectacle we and our forefathers have created. Am I, like these Chinese visitors, now complicit too?

Monks walk silently, diligently, their hands turning ornate vertical cylinders. *Prayer wheels.* I draw closer. According to the *LP*, the monks walk clockwise and spin the sacred wheels in a precise tradition as a way to cultivate harmony, peace, and compassion throughout the universe. I watch them, falling in love with their endeavor, smiling at the sensation of being anonymously cared for. I imagine for a moment what it would be like to work so earnestly in order to grant others peace. Unlike teaching, perhaps I wouldn't worry whether I was effective, whether it was *working*. Two monks, then three pilgrims, then two more monks, pass before me, moving along the colonnades, and I file in behind them, softly turning each wooden wheel with my own fingers. I feel their painted surface, their creaky rotation, the grains of dust in their axles, and my heartbeat slows. Everything slows down. My thoughts float away, pass and separate from me on their own trajectory. I do a whole circuit, then another, unaware of the passage of time. When I grow tired, I stand back and watch as the monks continue.

A back staircase takes me and my curiosity up onto the monastery's hardwood porch, and I peer through fuchsia curtains into a room where several monks sit in a circle on a polished wood floor. I tiptoe to a railing and take in the view of the steep hillside behind the monastery. Two dozen tiny huts are perched on knobs of the slope, perhaps for solitary meditation. Higher up, a crowd of black mountain goats munch the grass. Then, way up, atop the summit, I spy a little tent, a white dot against the blue sky.

Inspired, I leave the monastery in search of a way onto the hillside. I try a small alley between two homes, and sure enough it turns into a path that leads back to the earthen steepness. Setting a foot on a thick clump of grass, I begin to climb, not going too close to the white huts, thinking people may be meditating in them. The incline is steep enough that I can no longer see the white tent up top, and I have to scramble at times, lunging for handholds, letting the rough grasses bite my fingers. I turn and gaze back down at the monastery and the village. My bag, camera, and water bottle swing around and throw me off balance, and I pitch forward, off the hillside. I grasp a protruding rock and catch myself. Exhaling, continuing upward, I decide not to look down again. The sun burns cosmically hot and close, and I feel lightheaded as I clamber up. Resting with a hand on the slope, I swallow the last of my water. The mountain goats have moved up and off to my left. Goldmund's words ring in my mind, over and over: "What else is there than to live and roam, to feel summer and winter, to taste beauty and horror, to experience the world?"

The summit. A grin ripples across my face, and my fingertips fly up towards the heavens to touch the exploding yellow sphere. I turn and gaze back down, over the brown brick town, and it's nestled so nicely in the hills, its roofs so close together, that they seem to be one enormous, flat, brown home. The sight is soothing, and my mind reels backward to Peizheng, to my students, to the concrete dormitories, to the memory of standing under a tree, to the sound of children playing basketball, to pure listening.

The summit is a grassy plateau ten yards wide; the hill declines more gradually on the other side. The white tent is actually a low-slung tarp perched a hundred yards away. When I draw close to the tarp, I see that two men in red robes sit cross-legged on beige blankets beside it: an older man under a black parasol, and a thinner man partially under the tarp. Both face down to survey the town and its spellbinding valley. They turn to watch me as I arrive.

"*Nǐmen hǎo,*" I greet them in Mandarin. The older monk, who has a flabby neck and big round sunglasses, smiles and motions for me to sit down. He speaks slowly, but I don't understand. I sit cross-legged beside them on the grass, letting a minute pass, feeling my legs gratefully relax. "How long have you been here?" I ask. The older monk replies, but again I can't comprehend. I smile in embarrassment when I realize they watched my foolish, flailing climb. The younger man, who has a flattened nose, ladles out a large mug of tea from a black pot and offers it to me along with a yellow roll sprinkled with dark scallions. I refuse, though I could practically kill for a glass of cool water. He insists several times, so I accept the tea and leave it to cool. I bite into the roll, and it's crusty, dry, and salty. The older monk, his head shaven clean, the sleeves of his robes pushed to his shoulders, smiles warmly at me again. The two men exchange words, and I realize they're speaking Tibetan, not a sacred, incomprehensible dialect of Chinese.

Silence falls, a complete silence, a silence that I probably disturbed. Breezes gently lift my T-shirt from my sweaty back, and I watch a feathery, flat-bottomed cloud come right for us. The air—the wind and our breathing—flows around us, in and out, endlessly surrounding this perch, pushing the grasses and the clouds in a harmonious, unified motion. My awareness heightens as it dissolves into the brightness and the mountaintops, the sky and clouds, the earth and grass.

Some time later I hear a child's voice. I turn and spot a woman's head bobbing over the gradual hillside behind us. The older monk looks at me with a laugh and points at them. I realize his point. *I climbed up the stupid way.* I nod and finally smile. The woman arrives with a child and some food; she places a green ceramic bowl on the ground and scoops bowlfuls of soup for the men and the boy. I decline forcefully, presuming the soup needs to last a full day or two for these men. A different temptation seduces me. My camera begs, beckons, beseeches me to snatch some of this experience, as if I might own it and hold it. I've decided to bring the device with me only every other day, but it's with me now, and the adorable boy waddles toward me in an orange floral shirt and cowboy hat, smiling at me with a mouth full of soup. *Snap!* The old master turns to look at me with his benevolent laughing eyes. *Snap!* It's like a duty I don't believe in, but I obey nonetheless. No one else seems to mind.

Perhaps this shame is as useless as the mistrust I suffered with Qiu.

The woman and the boy leave, and the great silence returns. The clouds swim in our direction and then part before me like a vast human torso opening its arms. Gazing at the clouds, I hear an internal voice whisper to go further, to be like these clouds, to let go of the fog and fear, to walk through the world this way I've stumbled upon: eyes open, trusting more things, trusting more feelings, experiencing the odd, delicious, concrete knowledge that whatever happens is good.

The easy path takes me down the sun-baked back of the mountain, winding around hills and through pastures, and I carefully avoid the countless brown piles of yak dung. Yaks are the sacred animals of Tibet, the creatures trusted in these mountains for food, fuel, transportation, and inspirational fortitude during long winters.

I descend on the other end of town. Three laughing Tibetan monks and two Hui men chat in the shade beside a restaurant. Two Han

Chinese women giggle at me, one shielding her face from the sun with a purse. I cross a small bridge over the Daxia River and wander into a shop full of shawls and cloaks that are made of black wool woven with bright oranges, lime greens, azure blues, and hot pinks. It's rougher work than the silk tailor's in Linxia. We're at a higher altitude. I examine other goods—fur-lined boots, cowboy hats, prayer flags, yak-butter pots, and fragrant piles of Tibetan incense. The shopkeeper greets me, and when I ask about a long brass trumpet, he steps over to it and sounds a deep hum through it. He laughs at me, at the idea that I, this *lǎowài*, could want to take it home. Further on, in the center of town, I come to a long row of extra-large prayer wheels painted with vivid images of friendly animals and Buddhist saints. Monks and laypeople stroll or shuffle by, chanting, spinning the wheels one by one. Three young women prostrate themselves in the dust, standing, kneeling, lying face down, kneeling, standing. They wear black smocks and use wooden paddles strapped to their hands to avoid getting dirty. After a few minutes, they stop and sit on the raised floor of the prayer wheel colonnade, eating watermelon in the shade, spitting seeds into the dust. One glances at me, smiling, and she motions me to sit beside her. I do, and accept a slice of watermelon. There's a chopping sound as they slice more melon on a cutting board. Biting into the sweet mess and swallowing the droplets of sugary pinkness, I answer her questions and point up at the tiny white tent. "I scrambled up there," I tell her. "I'm pretty foolish. It's a little tarp. There are monks meditating. The view is beautiful." She listens, catching a drop of juice at her chin. She drops her rind in the dust. "Why don't you pray with us?" she asks. I point to her wooden paddles and say I'm not equipped. She insists, so I go for it, watching her elbows as she prostrates, and then emulating her as best I can: I press my hands together by my nose, then by my heart, then I kneel, do a push-up, then I'm up again. On it goes, up and down, a rhythm overtakes my body, and I release into the mindlessness of motion. Growing tired, I wonder whether they do this all day long. I smile at myself, me, this confused Christian Buddhist, this pilgrim, this man attracted to and confused by another Chinese woman. I prostrate over and over. *Méi guānxi* (no matter), I tell myself, letting it go, disappearing again into the serenity of the movement.

Further down the street, I push through saloon-style doors into the Brilliant Café. The cool concrete room is crowded, and I spot an open back door onto a grassy courtyard. There, I find an unobstructed view of Labrang Monastery, and in a flash, I know this is the place Colt described when we sat under the willow at the Old Summer Palace. "A veranda," he mentioned, and it's in a small grassy yard under tall cedars that I find an open table. I snack on noodles with radishes, scallions, and lamb. It isn't exactly what I ordered, and buzzing flies descend to share my meal, but my frustrations and expectations seem to ask to be released with the rest of my ego. A bearded white man and a robed monk emerge and sit at the table beside mine. They discuss Hong Kong and the *huígui*, and I listen a while before interjecting my own comment—that the *huígui* was like a wedding where everyone was happy except the bride. They laugh at my joke. The Frenchman explains that he's here to study the art and history of the monastery, so he and I listen together as the monk recounts what he knows about it: Labrang Monastery was built in 1709 by Jiamuyang, the "Living Buddha," who was born nearby. It became famous quickly for its beauty and tranquility, perhaps because of its surroundings, and the monastery grew. After just two hundred years, Labrang had become a Tibetan Mecca with over four thousand monks in residence. "During the Cultural Revolution," the monk sighs, his voice softening into the Mandarin syllables, "the PLA bombed the buildings."

Two Han Chinese tourists join us, a man from Beijing and a woman from Hong Kong.

"Many people were killed," the monk continues, watching them sit. "Labrang was reduced to 250 monks."

I shake my head, murmuring. The Frenchman pounces on me, claiming America has done things far worse over the last century. He attacks me about bombing Japan and Vietnam, about invading Iraq, about ignoring Rwanda. The group polarizes, and I'm pushed into the role of representing the U.S.'s self-righteous might. The Frenchman is the conceited European who has everything figured out. The Hong Kong woman is a surprisingly fierce defender of China.

"OK," I finally admit. "Still, it's horrible what happened here."

"The Monastery is doing well now, right?" queries the Hong Kong woman.

The monk nods. "In 1985, a fire burned down the main Prayer Hall. The government helped us rebuild it in 1994."

"That's ten years later," I say.

The monk adds that the government still won't rebuild the nunnery—so the nuns fend for themselves in the teensy huts on the hillside. But Labrang is now back up to 1800 monks and is thriving again as a major monastery of Tibetan Buddhism's main sect, the Yellow Hat; Xiahe is once again a magnet for pilgrims in vivid raiment.

"It always looks like a festival here," exclaims the *Beijingrén*. "It's better than Lhasa."

The monk tells us that the government doesn't harass Labrang anymore, and that the community observes every festival and offers an undiluted Buddhist education in five departments: Law, Medicine, Astrology, Theology, and Mysticism. "No politics, though," he says, and smiles.

We step inside, reconciled, and feast together on pork dumplings, peppery tofu, potatoes, lamb sautéed with bamboo shoots, fried rice with bean sprouts. Sharing food fosters amity in no time.

Stuffed, I wish them well and return to the streets. The monastery's gold spires glisten in the late afternoon light. I marvel at these different feelings—politics stirring the waters and meditation settling them.

"Fried dough twists," a street vendor calls out. "Sweet and warm. Four mao apiece!" I watch a pair of girls buy two golden cakes while behind them a mountaintop nibbles on the orange sun. When I look again, the sun has been consumed completely. The twilight around me fades from transparent to dark, and I wander back into the Brilliant Café for a mug of tea. In *Narcissus*, Goldmund has become a sculptor with precocious skill, ready to ascend to mastership in the guild. On a walk in the countryside, however, he rejects what he sees as the pitiful ability of human hands; only that mystery behind the best sculptures still amazes him, whereas "the fame and settled life of the sculptor seem to lead to a drying up and dwarfing of one's inner senses…The gold in the eye of a carp, the sweet thin silvery down at the edge of a butterfly's wing are infinitely more beautiful than sculptures." And in that instant he changes course and leaves the guild, the town, the women he has loved, the art into which he has poured his spirit, and he sets out again alone on the road in search of a more formless beauty.

"Can I sit with you?"

A young woman is speaking accented English. I nod, and she shrugs off her purple backpack and sits in one of the last open chairs in the restaurant. In Mandarin that is better than mine, but not fluent, she orders noodle soup. I ask in Mandarin whether she's traveling, and she looks at me curiously. Michiko, from Kurashiki, Japan, nods and unleashes her hair from a bun. She tells me she's between semesters at *Běidà*, Beijing University, the country's most prestigious university.

"I haven't seen any other women traveling alone," I say.

"Not many," she nods.

"You must be brave."

"Brave?" She smiles, as if trying on a hat. "Maybe I'm not as scared as I should be." She laughs as her soup arrives. I watch a waiter stuff logs into a wood stove in the center of the restaurant, and I feel the air suddenly, palpably change. The day's warmth surrenders completely to a bolder coldness than I've felt so far in this country, touching me through my one and only long-sleeve shirt. "We *lǎowài* need warm clothes up here," I remark.

She nods, intent on slurping the rest of her noodles. When I ask whether learning Chinese is easy for Japanese speakers, and whether Japanese would be easy for, say, me, she stops and smiles. "Your Chinese is good! I bet you'd pick it up quickly." Pronouncing Japanese is easier than Chinese, she explains, but Japanese grammar is much harder. She drinks the last of the broth, and asks if I'm staying for another cup of tea.

After noticing that she too wears just a thin shirt, I suggest we go on an expedition for warmer clothes. She agrees, and we wander down the street together. A wooden hut is crammed full of black coats embroidered with the distinctive Tibetan hues: bright pink, sky blue, pumpkin orange. They're woven as thick as blankets, and she briefly models the day-glow fashions for me and other passersby. I give her a connoisseur's glance and ask her to turn, and her smile cuts through me. I feel self-conscious and wander outside. She doesn't buy anything. We move on, passing a store of real, fresh furs, and as the wind whistles around us, we stop to browse at an outdoor stand of wool sweaters. She likes a dark green sweater, but there isn't one small enough for her. She really is quite small. I find a perfect blue turtleneck for me and haggle with the young salesman, referencing food twice, settling on 65元, and giving him a high five when I pull the thick wool over my head. The insulation feels fantastic. Michiko dances from foot to foot, visibly cold, and decides to head home. I rub a palm up and down her left arm, rapidly, to warm her, and a thrill like electricity charges up my own arm. She grins like a cat. "At least one of us is warm."

Her rate at a hostel is 20元 more than mine at my inn, so when she steps away I invite her to check it out. "It's out in the countryside," I explain. "The place used to be the summer home of the Head Lama. The Chinese rebuilt it as a hotel after the Cultural Revolution. It's gorgeous." She hesitates. I hail a motor-tricycle. "There are pretty paintings, and the river will lull you to sleep." She finally climbs in, saying she might as well have a look, and I'm caught up in delight and fascination and anxiety. My mind races around, and there's Lu Lan, and there's Lauren, and farther back, there's my college girlfriend, Danielle, and there's a sharpness there, a splinter stuck somewhere inside my chest.

Three children race their bicycles alongside us in the cold night. "*Lǎowài!*" they call out.

I unlock my room. Stepping in, I sit hesitantly on my bed. She sits beside me as we continue what we were doing—comparing Mandarin study techniques. We use a dictionary to quiz each other on vocabulary, and she beats me easily at this game. We open the *LP* to get tips on the places she's going, and when she leans over to look at the pictures as I translate the English for her, her round cheek comes close to mine.

There's a fragrance of honey when she sweeps her hair from her face. Our eyes meet.

"I'll get a room here," she says. "Tomorrow…"

My arm goes to her shoulder, and she looks up at me. Her lips part slightly. I lean down, and we gently touch noses, then lips.

Electricity buzzes through me sweetly, and she turns to me like a magnet. I trace my fingertips along her cheek, slowly, feeling every millimeter, from her chin down to the place where her jaw softly flows into her neck. My other palm holds the small of her back, and our eyes are waiting, watching, speaking again, and she leans into me, answering. I pull her all the way onto the bed, beside me, and we sink into it together, just touching. She lies on her back and we kiss playfully, her lips curving into smiles. We kiss longer, and she licks my upper front teeth. I duck below her mouth and run my lips along her chin and the softness underneath. I inhale her fragrance again and smile at the thrill, unworried. I pull off my new blue sweater. Neither of us wants to stop, and it seems to take forever as we remove shoes, socks, almost everything, and extinguish the light. Finally, her pale skin in the faint light rises to my lips. Her bra looks whiter than snow, her neck tastes salty. She removes the whiteness and there's nothing left. I see with my fingertips—tracing down her ribs, her navel, her thighs. She sighs. "*Wǒ zāng*" (I'm dirty), she says, the first words in forever, but it's only the word meaning dirt, earth, dust. I whisper to her. "*Méi guānxì.*" It's OK. She relaxes. We kiss more deeply still. She holds my penis a moment and her legs spread and I launch into a different world, one we create wholly, a new landscape of clouds, sunlight, mountains, and rivers.

❀

A SHAFT OF light parts the darkness. It's Shaun opening the door, awakening us. He gets into his bed, settles, and stops moving, asleep perhaps. Michiko and I curl into each other again, touching toe to toe and nose to nose, and I massage her thighs, the hook of her hips, the outside of her vagina, dipping a finger inside her. She inhales and arches her back languidly. My body climbs up hers again and the union and the friction set us quickly ablaze.

I drift off, thinking I've never been this one—the one returning home with a woman and keeping his roommate awake. The thought brings neither pride nor shame, just a strange letting go.

CHAPTER 27

The Brief Tibetan Sunshine

Of course Goldmund had only too often been one of them,
had felt happy among them, had pursued their girls, had gaily
eaten baked fish from his plate without being horrified. But sooner
or later, as though by magic, joy and calm would suddenly desert
him; all fat plump illusions, all his self-satisfaction and self-impor-
tance and idle peace of mind fell away. Something plunged him
into solitude and brooding, made him contemplate suffering and
death, the vanity of all undertaking.

—HERMAN HESSE,
NARCISSUS & GOLDMUND

FREEZING WATER runs down my body, yanking my senses into
a thorny paradise. Joy fills my lungs as I improvise a deep, chest-
buzzing anthem and sing it loud enough to remain under the cold
shower, lather up, and rinse.

On the railing outside our room I dry off and hang my towel. The
fiery sun has returned, and I linger awhile in its rays, knowing that the

high peaks crop its path here and that, well, you enjoy the heat while it lasts.

Shaun leaves, bidding me goodbye. Michiko left at first breath of dawn to check on bus fares, and we agreed to meet at the Brilliant Café at eleven. I take out my journal, and it feels like eons have passed since I last wrote. *Making love—what can I write? My second lover, but it felt like my first time all over again. It was wine when all I knew was water. I wooed her in Chinese.* I laugh as I scratch the pen across the paper, feeling both uncomfortable and delighted at writing with bravado. *Is she a typical Japanese girl? Or are those stereotypes more myths? She does seem submissive, ready to go along with what I put forward.* I catch myself imagining her body as I write everything, pouring out my thoughts: trust and openness and this strange wonderful way the world is unfolding everywhere. *I can choose—we all choose—to live trusting others and the world, or to live fearing others and fearing everything. When I choose trust, the very essence of trust blooms within me, and in countless manifestations around me, and I trust more my own deeper self, my instincts, my intuition. I followed my intuition to leave Lanzhou for Linxia, to leave Linxia for Xiahe, to trust Qiu, to climb the hillside.* My mind drifts over yesterday. *I feel free now, so free, more free than I ever have.*

A man in a yellow polo shirt emerges into the courtyard, approaches, and commences the standard litany. But his English is good, and after I compliment him he actually thanks me, demonstrating an uncommon grasp of the language. He's a businessman with a joint-venture export company. Chinese businesses, I've learned, are fond of joint-ventures, which allow them to utilize foreign brand names, to gain foreign expertise, while still taking the dragon's share of the profits. Most joint-ventures are with Japanese firms, and I've never figured out precisely why. "Do you like Japanese people better?" I ask.

He shakes his head and tells me more than I want to know right now. It's the opposite: Ever since the Japanese invaded China in 1931, the Chinese have held a special, unrivaled hatred for the Japanese. But today the Japanese do business better, he says. They wine and dine, buy gifts, even grease palms when necessary. Americans are too proud and too righteous, too concerned about doing anything illegal. What's legal here is whatever the local officials want.

I ask him about war, and he gives the awkward smile that means he's returning a favor. He's talking about something he doesn't want to talk about in return for me talking to him at all. "The Chinese realize that America wants to rule the world," he explains. "But more and more, when Americans expect their voice to be the only one, there's another voice: the Chinese voice."

"But would you say the Chinese people are generally peaceful?"

"We're the most peaceful people in the world, but China will not be pushed around any longer. And of course we're not afraid of America. We've already beaten America twice. We know how scared Americans are to die. If a few Americans die, your government will stop fighting. You might not know, but in Korea, it was the Chinese fighting the Americans—the Koreans weren't really doing much—and thousands of Chinese bravely gave their lives. We won. It was the same thing in Vietnam. People don't know, but most of the Vietnamese soldiers were actually Chinese in disguise, and that's why we won."

"Yes, I am scared of war. I think it's awful." More than ever, this very morning, the thought of so many people needlessly dying horrifies me and saddens me.

He's a pacifist himself, he reveals. "But it will be difficult for China and America to become friends. First, America wants to rule the world, and China will accept only equal friendship. Second, America loves Japan and Taiwan—two problems for China."

"Why not forgive Japan, trust the Japanese, as neighbors?" I ask, unable to help smiling at the word *Japanese*.

"That's impossible now. Taiwan must return to China soon, without America's interference."

"If the Taiwanese don't want to return to China, Americans will feel compelled to protect Taiwan—we support democracies."

"No you don't!" He smiles at me awkwardly. "Chile? What about Greece? Indonesia?"

And like yesterday at the restaurant, I defend America: We are not trying to run Asia from overseas; we are not trying to take over the world.

I return to town along the river. The morning air is bracing and pellucid. America is not perfect, but our interests are human rights and democracy throughout the world, and as a democratic state subject to the will of its people, America seeks, perhaps clumsily, what is right in the eyes of Americans. I'll have to learn about Chile and Greece, as every American should. Every American should see his or her country from abroad. So many people are mired in mistrust. I pass a woman crouching by the river to wash a dozen bowls. "*Zǎo ān*" (good morning), I say to her, smiling. She smiles back. I continue, wandering into town, thinking that if the Chinese covet an opportunity to prove their might, to reclaim international honor, there will be war. What is, is. Taiwan could be the spark.

"Yup-pee!" two smiling, ragged-clothed children cry at me. "Yippee?" inquires another. I ask if they want money, but they shake their heads. One boy writes on his palm with his finger, and I ask if they want my address, but they shake their heads again. Michiko would know what they're saying. An old man pushes a huge cart of ripe melons, and I put my shoulder beside his and help him roll it into town. We smile at each other as we push, and I enjoy feeling useful. I stop at the Brilliant Café, and Michiko walks up a moment later in blue jeans and an orange T-shirt, and now I don't think she's pretty. She's too small, with glassy skin, a kind of awkward nose that looks too tiny under big glasses, and her mouth is too narrow, or her cheeks are too round. Something inside of me closes. My throat tightens for a moment and I can't talk. My mind races back again, and the splinter in my chest explodes into a wall shoving my lungs into my heart. *Chinese,* I remember. I touch her arm. "*Zǎo ān.*" We don't kiss. She returns the greeting with just a smile. We relax and start talking, and suddenly I like her again, how she walks, how she speaks to me. *I've never let anything through this wall.* She leads me down a side street to another place, a travelers' café called the Heavenly Kitchen, and seated there we share pancakes dripping with honey. They taste so divine that we decide that they really have come from heaven. I smile at the simple delight she takes in swallowing a spoonful of yogurt. And there we are, Michiko and Tony, looking into each other's eyes.

"Have you done the long hike around the monastery?" she asks, referring to the two-mile-long outer circuit around Labrang Monastery. I haven't, and she hasn't, and it seems to us both like the perfect way to start the day. So we hike around the monastery, spinning the sacred wheels, sharing our physical contentment, sending it out to all creation. We stop for a rest beside the river, under the ornate rafters of a temple, and kiss once, twice, discreetly, until a trio of exuberant young monks pass by, chanting mantras, palming each green and blue prayer wheel solemnly. A disheveled old woman comes next, barely touching the wheels. Then two villagers come by, and they stop near us to rest in the shade of a bridge. Michiko wanders over to talk with them, and I watch her, admiring her. Connecting with her is awakening something new in me, planting some seed, grounding me in this unfamiliar place.

A woman from Shanghai and her teenage son stop beside me, and they chat with me about Xiahe, Tibetan Buddhism, and the Yellow Hat. They know a lot about Tibetans, but to me they seem racist, and it makes me think of America in a different way, as conquerors of native peoples. Uncle Sam is not trying to take over the planet, but we did this too. We talked this way about "the Indians" not long ago—as savages with childish ideas, primitive religions, and bizarre, animal-like customs. I ask them how much Tibetans have to teach the Chinese, and they look at me with utter confusion.

A German man passes by next, and when Michiko rejoins me we ask him to take our picture for us. He kindly obliges, and as two children approach us he tells us about a German couple who visited Xiahe two years ago with boxes of pens. The couple had heard that Xiahe's children had fine teachers and textbooks, but lacked writing implements, so they brought hundreds of pens and handed them out to children. Now every child greets foreigners by begging for a *yóubĭ* (ink pen). He reaches into his shoulder bag and hands each child a pen.

Alone again, she and I continue all the way around, once, twice, three times, before finally stopping when the sun vanishes and the temperature begins its plummet into another Himalayan night. We return to town and share a dinner of flatbread and Tibetan dumplings called *momos*. After eating, we get her things and move her to the Labrang Guesthouse—into the dormitory, a stone's throw from my room. I don't ask her to move in with me. Sitting on her bed, we play some translation games and talk about our morning plans. We decide to ride north, up into the grasslands. Her eyes stop inside of mine. We shift, closer, and a pressure grabs in my chest again, commanding me to retreat. But there's nowhere to go. My brain shouts. *Don't do this again, don't be stupid, don't give in, don't wait for skin to touch skin. Resist this, for both of us.* She admitted, I think, to two previous lovers, and there's also God, pregnancy, and diseases warning me. The idea of condoms drifts in from far away, but we don't have any. She looks confused, but I can't bring myself to say anything. I stand up, and we embrace at the door, holding each other, feeling each other's warmth. I leave, and leave myself alone outside in the cold.

✿

THE MOUNTAIN valley unfurls another sweet morning. The innkeeper pulls two ancient, heavy bicycles from a shed. Michiko and I are heading to a village called Sangke, and he tells us that in the grasslands nearby there will be a festival in two days, and that Tibetans will come from the surrounding mountains for horse races and parades.

"We'll be back before that," she assures him with a smile.

We set out on the paved road, pedaling up and down the slopes, beside each other. We leave the town and its people, buildings, and markets behind, and soon the entire Daxia River valley seems to be our own. At one point a stream cascades down the green hills and washes the road away; we remove our shoes and step barefoot in the icy water, walking our bikes across. The pavement resumes for another mile, then turns to gravel, making the hills pull harder on the weight of our bicycles. We climb further uphill as the sun soars higher and higher, lashing our necks with hot rays. We pause to apply sunscreen and strip down to T-shirts and shorts. Onward, we pedal, up a long hill, and finally we discover a cluster of adobe homes. But it looks too small to be Sangke, or even to have a name. Just to be sure, we roll down the dirt road through the village. There's not a soul in sight. The road dead-ends at the river, but there, finally, at a distance, we spot humans: A hundred yards upstream men in cowboy hats are holding plates and eating while their horses nibble the moist earth. Two hundred yards downstream men are erecting a large white tent. These are the grass-lands—miles and miles of ankle-high emerald grass—and they stretch all around us. Right before us the river overflows its banks and blazes new channels on the lush meadow grasses. We drop our bikes and re-move our shoes on the swollen banks. Laughing in delight, we wade into the gelid water that was probably snow an hour ago. We dunk our heads happily. Shivering, we lie back on the bank beside each other and relax our wet, refreshed bodies. First her hand is on my shoulder, then we're holding hands, then my head is in her lap and I'm staring into the sky. She tells me about playing in a river near her grandparents' home, where she caught *qīngwā*—frogs, I guess, as she hops her fingers around on my chest. She let each one go so she could try to catch it again the next day. Her breasts are two soft planets in the sky above me, and I feel drunk with contentment, being so close to her, being so far from everything else.

Our ponderous bicycles carry us another hour up the dirt road to an arid little village with a handful of people out on a single street. We've arrived, we decide. This must be Sangke. We park in front of a dark restaurant featuring saloon-style doors. Inside, the shadows are thick and the shelves hold warm cans of Pepsi and Pabst Blue Ribbon. There's no electricity and nothing cold, not even water, so we settle for hot tea. A man in a cowboy hat, a white coat, and brown boots agrees to rent us two horses, and he takes us to musty stone stables. A thin red scarf and silver beads decorate this Tibetan cowboy's hair—and the hair of many men around us in the street. He leads two steeds out into the sun: a chestnut brown and a dappled gray. After helping me onto the brown horse's hard saddle, he helps Michiko onto the smaller gray steed. The horse's mane feels coarse between my fingers, its body sturdy and muscular, and I try to relax, realizing I haven't ridden since I was twelve. I squeeze with my ankles.

With a jolt, I'm walking, then trotting, and then galloping out into the grassy landscape. Gusts of mountain air massage my cheeks. At ease, giddy from the thrill of speed, I gallop toward the river. Michiko begins galloping too, and she rides past me, climbing a knobby hill at a bend in the river. A village of white and blue tents with red flags comes into view. She looks at me, and I look at her, and I consider staying, to see this festival, to see what's next. Both of us know that both of us plan to leave the Xiahe region tomorrow, in opposite directions. For now, the future is further away than the sea, and we race back and forth across the grass. Out to the tents and back, we chase each other, pass each other, slap each other's horse, reach out to each other, and finally hold hands for several moments. We let go of each other's fingers, and in that instant I feel something travel up my arm and between my shoulders, and a relaxation opens up behind my lungs. Deep breaths of the mountain air taste like honey. My tan cap clings to my head. Her hair streams behind her.

❁

BACK HOME, after showering, we hike into the hills as the day fades to twilight. We scramble up onto a choice ridge above the grassy slopes. Xiahe lies below us, twinkling and peaceful. Michiko rests her head in the crook of my shoulder, in the warm blue wool of my new sweater, and we breathe together, recline together, and watch as the sun approaches the peaks like a lover. We watch the consummation, we watch until the fireball is gone and darkness envelops everything. The moon's cold coat of ivory shines brightly. Michiko takes my hand as we descend back to the road.

When we reach the inn, she writes her address down for me. We sit on my bed, side by side, thighs and shoulders touching, and all I know is that she's leaving in the morning on a bus for Lanzhou. I see that the characters in her name mean "Little Forest, Pleasing River." In her book, I write my name, Bao Tongning, which means "Shared Peacefulness." She sighs, leaning back into me, murmuring something about gratitude, and there's a wistfulness in her voice I can't read. *Should she come with me?* My breathing catches. *Why does my heart always whisper no?* I say nothing and just hold her, her cheek in my chest, my lips traveling through her hair. I kiss her forehead, and her skin is still warm from all the sunlight and exertion. She looks at me and there is a sheen like porcelain in the glow above her cheekbones. I kiss her beautiful lips. Her neck radiates heat, and she lies back on the bed and looks up at me as I lean all the way down so we can touch noses. Like a horse, I nuzzle her ears and neck with my nose, then her breasts. She smiles, giggles, arching her back and running her fingers through my hair. I feel the mild cut of her fingernails on my scalp. As clumsy as before, we remove our clothing, wiggle, shift, and laugh. There's a moment of hesitation, a fork in the road. The touches become caresses, and I align with a deep longing, the slowing flow of time, the unfolding of the obvious, the letting go. I descend from above to meet her. We challenge each other, accept each other, unwind into each other, fall and rise with each other. The light of the moon pours in through the window.

❁

SHE KISSES me awake. The morning is already crisp and bright, stunning my eyes. She pulls on one small white sock, then the other. She kisses me again, and this time it's goodbye. My lips feel sunburned as hers push against them. "*Yī lù shùn fēng,*" I say. She smiles and repeats my words.

She's gone. A storm swirls up in me as I surrender again to sleep.

Several hours later, I rise and pack my things. I hike slowly into town. My destination, Hezuo, is nearby and there are plenty of buses. Emotions sweep through me in sudden gusts. Anger comes first—at my lack of control. *I'm an idiot.* Pleasure comes next, at my renewed freedom, but it's tinged with a numbing sadness about solitude and abandonment. Finally I feel frustrated with a sense that I'm pushing everyone away. *Am I really free now?* What occurs to me is that she's probably not on birth control. I remember hearing they don't even have the pill in Japan. "It's possible," she replied, when I asked about pregnancy, and I miss most subtleties in Mandarin. *What about sexually transmitted diseases?* God, I'm an idiot. Why did I let her in? Four times, unthinking, unhesitating, unprotected. *Unbelievable.* My whole face is painfully sunburned from the biking and horseback riding.

Perhaps every delicious taste coats a poison, every dessert conceals a stupid choice. Excruciating pain cries out from where the saddle chafed my butt, right at the top of the crack of my ass. Saying that phrase—"the crack of my ass"—makes me smile for some reason, irreverent in spite of myself. But it feels serious, burning, jagged, like it could be an open cut. The stirrups were too low. God, I'm an idiot.

The puny bus station has a filthy floor. The ticket man argues with me, so I pay double the locals' price. Onboard, I have breakfast, a banana. Soon the bus begins to bounce and to pummel my bruise on the crack of my ass. Goodbye Xiahe, exquisite Xiahe, tragic Xiahe, magical Xiahe, a place of dreams, of heaven, of hell. I open *Narcissus*, and Goldmund comes upon a strange village where the people don't welcome him—they attack him. Perplexed, he learns that the Plague has invaded the German countryside. He wanders about in horror, not making love anymore or carving masterpieces, but fleeing, running from town to town, clinging to his own life amidst death and ghastly diseased flesh.

We climb mountains and reach rain. The bus parks in a village, a scratch in the map called Hezuo. I step out into a downpour to look for a bus to Luqu, an even smaller town further south. Onion pancakes sizzle on a street vendor's greasy box, and I slide one into the belly. The words on my lips are *pregnancy, marriage, abortion, disease.* This is what all that openness brings. Stupidity one day, regret the next.

On the bus to Luqu, two Tibetan boys laugh at me and call me names. I call back at them in Mandarin: "Little nose! Native!"

They giggle and approve and sit by me, handing me bits of a strange, delicious ginger candy.

CHAPTER 28

A Mandala's Permanence

不為一陣寒徹骨
那得清香撲鼻來

Without enduring bone-chilling cold,
Could its delicate sweetness so assail the nose?

—POEM ON THE CHINESE WINTER PLUM BLOSSOM

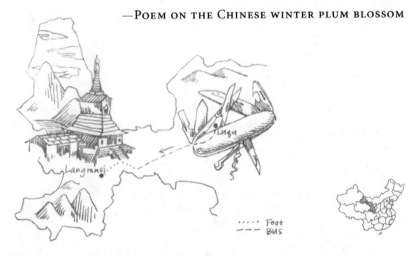

RAIN FALLS steadily as I trudge through the twilight and puddles on Luqu's only street. I step into the lobby of a cheap hotel. The woman informs me it's full. "Go to Hotel Luqu," she orders, pointing to the door. Back in the rain, I find this other hotel, which, with three stories, is the town's tallest building. It's a modern, white, concrete box in a Tibetan village that is only just starting to be "civilized." The lobby boasts the new, pseudo-luxurious style common in Guangzhou and Beijing: broad fake wood surfaces and lots of mirrors. Behind the counter is a shelf of toiletries. 3元 for a comb. 1元 for a bar of soap.

55元 for a foreigner. They don't rent beds individually, so I have to buy an entire room. I argue again that I'm a resident of China, a poor teacher, one deserving a discount. The young woman is not interested in my sad Mandarin or my logic. I fill out the form, and hand her 56元, since I'm out of toilet paper.

Threadbare pink carpet covers the floor, stained white blankets cover the bed. I sit on a red vinyl chair by the window and stare down at the cold street below, where the falling rain stabs repetitive concentric circles in the puddles.

I leave again and walk through the rain to a diner on the corner. The diner has three tables, all empty. The mom of the mom-and-pop welcomes me. "Where are you from?" she asks. "How old are you? How is Guangzhou?"

"Everybody wants to make money," I say.

"Are you traveling alone?"

"Yes."

"You must be very lonely."

"Sometimes."

"How is your family?"

"I don't know."

"It's so cold and rainy today," she shakes her head. "You should have some soup. We just made it."

"Fine. Soup. And some fried rice."

Her rail-thin husband greets me from behind a curtain that hides the kitchen. The plump woman brings out a steaming bowl of soup—tofu and some dark leafy greens—and sits down to chat. They've just moved here from Lanzhou because he finally lined up a job as a math teacher at the middle school. Problem is, Luqu #1 Middle School changed its mind and doesn't need another math teacher. Not for at least two years. Or they hired someone with better *guānxì*. "So we opened this little restaurant," she says. The bok choy and broth warm my belly, tingling like anise and soothing like rum. "It's delicious soup," I remark. I eat every last grain of the greasy fried rice, too. A glass cylinder holds long, soft golden sticks, and the woman follows my eyes.

216

"*Yoútiáo*, tasty and sweet," she jabs her finger at me happily. "Five mao apiece." I buy two of the honey-sweetened fried dough wands, eating one on the way home and saving one for later.

In *Narcissus*, Goldmund settles happily in the wilderness, away from the Black Death. He has two companions: a cheerful boy and a melancholy girl. It is the girl who asks him one bleak afternoon about death. "How can one ever be happy," she asks, "when one knows that soon all will be finished and over?" Goldmund pauses before answering. "About that, the wise men and saints have wracked their brains. There is no lasting happiness. But if what we now have is not good enough for you, if it no longer pleases you, then I'll set fire to this hut this very minute and each of us can go his way."

I drop the book, lie back on the bed, and stare at the peeling ceiling. *Set fire to this hut this very minute. Forget everything. Go my own way.* There's a big brown stain up there, probably from an old water leak. Silence envelops the room completely, like miles of cotton. I imagine a travel agent's brochure: *Cold, Wet, Silent. Visit Luqu.*

How beautiful it was with her. Would I regret anything had it been just one night, one risk? I pull out the blue pocket atlas, the one Lu Lan gave me, and I think of her: her distant smile; her predilection for orange velvet; her conservative, meandering, elusive sense of romance; the safety of her demure standoffs. Gansu Province is a pale blue vulture on page 125. Langmusi, another Tibetan village, lies fifty miles south, and it has an alluring ring to it. Better to keep moving.

In the bathroom, to brush my teeth, I turn on the sink faucet, and a powerful spurt of water soaks my thighs and crotch. I look under the sink and find a whole pipe joint missing.

I sleep solidly, corpse-like, in the utter noiselessness.

✿

LUQU SPITS out a brisk, damp morning, and the wooden bus hut is devoid of customers. Its sole occupant is a bullish ticket man, and I ask him about Langmusi. He's never heard of it. When I ask a second time, he snaps at me: "The bus doesn't go there." He unbuttons the top of his thick green coat and launches into a rundown of every car and bus that comes or goes for a week. His neck looks fatter than my head.

"I want to leave today," I finally say.

"Rouergai or Hezuo?"

"Does the bus to Rouergai stop at Langmusi?"

"No!" he says. "There's no bus."

"What about Maqü?"

"You can't go to Maqü. It's closed to foreigners."

"But there is a bus to Maqü?"

"Yes."

"And on the way, it passes Langmusi, right?"

"Mm."

"Where does that bus end up?"

"Rouergai."

"OK, one ticket for Rouergai."

He stares through me. "18元. Do you have insurance?"

"Yes," I lie, pulling out two 10元 bills.

"It leaves at 9:15, in one hour," he says. "There's a foreigner."

"What?" I look back at him.

"A foreigner."

"Me?" Getting no answer, I pick up my pack and step back outside as a gale blows down the vacant, colorless street. Water and the leftover *yóutiáo* treat become breakfast as I sit my bottom on the cold concrete curb, wincing when I graze my bruise. Looking around me, the town's rawness and slow transition to Han China are on display. The "minority" Tibetans still outnumber the Chinese here, and it was probably off-limits to foreigners until, who knows, last week.

Back in the bus hut, a pale face, an aquiline nose, blond hair, blue eyes, a huge lime green backpack—the shock never wears off. We gape at each other, and then Anton and I are talking about California and UC Santa Cruz, and we're friends. Maybe back home we'd hesitate, but here—two Americans in Luqu, Gansu, China? The ticket man was right. We carry our bags to a gravel parking lot riddled with mud puddles, and Anton groans that the bus only comes through on Tuesdays and Thursdays; he arrived Sunday night and coincidentally intends to visit Langmusi too. After studying Mandarin in Beijing for the year, he's now on a traveling kick. *Just like Michiko.* I sigh and step into a lushly overgrown corner of the lot to urinate, enduring a stench of rotting cabbage mingling with the odor of motor oil.

A long square bus pulls in and turns around as tightly as it can, scraping tree branches. It's nearly full, and Anton and I have to sit near the back. A strange frisson of elation overtakes me as we roll out of the town and climb higher into the misty hills. We wind on a circuitous road that grows muddier and more treacherous with successive switchbacks. Tibetans fill the seats around us, and I comment to Anton that they as a people remain here in their native lands rather than try to assimilate into some "melting pot" because they're not immigrants and, since there's a little more tolerance here, they still own the land. Anton looks out the window. "Well," he begins, "communism says the government owns the land, right? Also, if you haven't noticed, the government is moving Han Chinese into these Western areas continuously, like an ongoing conquest. From Xigatse to Turpan, Han Chinese settlers are here, everywhere. They rise fast through local government and business because of racism or corruption or Beijing's deliberate strategy to dilute independence movements. Every city is becoming a Han city."

I look at him, impressed. "Last night I met a Han couple who had just moved to Luqu."

"I'm not saying they're racist. It's just not a coincidence that they're here."

"At least China still has its native peoples to mistreat, right? We Americans slaughtered most of ours long ago."

"Right," he sighs. "True."

Behind his head, the sun inches over the green mountaintops. "What I've noticed about both the Tibetans and the Hui," I say, "is that they seem to be accepting it and doing better, to be more at ease, than American minorities who live in so many poorer parts of the United States."

"But these folks aren't immigrants—they've lived here for centuries."

"Well, so have lots of minorities in the U.S."

"In some cases," he replies, studying me for a moment. "No, what I've seen is that the peace here is from resignation, not contentment, and still not everyone is accepting it. This doesn't work for most people. The empire could crumble or become a superpower, there could be a civil war any day."

"Don't you see a longing here to forget the decades of suffering? I think the people sense how much is changing and dying, how much is being created, reborn, how much could happen."

Two Tibetan men are watching us. The skin on their cheekbones is wind-chapped a dark bronze, and they both wear white work shirts and brown denim jackets. With a broad smile that exposes his teeth, one asks where we're from and where we're going. They haven't heard of Langmusi, which is troubling. They ask a shriveled old man whose hair is almost gone and who apparently speaks only Tibetan, and he does know Langmusi. "It's up ahead," the young men report. "Not far. You have to get off and walk."

"Walk?" asks Anton. They consult the aged man again and promise to tell us when to disembark. Everyone on the bus is now watching us. One large man comes over and tells us he's going to Lande but occasionally stops in Langmusi. He's another Tibetan cowboy who wears beads and a red headscarf in his hair and a pea green coat with flamboyant red, white, and orange lines twirling up the arms. Most rural Tibetan men seem to be either cowboys or monks: they ride horses or sit on a prayer cushion. The latter seem the more esteemed. "Langmusi is small. It's mostly Tibetans, like me." He has a deep laugh. "Why do you want to go there?"

"We've heard good things," replies Anton, whose Mandarin is excellent.

A monk cuts in: "Langmusi is preparing for a big festival."

The cowboy nods, accepting a festival as a reason two *lǎowài* might visit.

"The festival is for everyone," adds the monk. "Tibetans all over the world."

"Even the Dalai Lama?" I ask.

"Of course," he replies, saying something about His Holiness. I flip to a picture of the Dalai Lama in the *LP* and show him. He puts his hands together and bows solemnly to the picture.

"Pictures of the Dalai Lama are illegal here," Anton murmurs in English. "Be careful." Another Tibetan rises from his seat and asks to see the picture, and I hand it to him. He hands it solemnly to someone else, and the book travels the full length of the bus. So much for safety. The ice broken, the passengers now want to see *all* of our possessions. I hand my knife to two youngsters who eagerly finger its assorted blades. Others take my watch and flip its leather watchband then flash its purple light. I sigh and trust them all, their curiosity. A sensation flashes through me, a shudder of relief, and I breathe it, savor it, seeing in my mind's eye a vision, a grassy hilltop different from these, with water and a lake, and in that place I'm opening my heart, pouring myself out, gratefully, uncontrollably. It's like honey to my mind, and I smile—before I remember how that opening up betrayed me. *I have to learn to control myself, my heart, my stupidity.* The youngsters enjoy my knife more than I ever have, and I'm tempted to let it go, to give it to them. The cowboy tells us to prepare. We roll down into a grassy valley, and at a bend in the dirt road, a smaller road splits off to the right. The bus pulls over. We thank the cowboy, the monk, the driver, and everyone else, and disembark. A dozen hands wave to us through dirty windows, and then those windows roll on down the hill, around a bend, and out of sight.

We're nowhere. No town, no people, no animals. No sounds, no movement. Huge sky, green hills, muddy road. Anton stands beside me, taking it all in. He points and we start up the smaller road. He's a tall, sort of wiry fellow, slight but strong, with fine blond hair he parts on the left. Calm and quiet, he—*Does he open himself to what the world brings? Does he trust himself, others, strangers, women?* I don't ask.

We round a hillside and cross a vast plateau of lush verdure, and with each step I feel my limbs awaken and my lungs fill with sweet, sharp air. Ahead, we spy towering rock walls that are half sedimentary strata and half lava-like igneous formations. We stare at the shifting shades of burgundy, orange, and black rock but have no theory for what geology formed it. We're at the very confluence of China's greatest mountain ranges: the Himalaya, Daxue, Kunlun, and Qinling.

The road runs alongside a river, and our feet sink an inch into the road as it turns to mud. We crest a hill, and the village of Langmusi lies before us, a small hamlet with crisscrossing dirt roads, houses made from wood beams and adobe brick, and crescent moons astride tall spires. High on a hillside, across town, a small Tibetan monastery perches, crowned with red, gold, and green tiered roofs. Hui Muslims and Tibetans seem to share the town, as they did the larger Xiahe. Apparently Tibetans predominate here in Langmusi.

Children rush up and walk alongside us as we enter town, touching our legs and our backpacks, but they don't ask for pens, or for anything else. Passing a blocky concrete hotel that is even more out of place in this venerable town than the one was in Luqu, I realize there are essentially two architectural styles in China: the old style, which is hand-crafted, thoughtful, and ornate; and this one, the new style, functional, Bauhaus, anonymous, glorifying modernity without frivolities. Thanks to the Cultural Revolution, 95% of China seems to demonstrate the new style. Two Tibetan cowboys wearing the traditional beads and red headscarves step out of the door of the hotel.

Anton and I continue on and step into a low-roofed Hui restaurant. Its sign indicates it's *qīngzhēn* (Muslim), a place in which the meat is prepared scrupulously in accordance with Islamic law. The tables are made of a chocolate-hued wood, and bright tomatoes and clumps of scallions hang on the wall beside the kitchen. Coal smoke hangs in the air. Old men wearing white skullcaps look up as we take an open table by the door. Before long a cook brings us piping hot bowls of noodle soup, and thick steam redolent of garlic and lamb rushes into my face, cleansing my sinuses. I grab the chunks with chopsticks and hold the bowl to my lips to drink the broth. Anton orders a pot of Eight Treasures Tea, a tasty blend of fermented tea, rock sugar, chrysanthemum flowers, and dried fruit. The meal feels like a private banquet.

We discuss politics and war, and Anton too suggests I look into the history of America and its military. "Is there a blameless land?" I ask.

"There are a couple," he says. "Not many. But there are a few that deserve most of the blame."

"Maybe love and war are man's only real passions," I say. There's a long pause.

"*Man's*, maybe," he says. "Women seem to have other ones."

"And maybe they're also man's only real fears?" I ask.

Anton turns reticent, and we leave the restaurant and climb the winding road to the monastery. The white walls are covered by gigantic brown tapestries, each of which is embroidered with mysterious white symbols: twin fish kissing in an upside-down heart, interlocking diamonds with wings, a compass wheel with eight spokes. We climb the stone steps tentatively, and pause below the tapestries, not wanting to trespass or interrupt. A slow drumbeat rises from within, like a heartbeat, and it grows in volume until a deep human chant joins in. We sit on the stairs to listen. Haloed by the sacred sounds and the scent of incense, we gaze upon the valley stretching before us: Below on our right stands a *stupa*—a sacred Tibetan stone tower that resembles a chess pawn; further down, nestled in a crease in the terrain, the village's hundred peaked wooden roofs huddle together; beyond the homes, jutting into a dazzling sky, naked rocky mountaintops touch the clouds. Behind us, the chanting continues. I notice my breathing slow down, down to the pace of the drumbeat, down to the pace of the clouds. There in my inner silence is regret, welling up inside me, whole, full, abiding, staining everything, like the saddle bruise.

Two monks in burgundy robes step through the tapestry above us and sit on the top stair quietly. The chanting fades to a hum, then to silence. One monk gathers his robes, stands, and invites us in, so we follow him up the stairs, through the tapestries, and into a large, candle-lit chamber of Buddhist paintings and sculptures. Giant trumpets and a gong stand near the door. Enthroned in the center of the room is a statue of the Buddha, showing a broad, peaceful, welcoming palm to us. The monk guides us through a curtain, into an area where five monks kneel around a low table. They huddle over something resembling a blueprint.

When we get close enough, we see it's actually a giant sheet of white parchment covered with piles of bright red, blue, yellow, and green sand. The monks are carefully scratching sticks on long wooden pens in order to sprinkle sand onto the paper a few grains at a time. We watch for a while. It will take years to cover the whole sheet. Anton asks about this, and amazingly, the monk says it will be finished for the festival on Friday, two days away. "It's a mandala," he explains, "a map of heaven." Lines of colored sand make concentric circles, leading to the center, but there are all kinds of geometric interruptions: flights of fancy, lions, dragons. I watch grains the hue of fresh spinach fall into place, one at a time, becoming part of a diamond. Each grain commands its own moment. Beside the diamond is a yellow lion, then a blue tree.

One monk tells a joke in Tibetan and looks up at me with a smile. A young monk with a flattened nose motions me over and asks if my shirt is silk. I shake my head, letting him touch it. I ask him how the mandala will be used in the festival, but my Mandarin must be wrong, because he tells me instead how they make it. He gestures for me to kneel next to him, so I place my knees on a red cushion, and bow my head beside theirs, barely a foot above the exquisite map. He takes one of the ridged straw-like implements and hands it to me. I point to my untrained hand, shake my head, and chuckle. Again, I ask about using the mandala at the festival, and he finally nods and says it's important, something to do with prayers and blessings.

"And the mandala?" I ask.

"We dump it into the river."

"The river?"

A monk sprinkling blue looks up at me. "To remember the transience of human undertaking."

His words ring in my brain. I try to imagine an American spending days on something and then destroying it, but all I can see is how different an hour with the mandala is from an hour at an American college or business. Most Americans are guided by something they're chasing—pursuit of achievement, pursuit of pleasure, pursuit of happiness.

This is about something else, a different happiness, a happiness not bound to the fulfillment of desires. It's a happiness bound to something that already exists.

The grains continue to fall from their wands, and the mandala takes shape, comprising four artistically distinct quadrants. Nothing but this world—this mandala—will occupy the minds of these monks until it is completed; they follow their life's path with an acuity I've never before seen.

Some time later I step back outside with Anton. The sky is split between good and evil. Thick, dark clouds have rolled in right next to the deep blue we admired before, and the rocky crags now appear black and menacing. Yellow sunlight still glints off the green and gold eaves above us, and we hike up the hillside behind the temple onto a grassy plateau at the same altitude as the fat honey sun. A white tent stands at the far edge of the plateau, overlooking Langmusi and its valley. We cross the plateau towards the tent, out of which a crowd of young monks rush en masse. They approach us, surround us, and with curious smiles on their faces pelt us with questions. We answer as best we can, watching their eyes search to understand. They look about twelve, but they're already in robes of fiery crimson, brick red, and day-glow fuchsia. Their heads are shaven. All of us sit down together in the thick grass and white wildflowers, but of course we can't convey the other world. "Are you Christian? Is college difficult? Are cars expensive?" Like everyone, they assume Americans are very rich, so I say some Americans are poor and explain many need loans to go to college if they can go at all.

They show us their campground. With just a tiny campfire to battle imminent night, it reminds me of camping I did as a boy, carefree. This may be their obligation. The youngsters find the same pleasure the teenagers on the bus did in tinkering with our watches and wallets; my Swiss Army knife mystifies one mischievous young monk; another flips open the lens of my camera. My mind is suddenly invaded by Michiko—that honey in her hair, the taste of her skin—and I feel her presence and see her suffering, pregnant, missing me. My mouth goes dry. I blink and silently make myself a teacher for the young monks.

How about a skit? How about if we do a skit about freedom, about choices, about women?

Anton produces a photo of the Dalai Lama, and the boys rejoice so openly that it forces me back into the moment, *now*. Ah, my lungs open, and I could give away everything, all my possessions, just to share, just to keep breathing, just to keep giving and receiving. Perhaps I could even give away this anger, this regret, as if it were a thing. They toss around my camera, and I feel a different, materialistic anxiety, and I voice it. I ask the one holding my camera if he's ever taken a photo before.

His face is pure innocence. "No."

Everybody laughs.

"Look through here," I point. "When you can see all of us, push this button." The sun is sinking behind the distant peaks, but its last rays shine fiercely, striking us between the eyes. The young novice takes a photograph of...heaven only knows. "Thanks," I say, grateful for the picture, for the honesty, for the reminder of so much I'd forgotten. Months into my future, in a different land, at a different elevation, I will discover this monk's magical, perfect, innocent photograph.

A cold wind whips up, and the boys tell us an address to use when sending Dalai Lama portraits, and then we all embrace and shake hands. They show us a steep shortcut down to town. Anton and I wish them well and descend the path. I remind him of his words about caution, since pictures of the Dalai Lama could be caught in the mail inspection and get the monks into trouble. He eyes the piece of cardboard scratched with Chinese characters. "I can't really read this address anyway. Too bad nobody out here ever has a pen."

Thick, orange mud cakes our shoes, and when we reach the streets we stop to kick it off in a village square. Kids of all ages are playing, chasing a soccer ball, playing cards, or just sitting in the dirt; a gaunt, smiling, toothless man sells soft drinks. One by one, they all stop to wave at us as we pass by.

"Would you live here?" I turn to Anton.

"It's nice," he murmurs, as we stop at a water wheel where the river runs through town. We watch the current turn the wheel.

"Living right in the middle of town might be trouble," I say. "But who would know if some guy just pitched a tent up in the hills? How long would I last?"

He smiles. "I doubt China has much of an immigration policy. They wouldn't know what to do. I mean, how many immigrants has China had in the last fifty years?"

I peer up at the hills.

"A few Koreans, I guess," he answers his own question.

"I could live here, though. What worries would I have? A bank account with a few thousand dollars, and I'm set for a decade."

"It's beautiful now, but what about the next revolution? As they say, 'The Kingdom long divided must unite, the Kingdom long united must divide.'"

"Good point. I guess in America I could live a peaceful, inexpensive life too, people just don't. People want to get rich and have everything. We're so stupid."

"*Free*, I think, is what we say."

"Free." I try out the word. "Free. The advertising makes us want big cars and homes and perfect spouses and all of that, and to get enough money we take jobs that stress us out. We'd be a better country if everyone came here for a while."

Raindrops test the air, and we step into the Bauhaus hotel to get a room. I climb into one of the two beds and listen to the precipitation ring on the metal roof for an hour before my mind dissolves into sleep.

❁

ANTON IS on a tight schedule and decides in the morning to leave Langmusi. I consider my alternatives and opt to move on with him. The woman at the hotel desk informs us that a bus usually swings by that curve in the road "around two in the afternoon."

A man near the front door shakes his head. "It comes around noon."

We breakfast at Momma Jun's, which has only two tables, and we ask Momma Jun herself. A sturdy woman in a traditional Tibetan woman's black dress, brilliant sky blue apron, and scarlet headscarf, she says, "Ten or eleven." Anton and I chuckle at the disparate intelligence we've gathered. She serves us fruit, tangy yogurt, Eight Treasures Tea, and husky slices of local bread. Onions, eggs, and tomatoes sizzle in her big black pan, then land on our plates.

Bellies warm, we leave right away. Children run alongside us, screaming goodbyes, petting or punching our legs. The river, swollen from excessive rain, has forgotten its banks and rushes along carelessly beside the road. A truck barrels by and kicks fistfuls of wet earth up at us, making us dodge and slip on the bank. Anton nearly falls into the stream. I throw him a hand, and he regains his footing.

CHAPTER 29

Storms, Death, and Six Dollars

When the breath ceases...
the knower will experience the clear light
of the natural condition.
—TIBETAN BOOK OF THE DEAD

R AIN RUNS down the Himalayan foothills, carving little paths in the orange earth at our feet. Anton is shivering. There are others here too at the bend in the road: A Tibetan family of four—father, mother, daughter, and son—huddle under a translucent sheet of plastic. I hold my poncho close as the downpour pitter-patters to me about the long journey north these summer monsoons make from Bangladesh.

A white bus bounces down the mountainside. The Tibetans remain on the ground, but we *lǎowài* practically do jumping jacks in our ponchos. The bus approaches, passes, never slows, and the Chinese tourists behind the wet windowpanes apparently don't even notice us. To amuse myself I call them "Taiwanese," a word that connotes "foreigner." In Beijing, this was blasphemy. *Taiwan is a part of China; all Taiwanese people are renegades who fled the mainland; China must fight to defend its unity and sovereignty.* But out here, who cares? Who cares if there's a world war over Taiwan? In the middle of this cold muddy nowhere, as the bus flees from sight, I blaspheme freely.

At least it's gorgeous. The hills around us are ridiculously green from all the rain, the road is a stripe of dark mahogany, and a silvery river dances down a nearby hillside. An hour passes by, and I hike fifty yards to where the river crosses beneath the road, discovering a dry hideout under a stone bridge. I call to Anton, suggesting we take turns at lookout, and he yells back his approval. I doff my pack and rest in the dryness, listening to the rush of the monsoon overhead, letting my eyes and mind flow with the stream. The quiet artistry of the monks replays in my mind. I picture the red, green, yellow, and blue sands slipping off of the mandala, falling into the currents, swimming by, carrying away my troubles, their troubles, everyone's troubles. Today they will finish the enormous mosaic, and at a festival tomorrow they will bring it to this river. The vision of this dispassionate destruction, this earthly consecration of a map of heaven, captivates my mind as the water becomes my world. *Now.* It happens *now.* Everything, *now.* The end, *now.* The beginning, *now.* The present expands to envelop me, to envelop all possibilities, and I'm floating in the clouds, swimming in warm seas, doing everything I've ever done, simultaneously, right now. Hours, weeks, months go by.

Anton switches places with me; he's almost ready to give up. I can see why when I'm back up in the storm, the cold shoving my mind into *this* moment. This blue sweater scratches my neck but keeps me cozy while it reminds me of her. I wear it every day now for its closeness and insulation, but it seems to chain lodestones around my neck. *Do I have a disease? Is she pregnant? Am I bound to her forever? Am I bound to be alone?* It hugs my chest, constricting, loosening, constricting.

Through the rain, a huge sky-blue truck crashes down the slope and blows its horn. I flail my arms and legs and call to Anton. The behemoth with a wooden trailer actually slows down on the bridge, sending my spirits soaring. It lurches to a stop right in front of me. A boyish head shoots out of the passenger-side window. "Hello?"

The tired English word melts my anger, sweeter than the *yóutiáo* honey wand in Luqu.

"Whither dost thou go?" I use my most polite Mandarin.

"Lande," he says.

Not that it matters. "Old master," I say. "Could we possibly get a ride?"

He throws open the door like the gate of St. Peter, and we pull ourselves up into the cab as he moves to a small back seat. Anton and I sit in front, too delighted with the warm and dry to follow what he's saying about some "crazy brother." The musty air and cigarette smoke smell comforting, almost refreshing, as we arrange our bags and ponchos on the floor, trying not to slog in too much mud.

"Where are you from?" The guy leans forward. His Mandarin has a heavy Tibetan accent, and his white work shirt is unbuttoned halfway down his chest. He looks about twenty. Beside him in the backseat sits a young woman with a calm, noncommittal smile.

"America," I say, sighing, invoking home for the thousandth time. "A long way away." The driver's seat is empty, and the door stands wide open.

"He's checking the wheels," the young man explains. "It's a heavy load today." Leaning back, he extracts a cigarette from a tan pack, lights up, and offers us the pack.

Anton shakes his head. "What are you carrying?"

A smug stream of smoke shoots from a corner of his mouth. "Bricks," he says. "Heavy."

I look outside, and the Tibetans who were waiting with us are nowhere to be seen. A teenager vaults up into the driver's seat and greets us with a broad smile. His navy blue pants are rolled to his knees and his shock of black hair stands on end. He says something in Tibetan to his companions. His elbow pierces my thigh as he throws the enormous gearshift down and over. I rub my leg as we ease into a downhill roll. Everything feels incredible: to be dry, to be warm, to be moving.

The driver asks to see my watch—not to learn the time, just to see it, as the young monks did. He asks how I like China. I gush about the kind people, especially the truck drivers, and he laughs. With one hand still on the wheel, he pulls a cigarette and lighter of his own out of his shirt and lights up. I look straight ahead at the emerald hills sliding by, obscured by the spattering drops and the windshield wipers' rhythmic tick-tock. Deep potholes bounce the hard middle seat up against my wound, which I again earnestly pray isn't infected. The young driver puffs away, and the cab slowly fills with smoke as we wrap around downhill curves.

"This is amazing kindness," Anton says. "Thank you."

I whisper to Anton in English about offering them some payment.

"I like to give dollar bills," he replies, not whispering. "Not for payment but more for good luck. Everyone seems to love it." He hands me a dollar bill and I find five more George Washingtons in the bottom of my Dry Ice pack. Six dollars. I fold the notes up in my pocket for later.

The cigarette smoke gathers thick, and sheets of rain conceal the world outside, but our young pilot guides the wheel with a single nonchalant hand. I focus my attention on the green and red prayer flags that hang from his rearview mirror. I breathe and meditate. I pray for Michiko, that she is happy and safe on her own, and it all replays: horses, monastery, bliss, beauty, regret. *Maybe I'm learning something in this new classroom.* I pray for myself, that I gain wisdom about this anger and frustration, that somewhere some new insight awaits.

And I pray for our driver, that he is somehow an old hand at these Himalayan roads. He looks sixteen and too confident. He opens a beer, wrestling its cap free while bracing the steering wheel with a knee. "PSSHT!" cries the large brown bottle. He drinks as he whips us around a muddy bend. He passes the bottle to me, and I hold it a moment, then take a deep swig, wanting to leave less for him. It's a sweet, heavy, raw barley brew. I pass it to Anton, who samples more slowly but wisely holds on to the bottle. Not to be outwitted, the driver points to the glove compartment, where we find two more bottles. He cracks into one immediately and keeps it for himself. "How old are you?" He glances at me between a puff and a pull, forearms taking turns on the wheel. On an uphill slope, he yanks around the mighty gearshift, leaving the wheel unattended. The engine roars.

"T-twenty-three," I stutter. "You?"

"Eighteen," he grins. His name is Lamdo. His brother in back is Jamyang, twenty-two. Ranjie, the thin woman, is twenty-four and a schoolteacher.

Jamyang leans forward and chuckles. "Don't you worry, my little brother's a good driver." On cue, Lamdo leans back and rests a foot on the dash.

"You're all Tibetans?" Anton asks, looking back at Ranjie. She nods, smoothing a wisp of glossy hair. Her classes are over for the day, and she's hitchhiking to her parents' home. Up ahead, a dead end fortunately turns into a hairpin turn, and we learn that the Tibetan family who waited with us is above us now, on top of the open trailer. We veer around the hairpin, and I picture them up there, clinging to the wet bricks. Goldmund's words dance through my mind: "Travelers accept what heaven's hand gives them: sun, rain, fog, snow, warmth, cold, comfort, hardship..."

We wind higher, entering the clouds, and under my feet the engine grows hot. Mist gathers around us like a scarf. Lamdo flicks his cigarette out the window, grabs a towel, rubs on the windshield, and cuts a momentary hole in the condensation. I want to help in some way—wipe the window for him, maybe, or just take the damn wheel. But instead my knee collides again with the gearshift as we roar around another bend, and I'm saying something about the driving rain when another tractor-trailer appears out of the mist, coming right for us. It's twenty feet away, ten feet away, ten inches away, passing by, on our right, gigantic wheels skidding and spitting mud off the edge. Lamdo shoots me a smile, and for a moment he looks like a devil, a giddy, mischievous agent of death. I swallow my breath and leap forward to wipe fog from the glass with the arm of my sweater.

"Sing us a song," Jamyang says.

Ranjie suggests we sing our "national song," and it seems plausible, so we launch into the *Star Spangled Banner*, giving it our full voices. Anton's a better singer than Byron and we're able to find the melody. They applaud and respond with a punchy Tibetan song. The singing seems to warm this little chamber, to make it safer. When it's our turn again, we sing, "Twinkle, twinkle, little star…" We apologize for choosing a children's song, but they're delighted, and they hum the melody and ask for a translation of the lyrics. The brothers launch into a Chinese drinking song, but their tune is cut short. Lamdo curses and strips the gears, repeatedly ramming the stick into place. Jamyang whispers to him anxiously in Tibetan while the engine growls like an angry lion.

"How high are we?" Anton asks.

"3300 meters," mutters Jamyang. "4000, soon."

This is 13,000 feet, a new record for me. Jamyang says something else, louder, and the brothers disagree. On a steep incline, the truck stalls and dies. It's over. Lamdo kicks down the brake. We all climb out. Lamdo and Jamyang recline under the front axle and pound with hammers. Anton and I eventually scramble up the grassy mountainside for the view: The trailer yoked to our blue cab contains pink bricks and a family of hardy Tibetans; behind it, below it, black Tibetan yak-cows called dzo dot the hillsides; beyond them, through the mist, mountains stretch inexhaustibly, like massive green sand dunes. The little girl on top of the truck peers up at me, and I realize that if we ever move from here, I should change places with her. Yes. Although… all huddled together there, caring for each other, they seem to have it figured out. Why did the brothers give us the warm cab and give their own countrymen the cold bricks? Is it my place to question their decision? As if hearing my thoughts, the brothers drop their hammers and climb to our vantage, and they smile with us at their beautiful land. On official Chinese maps we remain outside the Tibetan border, but culturally and historically we're well inside the Land of the Snow Lion. To our companions, this is the Tibetan province of Amdo.

Fierce gusts whip at our clothes, and the rain returns. Unbelievably, as if cured by some visiting spirit, the truck roars to life like a hungry beast, and all is well—we're climbing the sides of mountains again. New smokes for Jamyang and Lamdo. We learn, through a roundabout conversation, that the weight of the load has cracked the wheels. But up we go, climbing, spiraling to some invisible apex, riding a slippery shelf above the world. Patches of clarity reveal a hang-glider's view so boundless that for a moment I forget the road entirely.

Then we start to go down. We roll easily and freely, helplessly accelerating, skidding on mud around the bends, and death introduces herself again to the architect of my thoughts. People have existed precariously forever in these mountains; death is the simple, swift consequence of negligence, foolishness, a tough winter, or, perhaps, cracked wheels.

We roll faster—too fast—into the next turn. HONK-HONK! Lamdo has to take the middle of the road and blow his horn through the mist in case another truck is coming. I clench closed my eyelids, feeling every molecule in my body tingle. "Don't be afraid," Jamyang touches my shoulder. "Lamdo is a race-driver." Around another blind hairpin, Lamdo blows his horn, taking the whole road. Race-driver? Race-trucker?

Rolling down his window, Lamdo flicks a cigarette butt out into empty space. He throws a leg up on the dash, pops another beer, and relaxes, but now he doesn't have a free hand to sound the horn. We roll faster toward the edge, toward a tight curve, and he whips her around—with just his right forearm. We speed down a steep stretch towards another no-look left turn. We draw near the hairpin; Lamdo waits. We reach the turn; Lamdo waits. At the edge, he whips his forearm across the steering wheel, but it slips. Instead of turning it, his arm slides all the way off the steering wheel. We roll straight for the edge. My mind flashes a vision of a childhood soccer game bathed in sunlight. My heart fills with gratitude for all of these years I've had, these highs and lows that make a varied life and that suddenly collapse into a single bright dot.

Lamdo brings his arm around. He places an open palm on the wheel and turns with all his might. A skidding sound. Death disappears off to the right and is replaced by another stretch of muddy road. My heart beats again.

But no one speaks for several minutes.

❀

THE ROAD winds hurriedly downward, oblivious to who might be traveling its muddy thread.

"Race driver?" Anton finally asks.

"I race trucks," Lamdo replies.

"One of the boldest around," adds Jamyang. "Because he's so fast."

"Where do you race?" Anton asks.

"Usually on long straight roads. Sometimes right here." Lamdo grins just as the road flattens, straightens, drops into a valley, and runs as fast as it can from the peaks and the storm.

"Is that how the wheels get damaged?" Anton asks.

Jamyang shakes his head. "It's these bricks—the heaviest load we've ever carried."

Death. It's startling to watch it pass on your right or left or reach for companions on top of your truck. The worst is that moment of its arrival, that moment of breath-stealing fear, that moment that is…useless. Without the fear, death might be just another arrival, another serendipitous experience, another conclusion; painful perhaps, but many things are painful, and it might be pleasurable, like a dive off a cliff into a cold lake where the fear freezes you at first, but the shock of impact is brief and the water soon turns warm and familiar.

Anton asks about the Tibetans on top, and Jamyang peers through the tiny back window. "Still there."

"Did you know them?" I ask.

Jamyang smiles. "Did we know you?"

Lamdo looks at me. "Did you know us?"

"You're very kind to pick people up," I say, after a pause.

"They only pick people up sometimes," qualifies Ranjie.

Storms, Death, and Six Dollars

Lamdo pulls over in the middle of a grassy windswept plateau, and everyone climbs out for a rest. My feet touch the ground—oh, fertile, solid earth, forgotten friend! I stroll out greedily into the chilly air, into a vast emptiness that unfurls like a green prayer flag all the way to distant mountains. The gray maze of mist overhead parts, and the sun emerges like a symphony, serenading everything with its radiance. I close my eyes and inhale deeply to taste this change, this light-switch movement of Tibetan darkness and light. My eyes open again and everything seems weightless, like colored sands falling into a river.

CHAPTER 30

The First Laughter

火要空心人要虚心

Fire burns only with space in its center,
Man grows only with modesty in his heart.
—CHINESE PROVERB

S UNLIGHT POURS through scattered holes in the clouds. The land
smoothes out and our cracked wheels hop onto pavement. Lamdo
cuts sharply on the wet cement. "We're entering Sichuan Province," he
announces. Sichuan, or Szechwan, is the California of China: the most
populous, rebellious, and diverse of China's provinces. Sichuan's cuisine is China's most famous, and its people number more than those
of any European country. The fertile valleys of its East are Han; the
sky-scraping mountains up here in the Northwest are Tibetan; and the
moist, culturally diverse South resembles Burma. Just this past March,
to reduce the province's size and power, Beijing sliced off its eastern
quarter and created a new province.

Lamdo whips down the first side road we come to and pulls over in front of an abandoned building. The truck rolls to a halt.

"Zöigê is just down the road." He points.

The Tibetans on top of the truck got off hours ago in a splendid, drenched nowhere. Now it's our turn, and we thank Lamdo and Jamyang warmly and hand them the six dollar bills. They refuse courteously at first, but then accept the exotic pieces of paper with wonder.

The truck disappears around a hill, and a cold drizzle falls gently down upon us. I stare up into the heavens, opening my mouth to catch a raindrop's blessing on my tongue, and its tapdance deepens the strange pleasure of being alive in the precise middle of nowhere. Anton starts in the direction they indicated, and I follow. Lot after abandoned lot of overgrown concrete lie on our left, while on our right a naked mountain valley unfolds. A bone-chilling shiver shakes me under my pack, and Goldmund's thoughts come again: "Time does not exist for travelers—they're children at heart, always living in the first day of creation." Travelers have always by necessity welcomed this magic, this fate, danger, and discovery. Travelers ineluctably live in the *now*.

A lone billboard depicts a hot mug of green tea, and the wisps of steam take me on a journey far away, fueling a desire not to be here, not to be *now*, to be somewhere else, to be warm, dry, *home*. Harried souls dart through the rain, not even wasting time to stare, and then we enter Zöigê, a collection of buildings in the new architectural style—solid drab concrete and blue tile. Every store and door is closed. In the truck, I made a note about a hostel, and I extricate the *LP* with my shivering fingers. The Zöigê Government Hotel is "filthy" and "putrid," I review, and the status of Zöigê as a whole is "unclear for foreigners… but don't worry, the police will find you if they want to." We locate our putrid destination at the far edge of town, and it's actually of the old style—covered in lovely, intricate paintings that seem to fade away with charming nonchalance right before our eyes. A rotund woman opens a metal gate, takes our money, and kindly shows us to a second-floor room that's covered with murals of mountain landscapes. Greeting us inside is the smell of mildew. Our wet packs fall to the floor, Anton hangs his poncho on the door and collapses onto a chair, and I fish my towel and soap from my pack and speed like a downhill racetruck to the shower. In a wooden shed, a nozzle sputters as I strip naked. Hot rivers stream, spray, pound, and soothe the muscles of my shoulders, back, and legs. I wiggle my toes and roll my neck, grinning, imagining every cell of my body diving into a warm pool.

Having finally washed my riding wound, I ask Anton to attach a bandage to it, realizing with an odd certainty that I would never ask a man to do this *at home.* "It really doesn't look too bad," he says, casually lifting a huge weight from my shoulders. "It's a cut, it's almost healed."

I pull my blue sweater over a cleaner T-shirt and for a moment I can't stop grinning, and I'm floating with a sparkling lightness back to the monks and the mandala, remembering that other happiness, that gratitude for simplicity, that pure uncomplicated awareness of existence. "Isn't it amazing?" I say. "This moment. This life. We're alive. Everything that we need already exists. Nothing needs to exist that isn't already here."

"It is amazing." He smiles at me. "Well, I could do without the rain."

H E GETS his wish. The Zöigê market peacocks a panoply of colors amid the town's baldness. Radiant in slanting afternoon light, fresh fruits and vegetables, so rare up here in the mountains, beckon to us: red peppers the size of pinky fingers, fat purple grapes, fuzzy kiwis, bright orange persimmons, white melons, long succulent green beans. People are everywhere now, leisurely buying and selling, conversing with friends, perhaps planning a family dinner. A man pushes a giant wheelbarrow of spinach past, and the smells of the green leaves and rich earth rise to my nostrils. Three children fly by on a bicycle, hollering and splashing through a broad puddle. It's already seven, but the lingering raindrops glisten in sunlight since the entire nation runs on a single time zone—"Beijing Time"—as if to remind us all who's in charge. The clocks say seven when the sun says four.

Anton craves fruit and insists we stop for a snack. We haggle gently with a vendor for bags of grapes and persimmons, and one of the fist-sized orange fruits soon surrenders its juices between my teeth. We stroll on through the town, passing between cinder-block homes. A horrific squealing pierces our ears. In front of one house, a small man holds firmly onto the large neck of a pig; the man repeatedly braces his knee against the meaty body as he brandishes a long knife. The animal shrieks again in terror, hurling its cries skyward, throwing wails off the walls of the homes. Then, silence. The door of a different home stands wide open as we pass by, and I see a family at a table: Two adults poke into bowls of rice, and a little boy sings, filling the air with a chaotic melody.

Dimness grows from the shadows around us as the sky overhead shreds into pink and purple. We stop into what must be one of the town's finer restaurants, and a man with smoothly combed hair strides out of the kitchen to greet us. He takes our order, and our choices arrive on artistically arranged platters: thin, smoothly sliced *tǔdòu sī* potatoes; fragrant, ginger-kissed bok choy; and sizzling *tiěbǎn niúròu* (iron plate beef). Everything looks unbelievably divine, and with the first bite, my eyes slide closed to savor the scents and the flavors, the spices and sauces intertwining their textures on my tongue. A frisson of pleasure courses through me.

Anton pincers a morsel of beef and asks where I'm off to next. I'm not sure what to say. He's made the decisions thus far, but he seems unconcerned as to whether we travel together or apart. He mentions Jiuzhaigou, China's largest national park, and coincidentally it's the place that Li Song, quite well-traveled himself, called China's most beautiful. It could be next for me, but Anton says he doesn't have much time. He still wants to see Xishuangbanna, a lush jungle region in the south that borders Burma, and he's leaving China in eleven days. We agree for now just to keep moving, together, to make a decision on Jiuzhaigou tomorrow.

He tells me about his year in Beijing. He was at *Běidà* too, like Michiko. "We had this amazing city of international students right on campus," he says. "Europeans, South Americans, Africans. And yet everybody spoke Mandarin."

"That must've helped you learn."

"Yeah, but with two non-native speakers, neither of you knows how the language is actually supposed to sound. We probably just made each other's errors worse!"

"Was everyone in dorms together?" *Does he know her?*

"Yes, all the foreigners. We were probably isolated from the regular students intentionally, since *Beǐdà* has been the center of so much activism over the years. The government wants *Beǐdà* to be prestigious and to be a place where foreigners come to learn Mandarin, but they'd love to do without any more democracy movements."

I can't tell him about her. I know that. I should just forget her, or I should just never have been with her, or, well, either way, it's something to deal with on my own.

"It was really different for us," I say, "down in Guangzhou. The gates were locked at night, but otherwise we were free to go where we pleased around town." I tell him about watching movies, dancing in discos, meeting dissidents for dinner, disseminating propaganda in parks, visiting cultural landmarks with attractive fellow teachers. "One of the teachers who taught at our school last year dated one of the local teachers, and everyone quietly knew, and my roommate dated that same teacher this year," I say. "I was good, though."

"Better to steer clear of the Asian Cravin,'" he agrees, with a casual grin.

We exit into darkness. The street is unlit, and a starry sky is overhead. The fading murals await us in our room, and as I climb into the cold bed, my mind wanders over the day, past the callous stare of death, past the swirling sands in the stream, back to the morning's sizzling omelets at Momma Jun's. In a minute my body warms the sheetless cot.

❁

AN ALARM buzzes in the darkness. It's already five-thirty. Anton snaps on the light. I stumble to my feet, reaching for a shirt and pants. We trip down the stairs onto empty streets. The wind whips around us as the first bending arrows of the sun illuminate the sleeping heavens.

Atop a concrete cube, Chinese characters declare "Rouergai Bus Station." The Chinese evidently renamed this town *Rouergai* in order to liberate it from the Tibetan language, which is not only difficult for them to pronounce but impossible to transliterate with characters. And as with the time zone, everyone in Zöigê seems simply to work around the imposition. Inside the cube, the bright fluorescent light and swirling cigarette fumes greet us. Yesterday, our waiter told us that there are two buses to Songpan: one leaving bright and early at six; the other, for those who cherish daylight and beauty sleep, departing half an hour later.

We slip out back, where a crowd is stepping past a ticket taker and squeezing their sluggish bodies onto a bus. The mountain dawn around us is frosty and beautiful. The stink of sweat and chicken excrement wakes us up as we push onboard and sidle between two cages of complaining birds, six tarpaulin-covered crates, a dozen sacks of potatoes, and countless human beings. We find seats at the back and push open a window.

The bus begins to roll. Several dzo perched on hillsides watch us rumble out of town under the periwinkle sky. Beyond the hills, the slopes turn deep green and then, for the first time, snow white at their peaks. The only sign of human habitation is a single chain of telephone poles running fifty yards from the road.

I ask Anton if we should ask the driver to let us off so we can camp over the first rolling crest.

He smiles, following my eyes. "You're really into this idea of living here."

"It's so beautiful. This whole land feels blessed. Why not? We could go months without anyone knowing. As if we'd dropped off the face of the earth."

"It's a special place," he nods. "Maybe someday. We'd need some serious gear."

I spot plumes of smoke curling skyward and follow them down to a village of tiny white dots that turn out to be tents. People *do* live out here. We pass close enough that we can make out an enclosed herd of dzo beside a mound of black dirt that might be a human home.

Miles of mountains push us downhill, and around noon we roll down into a valley and into Songpan, where the sun is high, hard, and scorching. On a crowded, shady stretch of sidewalk we wait four hours until the bus to Jiuzhaigou finally arrives. The bus is late, and we have to run alongside it, banging the dirt off the hinges of its rusty door. It never stops. Arrogant and packed to the gills, it just keeps going, right out of town, never stopping, never even slowing to confer with us. The hot dust stares back up at me as I pant, letting it go, feeling tired and frustrated. I suddenly laugh, and what spreads through my body is strange, sweet, and new: a recognition that every moment is like this—impossibly unpredictable.

The monsoons up north are bad, we learn, and mudslides have closed the road. There is no next bus.

A man loads boxes of melons into a large titanium-white jeep. He's the fifth person we've asked, but he is going to Jiuzhaigou, and if we pay for the gas, he'll take us. Flat-faced, middle-aged, he wears a frayed red T-shirt emblazoned with the Coca-Cola logo, but where the letters should spell "Coca-Cola," they spell "Cocaine." He doesn't speak English, so he's probably not aware of the wordplay. He assures us we can do the trip in five hours, which makes no sense with the monsoons and mud—and the fact that the woman in the bus station said it would take eight. But it's too tempting, and we close the deal and load our bags into the back. Ten minutes later, we climb in and roar out of town on a cliff-hanging highway.

"We'll beat the rain," he vows quietly. For the first time in China I find a seatbelt and fasten it. We turn onto a pitted dirt road which takes us northeast, through terraced rice paddies. We have to slow down, almost to the pace of a man in a broad-brimmed straw hat who steps along the terrace walls between puddles that reflect afternoon sunlight. The Swiss cheese road turns to soup, and the driver kicks down the four-wheel-drive and slaloms around knee-deep sinkholes. At twilight we hit a line of stopped vehicles, and the driver climbs out to investigate. "A stuck car," he reports. "The mud is like snow. We might... not... make it." He gives us a blank stare. There are no more places to stay before Jiuzhaigou, so it's a gamble, and Anton and I glance at each other. "Go for it?" he asks, raising a fist. "Double or nothing?"

I nod and smile, and we tell him. We forge on, steering around trapped vehicles, climbing hills of thick ochre mud. Darkness drops like a curtain. We roll down a slope and around a bend, and there below us, lit up by our headlights, is a long queue of parked vehicles. The narrow road is soft, velvety mud. Buses, trucks, and jeeps idle, pointed down, while others, below them, are stranded and point up. At the face-off, in the center of the road, a broad rut bisects the road, and a truck is mired down in it. On our right, a steep, wooded mountainside rises abruptly; on our left, the viscous soil shelf drops off sharply. People mill about in the halo of headlights, waiting to try their luck.

Obviously it will be a while before we can move on, so I hop out into the cold. After just two steps my shoes are caked in an inch of the orange-brown glue, but I trudge on, past the people, up into the woods. From a steep outcropping I gaze down at the writhing truck, its frantic roar now distant enough that I can also hear the crickets sing to the milky moon. I have a disease and a wife and a child, all three. I did everything wrong. I allowed her in. I surrendered my freedom. Death awaits around the next bend.

A sigh emerges slowly from my chest, a whisper, and I breathe deeply for many minutes. I contemplate the moon and lose track of time.

Our "Cocaine" driver sits motionless in the jeep as I climb back in. The four cars ahead of us are gone. The driver who's parked behind us raps on the window and demands we go or move aside. Cocaine listens, does nothing. A full minute later, apparently having saved sufficient face, having said to the world, "no one tells me what to do," he starts our engine. I can hear his stuttering anxiety, smell his metallic fear. We begin to roll to the right, all the way right, alongside the mountainside, and watching his face tense, I wonder if mine looked that way yesterday when I saw death. Down we go, bouncing along the slippery edge of the rut. A bus is down in there. THUD! Our right front wheel slips down into it. Cocaine gasps. Our wheels spin, and we slide, creep forward, then rock back, spitting mud and gravel, going nowhere. Then, our momentum carries us out, over, and down. We pass five buses queued for the ascent.

I drop in and out of dreams. Dazed and dim, at two in the morning, I realize we're parked in a dirt lot. The only building around has a sign: The Jiuzhaigou Guesthouse. We made it. The driver nurses a beer on a bench, looking pleased. Anton and I groggily climb out, thank him, and split a room in the guesthouse.

THE MORNING sky unfolds above us, royal blue and vast, spanning the space between the upward stab of glorious green peaks. The air darts into our lungs sweetly as we hike on a long dirt road, searching for a way into the national park. From nowhere, growling like thunder, shattering the beauty, kicking dust into our eyes, a steamroller and dump truck roll by. The din sends us to the roadside where we have to pick our way through stacks of cinder blocks and concrete-mixers amid what appear to be half-built hotels. Another roar approaches from behind. "Hello?" calls a voice. We shield our eyes from the sun and spot a thin driver on top of a tall red bulldozer. He waves his baseball cap jovially. "America!" he shouts, in what could be self-parody but isn't. He points to space in his cab. Perplexed, we climb aboard and slap hands with the young man. He has a sharp Adam's apple and filthy work clothes, and he pilots us along at a crawl. Anchoring one foot in the cab and the other on the rumbling right fender, I command an emperor's view of the forest, the construction sites, and the swift river racing alongside the road. The river seems to run directly below me. "Wom!" He shouts above the roar of the engine.

"What?"

"Wom-en!" He grins over his shoulder in Mandarin. "Do you like women?"

"How much?" Anton asks.

"150元 for a room and a beautiful, young girl."

Not bad. I consider something I've never considered before. Such a connection must feel meaningless.

"How do you know her?" Anton asks innocently. "What's her name?"

"You like girls!" The guy bursts into laughter, delighted at this simple discovery. "Her name doesn't matter!" he cries. "I'll take you. Now."

"Is she waiting in Jiuzhaigou Park?" Anton asks.

"No. It's right here."

"We want to stay in the park tonight," Anton apologizes. "Maybe tomorrow night."

The bulldozer-driving pimp looks crestfallen, but he takes us all the way into the little town. Jiuzhaigou Town is a ramshackle, hastily-built street of souvenir shops catering to tourists and building supply stores catering to itinerant construction workers. The name *Jiŭzhàigōu* (the Valley of Nine Villages) refers to nine ancient Tibetan settlements, but this surely isn't one of them.

We climb off the bulldozer, thank the man, and walk up to the gate of China's largest national park. Compared to the Bīngmǎyǒng, the gate is unimpressive and deserted, but we buy the requisite tickets, which promise a "Tour of Beautifulest Jiuzhaigou Valley Park in the Scenic Way." Sure enough, we're soon herded into a minivan alongside four Chinese tourists, and we zip up into raw pine forests and across plateaus of gorgeous blue lakes and broad sonorous rivers. The road wends high into the mountains before we pull over next to a few peasants' homes and a small inn.

Anton and I rent beds and immediately set out on foot to explore. The sun bakes our backs, and breezes whistle through spectacular pine trees overhead. We strike off the main road, onto a path that meanders down into a meadow nestled in the mountains. A river cuts through the meadow, and its rushing is soon the only sound we hear.

It should be legal in America, Anton explains, as we reach the middle of the meadow, where a small two-log footbridge spans the river. "Prostitution will always exist, and it's by nature non-violent, so why force its association with drugs, violence, and criminality?" He confesses that he almost accidentally partook in Tianjin: After a long bike ride, he and a friend saw massages advertised for 80元 and made arrangements for massages in their hotel room. Two girls showed up wearing tight clothes and makeup, and Anton and his friend enjoyed the massages but refused the girls' suggestive advances. The girls asked for 300元 anyway. "An older lady with a leathery face showed up to… clarify things," he chuckles. "There we were, haggling with the madam. We finally agreed on 150元 each." He sighs. "We were a little worried, I guess. But you know, they're probably just trying to support their families. It's illegal because of perceptions, because of media coverage."

We sit on the bridge, remove our shoes, and wash our feet in the razor-cold current. Anton did an internship with CNN while studying in Beijing, and his task was scanning newswire for bits about China. He says it was all about perceptions there too—to CNN, he discovered, delivering news is not about being fair, covering both sides, or giving voice to the unheard, but rather about entertaining viewers and affirming American stereotypes of China. "We shot scenes portraying China as poor and lacking human rights laws, as a place in profound need of— most of all—American influence." The experience may have put an end to his dream of being a journalist, he says. He hopes now to become a college professor. I watch the river flow around my feet and cut between my toes, imagining my own various futures, with and without freedom, with and without a Japanese child, with and without Michiko.

Back on the road, on the way back to the inn, the scent of frying soy sauce lures us towards a sign, down a path, through tall brown grass, and all the way to a cottage with three tables on a veranda. A couple is quietly eating at one table; laughter spills out from the cottage. We sit at an empty table, next to the couple, close enough to hear the man hulling sunflower seeds with his teeth. The woman, pregnant, stares at him thoughtfully, watching him hull, spit, eat, hull, spit, eat—the three actions all occur between his teeth, so it looks like just chewing and spitting. "Love," Anton says, watching them, smiling. He tells me that he had a girlfriend for most of the year. "A passionate and impossible relationship," he says.

"*Nǐmen hǎo!*" A matronly woman emerges from the dark doorway and greets us. Anton orders for us, and I sit in silence, wondering why I can't tell him about Michiko, wondering why I'm so dutifully silent. The woman returns with platters of what lured us here—spicy noodles swimming in a broth of scrumptious garlic, scallions, red pepper, and *huíxiāng*, a Chinese fennel that delectably numbs the tongue. Overhead, the sun kisses the mountaintops, and fresh, chilly breezes remind us of the speed with which this warmth will end.

"Actually," I close my eyes and watch the parting of the clouds on the windswept plateau, the singing sun emerging. "I just met someone up in Xiahe. She was from *Běidà*." I look at him. "We hit it off. It had been months, without even a kiss, for me, and we hit it off right away, and," I tell the whole story. He listens.

"You didn't have condoms."

"We didn't have condoms."

"You had sex four times."

"We had sex four times."

"Stupid," he nods. "But hey, you got weak. It happens to all of us."

My fists unclench under the table. My smile wraps around the planet.

"No need to kill yourself over it," he says.

"But I don't know anything. I don't know what's going on with her. All I have is her name and her home address."

"A lot of guys I know wouldn't even care and would have forgotten her by now. One guy I know in Beijing gave a girl money and said, 'get an abortion or do whatever you want, I just don't want to hear about it.'" He shakes his head. "Do you really think she'd want to get married if she were pregnant?"

"I was weak." I address my plate.

He jokes about his own moments—weaknesses and subsequent anxieties—and he's no monk. He laughs about it, "getting weak," and his laughter is contagious, infectious, delicious, and it finally ripples through me like the garlic and fennel, hot and sweet on my mouth and nose. Yes, my God, the truck didn't go over the edge.

"You should write her a letter," he says. "She'll tell you if she's pregnant."

"A letter? To her home address? What if her mother reads it? Here's

a letter from some strange American guy asking if her daughter's pregnant!" I laugh, and it's bliss.

"No e-mail address?" he asks, and I shake my head. "Well, *you* have
an e-mail address, right? Include it. Maybe she has the same fears.
You've got to do it, write her, man."

A wind rushes through the leaves overhead, and our empty plates
are stained orange from the spicy noodles.

CHAPTER 31

The Waters of Jiuzhaigou

Your joy is your sorrow unmasked.
The selfsame well from which your laughter rises
was oftentimes filled with your tears.
And how else can it be?
The deeper that sorrow carves into your being,
the more joy you can contain.
—KAHLIL GIBRAN, *THE PROPHET*

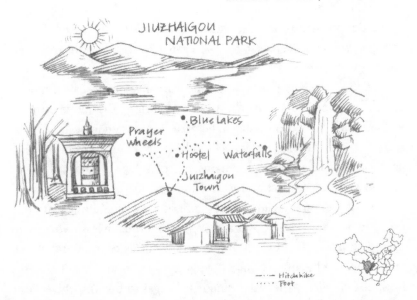

SUNLIGHT STREAMS in the window, awakening me. I arch my back, stretch, and smile. There's nowhere to go this morning—no need to pack, no need to leave. I rise, use a wooden outhouse, and wash at a spigot on the patio. Our breath is still visible in the air as Anton and I set out on foot to find Jiuzhaigou's famous blue lakes.

Trekking up the road, we share a breakfast of crackers, peanuts, and white salted taro root. The salt spreads its ancient satisfaction on my tongue, waking a deep presence in my body. I chew, moisten, crush the food, and propel my body uphill. Anton stops a green jeep carrying four PLA soldiers. "Venerable masters," he entreats them, and they wave us on happily, joking with us, reminding me of my soldier friend at Tiananmen. The jeep conveys us upward, then angles off the main road onto a brand new, steamrollered dirt clearing cutting through virgin woods. The soldiers let us off there, beside a steep incline. We spot small lakes below us that are the most brilliant hue—the blue of a blue jay's tail after a spring rain. Above us, peaks stand against the sky like torn green paper, and the splendor of the scenery takes my breath away. Summiting a small crest, we come upon a pond nestled in the woods, one we could swim across if need be, and we crouch beside it and dip our hands into the water. I make a fist, moving my fingers through the shallows, seeing if the cyan will transfer, but my hand comes out only wet.

We climb higher, and I admire the immense beings called mountains that stand like eternal hosts to everything. The mountains are what they are; they do not long to be perfect, nor even to be good; their truth is their truth, and they need nothing else. Our steps bring us to an enormous lake in the mountains, an inland sea, where tall slopes plunge straight into tranquil water. The sun's fierce reflection bisects endless ripples on a meadow of aquamarine. We could not swim this one. Moments ago, Anton was arguing that marijuana is no worse than alcohol and that, like prostitution, it ought to be legalized, regulated, and taxed, but because of lingering perceptions in the U.S., it can't be; now, he falls silent. The water quietly laps against brown pebbles near our feet. We rest and let the cool air drench our lungs.

"Everything is a matter of perception." I repeat his words.

He nods.

Two shoeless children appear, approaching on a dirt path and then wading in to their knees.

What Anton eventually says is, "It's time. I have to go." He's glad he made it here, he sighs, but he needs to leave, to be on the road first thing in the morning.

I nod and panic.

"This place really is amazing," he cranes up at the peaks, as if looking for the last time. He knows something about *fēngshuǐ*, the ancient Chinese geomancy, and he calls the mountains the permanent, energetic *yáng* force: the male, creative force. He names the water the flowing, nurturing *yīn*: the female, enduring force. He seems to be addressing the water. "This place has perfect harmony and flow. The duality—both parts are equally represented."

Yin and yang, male and female, life and death. Perhaps things are what they are but can only be defined by an opposite. Solitude and union, fear and trust: I could never truly know one without also knowing the other.

"Now? And miss the waterfalls?" I ask. "The legendary waters of Jiuzhaigou?"

"We don't even know where they are."

He stands. I nod, pull my battered tan cap lower to combat the midday sunbeams, and we hike down together. We pass a different set of cerulean lakes on the way down. We stop where a broad river connects two lakes and a gutter brings a stream of the river into a tiny wooden hut too small to stand in. Inside, we discover that the water spins a carved upright cylinder—a prayer wheel, alone here in the wilderness, turning constantly. I watch it rotate for several minutes, my mind spinning with it, and I'm at the prayer wheels of Xiahe again, caressed by revelations. *I am loved, we are all loved, always, from the ground to the clouds, from the start of life to the end.*

At our hotel, he grabs his pack. Further down, a long, rickety, plank bridge takes us across the river, and we hike silently on a path that snakes up and down the other bank, weaving over logs and under branches, through overgrown bushes, and over fallen trees that rest partly in the water. The air tastes rich and loamy. The forest breaks into a clearing where elephant-sized boulders are strewn about as if God had crushed chalk in his fingers, and I hop onto them, jumping from one to another, landing only on the pointy tips, joy and lightness gathering like sparks in my limbs.

Across the river, where the road is paved, we come upon people: a parked bus and a tour group. A man in a peach-colored polo shirt greets us while the rest of the group, all teenagers, explores a rocky riverbank. The group is from Guangzhou, we learn, and the friendly man, who is their chaperon, chats with me about the Five Ram City. He tells me a story about corruption and a patently false newspaper article, and his story is remarkably similar to that of Yang Youwen, the dissident camera repairman who bought me Budweisers. "I want to go to your country," he says in English, with a little laugh. His eyes are full of eagerness and frustration, and it reminds me of all that is Guangzhou, that huge pulsing hive of people wanting to be someone else. The fashionably dressed teenagers step back onto the bus, and he offers us a ride. Anton and I nod and climb aboard happily, and some of the teenagers want to talk with us and practice their English, while others withdraw into their headphones. At least no one has to ride on top. Anton learns that they're leaving in the morning for Chengdu, and he negotiates to ride with them. Thus he suddenly doesn't need to buy a ticket for a bus, and since I'm staying in Jiuzhaigou a few more days, it's already time for me to go. We embrace at the front gate, and I thank him for everything I can think of. The bus rolls away, he's gone, and I'm stranded on the dusty dirt road with the dump trucks.

My eyes wander from the ground to the sky. *Solitude and union. Trust and fear. I could never truly know one without knowing the other.* There's an alternative path on the other side of the narrow river, and a tree has fallen across the current, so I test its strength with a foot. It's solid. I step onto it, one foot after the other, looking straight ahead, and I'm balanced ten feet over the turbulent brown water, finding the same equilibrium—light, patient, never looking down—I found hopping on those boulders. Freedom and fear come in swift waves. Reaching the other side, I feel bolts of energy charge up from the ground through my feet to my legs, my thighs, my stomach, my chest. My mind clears as if it were a mountain pool after a rain. I'm alone. My fear stands naked before me like a vertiginous peak, and I observe it as I never have before. My fear isn't there to protect me from things that could actually kill me; it's there to protect me from confusion and dark places inside me. But, in fact, it doesn't protect me, it's not a mountain at all—it's a wall, it's the dark places themselves, and it makes me run away from people and from solitude, from illness and from singing at a wedding, from Lu Lan and from *gwailo* colleagues. Always, I just run from every unknown part of me, every aspect of life that I don't want to face. Nothing is erased by this escape! Life grows and changes shape and through the lure of curiosity or the slap of misfortune, finds me again, bringing its lessons again, again, again.

Branches overhead crucify the fading sunlight. The capricious path pulls me into thick underbrush, and I stop, wondering where my curious feet are carrying me. I'm about to turn around, but I spot a stick at my feet, and I take it in my hand and hack my way on through leaves and branches. I apologize to the branches. *I'm sorry if I cause you pain.* I think of Goldmund and smile, realizing these curious feet brought me this far—to Jiuzhaigou, to Songpan, into the truck, into the monastery, into bed with Michiko, to Xiahe, to Xi'an, to Beijing, to Peizheng. I smile. *I love this.* At the end of it all, this is what I love. Doing what confuses me, scares me, makes me suffer—as long as I don't die—and I never seem to die—I grow. My stick falls from my hand as I hold aside a young tree limb and spy a cottage in a clearing. I step up close to its dark windows, walk around it, and follow its driveway downhill onto a dirt road. Soon I'm through the woods and onto the pavement of Jiuzhaigou Town. Twilight envelops the village scene as I walk down its street. The sun breathes orange sighs on the tea green mountaintops above.

I eat at a sidewalk diner and watch darkness slowly touch everything: horses and trucks on the road, an ice cream vendor, the leg of the table holding a pottery bowl of white rice. I pinch up the last grains, and a pony-tailed waitress asks me about my Chinese skills while refilling my tea. It's been days since I've had a real conversation in Mandarin—I let Anton do all the talking—and I'm fascinated as her mother, the cook, sits down with us and recounts how the two of them came to this ragtag village in search of a better life but now abhor its lawless, get-rich-quick culture. Once they've saved a little money, she says, they plan to move someplace where the girl, who's sixteen, can go to high school.

"China is so beautiful," I tell them. "Don't stay here. Your food is delicious—you'll have no trouble saving money."

The mother smiles bashfully, and I watch her thoughts stray to greener pastures. She looks at me again and warns me that the park guards often close the gate at dark.

I heed her words, bid them farewell, and hurry away. Rounding the bend towards the gate, I see a floodlight on the gatehouse. Under the huge light, four PLA soldiers sit at a table in the middle of the asphalt road, playing cards. Behind them, the big gate remains ajar. "No more tickets," one calls out, as I approach. "Tomorrow morning. Seven."

I reply that I already have a ticket, but when they find out where I'm staying they tell me that it's too far and that I should come back in the morning. I pull my ticket from my pouch. "No, this was expensive." I want to make it home tonight. "I'll walk."

"Walk?" One soldier laughs loudly. He suggests instead that I sit down for a rest. A man in glasses pulls out the one unoccupied chair, and I hesitantly sit and answer their questions. Five jumbo beer bottles stand empty on the table, and when one soldier thrusts his handshake at me clumsily I can tell that he's drunk. Another leans back in his chair with his hands behind his head and shouts at me. "You better see the waterfalls of Jiuzhaigou! They're gorgeous! Magical! If you're going to walk seven miles tonight, you can walk a few more tomorrow!"

"I better get started," I say, and stand.

"Walk, foreigner!" the drunkard cries, and everyone laughs.

I leave the spotlight. A stimulating pine scent rides the night air, and the full moon and twinkling stars cast enough light to paint the trees across the river. I hike along the road, rounding bend after bend, accompanied by rushing wind in the trees and chirping crickets and frogs in the shifting shadows. The gusts blow stiff and chilly, and as my feet grow tired I look at my watch and calculate: Rigorous hiking could get me there by 2:00 a.m. if my legs hold out.

The road turns a lighter black, then gray, and a full minute before it passes, I know a car is coming from behind. Headlights flash, and I flag it down. "Wise sage, may I have a ride?" The man in the minivan blinks at me as if he's the one caught in the headlights, but he lets me in. And soon the wilderness is streaking by outside. Gratitude fills me, and fifteen minutes later, I'm at the inn.

❁

MORNING SINGS sweet and fresh, and a boy with a cart outside the inn sells me fruit, bread, and water. I hike off the road in a new direction, up through a sloped glade into a sun-soaked field of tall brown grass. A solitary tree stands guard in the center of the field, and I sit against its trunk. In *Narcissus*, Goldmund finds a sketchpad and pours onto paper the images of love and death that are burned into his brain—the magical countryside, the corpses slain by plague, a slender black-eyed girl named Rebekka. He draws himself too—as a curious wanderer, as an open-hearted lover, as a fugitive from death. His visions, one by one, incarnate on paper.

I lie back and gaze at the drifting clouds, imagining shapes and faces in the billowing heaps of vapor. What are the concerns of clouds? What are their fears? I imagine that they would say that matter forms and reforms, again and again, into life after life after life. The cycle is effortless, beautiful, and inevitable.

My gaze shifts from the clouds to the sun itself, and when my eyelids close to protect my sight, colored grains of sand appear there, falling in slow motion onto a mandala, and the four spheres of the mandala speak the same natural cycle as the clouds—life and death, creation and destruction. I see the mandala slowly turning. It is a cycle of four: four places, four phases, four spheres that cycle on and on. For a human journey, the first part is these *thoughts*, the mental permutations that playfully overtake my mind; the second is the *feelings*, these peaks and valleys of joy, frustration, and fury; the third is the flesh, the taste and touch, the sometimes delicious, sometimes diseased skin and bones and their *sensations*; and then there's a fourth piece, the patient wisdom in the clouds, a fertile and mysterious permanence of *awareness*. The mind, the heart, the body, the soul. Could it be so simple? Certainly conflicts arise along the fault lines that divide me in four—four different wills pull me apart. With Michiko, I went with my heart for a few days, and it was a sweetness, a love without the mind's fear, if only for a minute, an hour, a day. Then my mind retook the upper hand, telling me with its intimidating authority that I made stupid decisions and risked everything imaginable.

I open my journal to a clean page and write a letter. "Dear Michiko, I hope you're safe and well," I write. "I enjoyed deeply our time together." I describe the beauty of Langmusi and Jiuzhaigou, and finally, simply, clearly, I ask if she's pregnant. Unsure about the clarity of my Chinese, I add a paragraph of English to pour everything out completely.

Finished, I turn the page and drink memories of her freely, riding a horse alongside her, feeling her fingers hop on my chest, joining her body and mine. I write a poem on that next page. Skin, contact, touch, weakness, union; humans think so much, so carefully, but the luscious, thirsty skin rubs against itself—*may I experience that again!*—and thoughts vanish. The sweet skin, the weakness, the sweet skin, the strength.

I stand and hike farther, seeking the sight Li Song called the most beautiful in all of China, searching for the famous waterfalls of Jiuzhaigou, letting the drunk guard last night be my guide this time. After several uphill miles, a path diverges down into the woods, and I'm tired enough and hopeful enough to try it. Twenty yards down the trail I reach a broad river, and it splits into two ferocious channels, the nearer one switching back sharply. I spot a nook at the elbow of the deafening switchback, where I know that at least I can retreat from the sun. There, on a carpet of pine needles, I flip open *Narcissus* again, and Goldmund now woos a beautiful princess and rediscovers passion and the thirsty curiosity of his senses. But the fierce prince discovers him and sentences him to the gallows. He awaits execution in a dungeon. An image appears to him that replaces all his many other visions: a divine Mother, a presence who sees all life and all death with equal compassion. In tears, he tries to accept his imminent death, to bid fare-well to the sun and rivers, to the sweet taste of wine, to the smell of yellow leaves in the wind, to a young woman's song from a window. But he can't. His instinct to live impels him, and rather than be hanged, he plans to murder the priest who comes to confess him. At dawn, when the priest enters his cell, Goldmund steels himself to kill. The priest enters... and it's his old friend, Narcissus! Goldmund is saved. He rides off with Narcissus, now the abbot, to the monastery.

A gust of wind sweeps through the branches, and I rise and trek on-ward, between the channels of the river. Rounding a sharp bend, I hear a faint whisper. Around another bend, it grows to a roar. I step between two trees, and before me a magnificent waterfall gushes straight off of two-hundred-foot-high walls of stone. Outcroppings split, slice, and throw the downpour a thousand ways, and each droplet is a prism of sunlight dancing down to diminutive islands in a broad pool. Pine sap-lings quiver in the incessant rush of air. The noise and vapor envelop me and pull me into their timeless song, into their eternal white peace-ful violence. I kneel on the moist earth at the water's edge, and my hands fall onto knobs of rock. The water plummets and pounds, and in the clamor I hear again the entreaty that the sun sang to me on the windswept plateau. And this time the entreaty rips me open. Awed by the sparkling transience of creation, in its effortless beauty, I relinquish control and release. Tears roll to my cheeks. I am alive. Like everything around me, I too am this miracle that forms and reforms, again and again, into joy after joy, into suffering after suffering, into wish after wish. Each droplet dies, each moment dies, everything dies, as it must, as it longs to, to make way for the next form, the next moment, the next twirling leap in the dance.

CHAPTER 32

White Rabbit, Black Rabbit

Now he was part of the wide world.
It contained his fate, its sky was his sky.
HERMAN HESSE,
NARCISSUS & GOLDMUND

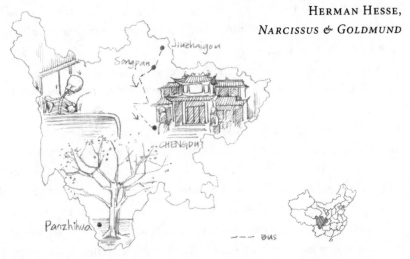

I CLIMB OVER a woman to get to the last seat. She gathers a pile of purple pomegranate rinds in her lap, and she gives me a friendly purple smile. The jam-packed bus rumbles and begins to roll, and slowly Jiuzhaigou Town slides by the windows. I think back to the mother and daughter in the diner. Wealthy Chinese people today make enough money to vacation, so the government now grooms these national tourist sites to satisfy them, and to cash in; they build ski lifts at the Great Wall, for example, and gigantic pink promenades beside the *Bīngmǎyǒng* soldiers. The PLA soldiers in the jeep said they were building a helicopter airport and paving all the local roads because Jiuzhaigou is slated to handle 300,000 tourists a year. For now the place is a motley mishmash of thieves, speculators, and opportunistic construction workers. The bus

263

bounces along, back the way the red bulldozer ferried me and Anton. Our tires splash through mud puddles and jump over huge rocks, throwing everybody into the air. The Greyhound-style bus is out of its element here in the mountains, and it's carrying way too many people.

A bone-crunching hour goes by, and I study vocabulary in my faithful scarlet dictionary. *Pùbù*, "waterfall;" *dúlì*, "independent;" *guānguāngkè*, "tourist." Late in the afternoon we charge through Songpan, and there's no room for new passengers. But it's different up here amid the bodies, smoke, peanut shells, and leaky bags of pork; now, the waving people running alongside the bus look desperate and silly. Leaving them behind, we climb higher, bouncing onto a tiny dirt road that ascends taller mountains. We shoot around blind bends. SMACK! The pomegranate woman's elbow punches my skull as she pulls a metal suitcase down from the rack. She looks at me without apologizing and gets off on a vacant hillside. I greedily try to occupy both seats, and it must be my selfishness that brings death upon me.

A thin, brown-skinned Tibetan in ragged clothes boards the bus and points to my seat. I rise to give him the window. He lands tiredly on the vinyl and wedges his ancient canvas sack by his knee. A deep cough convulses his whole body, and a disgusting stench wafts over my face. I turn involuntarily to the aisle to inhale. Glancing sideways, I watch his head drop between his knees as he coughs up something wet and fist-sized, like a spleen. He looks at me with bloodshot eyes and then stands to open the window. He expectorates phlegm laced with blood out into the day. With a moan, he crumples back into his chair, and slowly reaches into his jacket... for a cigarette. He sucks in smoke, exhales a gray cloud, and then doubles over and hacks violently. I'm torn between revulsion, compassion, and fascination—this isn't just *gǎnmào*, the ubiquitous Chinese cough; this is tuberculosis, lung cancer, death.

SMASH! The man's head crashes against the glass window like a wrecking ball. He holds his head rigidly erect again, eyes closed, trying to sleep. We bounce along and pitch sideways on boulders— BANG!—his head crashes again and his eyes fly open and dart about, then droop, then close. I wonder which will come first: death by bronchitis, or unconsciousness by concussion. He leans towards me, onto me, onto my shoulder. His filthy ear and hair roll around on me, and I shudder and shrug him off. He holds his head erect again. Instinctively, I realize something—others' death won't kill me. It doesn't work that way. I allow him to sleep on my shoulder. Past his head, out the window, there's nothing but sky. He won't last much longer, this dying Tibetan—one more dying Tibetan, after so many have been treated so horribly by the Han.

I switch seats with him, to make his ride safer and mine more relaxed, and his head lolls out into the aisle. Now I see much more: green mountainsides, the thin edge of the rocky road below us, and miles further down, a tiny river. I open *Narcissus*, and Goldmund is back at the monastery, the school, his childhood home, and the end is near. With Narcissus, he discusses the meaning of everything, the existence of God. He speaks with the passion of his heart and the honed acuity of his senses, while Narcissus speaks with the rigor and perspicuity of his mind. To Goldmund, God has created the world badly—full of blindness, suffering, and cruelty. But he sets to work carving magical images for the cloister pulpit, and a new joy and love of creation—and then a new wanderlust—overtake him. He strikes off once again, into the world, alone. This time, however, the world is too big, too hard, too cruel, and it breaks his bones and steals his health. He finally returns to the cloister to die. He lies spellbound, imagining without worry that his heart is being plucked from his ribs by the source of love and life, the eternal Mother. He accepts everything, releases everything, trusts everything. His last words are to Narcissus. "Love. Without love one cannot live, without love one cannot die."

The story ends, and with hacking and drooling Death beside me, and patiently waiting Death at my right, darting like a bird through empty space, I feel Goldmund's death inside me. A strength suddenly ripples through my body. *I'm still alive.*

Everywhere across the vast valley things are beginning and breathing, or ending and wilting. *Birth is everywhere; death is everywhere.*

Fear is new, created in every moment. My body, my animal, tenses at every bump that threatens to throw us off this narrow shelf, but my heart, mind, and soul worry not. The body's fear invigorates me unless it's repressed by the tension of the mind's fear. The driver at the helm whips the wheel around the switchbacks, focused but unafraid. Yet if he sneezes, we die. My body is scared, and I leave the window open so that if we go over I can lunge for an outcropping. My heart, mind, and soul fear other things, bigger things, lessons they long to learn. This is their paradox. We fear what we long for.

Up ahead, a dozen boulders speckle the road. It's road construction, and I recognize the method. Clever men set dynamite on the mountainside, run away, watch the explosion, then return and toss the resulting boulders over the edge. Voila! More road. But this stretch before us hasn't been cleared yet—or else there was an avalanche. Yet we hurtle headlong, unabating. The driver indeed seems unafraid. Or lazy. Or blind. We don't stop, we don't slow down. Our front wheels slam into the rocks and the whole bus leaps skyward, flying towards the edge.

In an instant of sudden silence, I die. Every molecule in me expands, explodes, and I fly—uprooted, unconnected to the world, free.

The seat below my body crashes down, and the pulse of force rattles my bones like twigs. My mind returns to my body, and I notice my heart bouncing around in its cage like a madman. Two wheels are down in the boulders, the other two are floating at the edge, and we're perched too close for anyone to leave through the customary door.

I exhale. Out my window, I can see only the hairline river miles below, but when I lean out and look down, I can see two men pushing boulders under the front wheel, which hangs about a foot off the ground. The driver climbs back in and fires the engine. The world shakes, our wheels grab, and we roll up onto stone, forward, towards the middle of the road, and—BOOM!—the wheels land.

Our descent carries us into a ragged, apricot sunset. Death gets out in a small farming village. Sichuan Province, looking like a bowl with serrated edges, welcomes our slide down from the mountains into the basin, the center, the capital city.

White Rabbit, Black Rabbit

❁

BLAND APARTMENT towers in every faded shade of pink, yellow, and gray; bustling boulevards with authoritarian metal-fence medians; screeching car horns, ringing bicycle bells, and sidewalks full of *gètīhù* vendors; cloying smells of garbage, sewage, and cigarettes; alluring fragrances of ginger, fish sauce, and roasting red peppers. I'm back in a large Chinese city.

I walk down the sun-baked streets, through the crowds, kicking out the aches of the long ride, remembering Xi'an and my meditation in the Great Mosque as if it were long ago, realizing that the mind measures time not by minutes or days but by new experiences. Xi'an only *seems* like a year ago.

This is Chengdu. Its broad noisy Liberation Avenue fades behind me as I turn onto a side street, hoping to find a hostel mentioned in the *LP*. This side street too is crowded, but it's quieter. Women fix shoes, men repair motorcycles, and children play soccer; many stare at me, and I smile and wave back. The street narrows, and people brush by my elbows, carrying crates of bok choy, bags of potatoes, and buckets of fish. I walk right into a market that welcomes me back to China's fertile lowlands: carts, piles, boxes, and barrels of oranges, pineapples, peanuts, eggs, eggplants, leeks, lettuce, yacote squash, bittermelons, and so much more. Hundreds of brown ducks with yellow bills waddle and quack in wire-fence corrals; thousands of silvery orange fish swim in countless shallow tin pans of water. Sellers call out to passersby, arrange their beans, nuts, or vegetables, or just lean back serenely in the shade. A pockmarked woman organizes bundles of green scallions on a cloth on the curb, and she waves to me vigorously. I stoop down, but I can't understand her dialect, and so we just smile at each other. She rubs her fingers together and points at my face. Wondering if she wants money, I lean down so far that I can smell the earth clinging to the little roots on the round white bulbs. She grabs my beard. I pull back, but she smiles wistfully, rubbing her fingers together again. So I let her feel my beard, rub it between her fingers. I haven't shaved in weeks. She beams at me, nodding up and down.

My backpack makes me clumsy and makes me sweat more profusely in the afternoon heat. I weave through the crowds, but the hostel evades me down alley after twisting alley. I double back the other
way, trying to decipher the signs. I can now read many of them: Dry
Cleaning, Hair Salon, Bakery, Tea, Medicine. The hostel is nowhere to
be found. I collapse for a rest on the curb, homeless, thinking back to
my faraway home in America. It's been forever. I go to a phone stand,
slap down a five-mao note, and punch the buttons. "AT&T," says the
god of telecommunications, smiling whimsically at me after a series of
otherworldly clicks. Then there's another voice. *Tony? My son? God, it's
so good to hear from you! Your voice! Where are you? Chengdu? OK, I'll
look at a map. Are you OK? Yes, I'm fine, too. Dad wants to talk too. We
all miss you. We're doing well. A flight home? Hong Kong? I'll try. Early
August? See what I can do. Are you safe? The connection is bad. Are you?
Safe? I love you.*

I put the phone down and let a sweet sensation work its way inside
me. My wad of colorful *rénmínbì* notes is thinning, but it's time for a
nicer hostel. Chengdu is home to the Traffic Hotel, "the backpackers'
headquarters of western China," according to the *LP*, and with a map I
navigate my way there. I step through its doors into the lobby, and for
the first time in forever I encounter a land of *lǎowài*. Big noses protrude
everywhere. To bring down the price, I share a room with a Danish
couple. I listen to a double-earringed Scotsman sing Bob Marley as I
shower in an immaculate bathroom. Everything is communal: a café
where strangers share tables, a bookshelf of English-language novels,
a bulletin board with friendly notes: "To Penelope Hudson, I left this
morning and took the box of digestives. See you in Kunming on the
28th. We'll conquer the elephants! Much love, Julia."

In the evening, after dinner, I find a note on my bed—from Anton!
"Find me in room 417, Anton DeSales," it says. I climb two flights of
stairs and knock on the door, and, yes, there he is. We grin and catch
up, and his roommate Dorjee, a tall Australian, ethnically Tibetan,
laughs as we describe our latest journeys. We both share our stories,
and, seemingly, a strange feeling of immortality, but Anton changes the

subject when I feel it going there—to the spiritual, to the dimension of the unfolding soul—and this surprises me and disappoints me.

Dorjee's first comment comes when we discuss Tibet. In his thick accent he denounces the exploitation of what he calls "Tibetan Chic." "People in Melbourne sell beads and clothes, and this whole…mystique. It's disgusting. It has nothing to do with Tibet."

"Same thing in America," Anton nods. "Rock bands work Tibet into their image. You should hear Richard Gere."

"At least people become more aware of Tibet, that it exists," I say, removing my shoes to massage my feet.

"But does it really help people understand anything?" Dorjee asks. "People just believe in the Tibet they're sold, and see it the way they want to. Of course Tibet should regain its independence, but let's be objective about it. You need to look at the States. You Americans lock up more people in prison than any other country. Work on your own oppression! Look at yourselves. You're seen as loud and self-righteous. It's the quieter people—people truly free who can look at their own shortcomings—who change the world." His ponytail is swinging as he looks from Anton to me, and I absorb his words and admire his conviction.

Anton brings up the other touchy T. To avoid war, he says, the island of Taiwan should just be recognized by the world as part of China. "It's time. But we should draw up a new political model. Taiwan's status should be more separate, more independent, and more secure than Hong Kong's. Taiwan shouldn't have to host any military, except maybe a tiny bit for national defense, and their own government should run everything."

"What happens to their democracy?" I ask.

"They keep it and elect their own leaders. It will be more secure that way, rather than in this political ping-pong between China and the U.S."

Dorjee considers this. "We could grant the same status to Tibet. There's a harmony to it. Taiwan's current situation is unstable. Partially freeing Tibet would balance the karma, if you will, of partially abandoning the Taiwanese. Right? The two provinces would be tied together by a common system, an autonomy. It would actually be decent, honorable."

"That would be amazing, to grant that status to Tibet," I say.

"It would actually be decent," repeats Dorjee.

Anton is leaving bright and early for Xishuangbanna, so we renew our farewells, and I return downstairs to my solitude. The Danish couple are out. I open my journal and in a free flow write of my gratitude for the journey; for seeing, learning, and surviving; for the opportunity to wander through this beautiful world with this variety of people—not just Tibetans, Chinese, Americans, and the rest, but the variety within each group. Every person, like a waterfall, has a story, a beauty, an unexpected twist to discover, a trajectory and a velocity. Before closing the journal, I remove the letter to Michiko. I seal it in an envelope. I take it downstairs and listen as it slips from my fingers into a green mailbox.

Sleep steals over me, and I dream of her. We are in some big, hot city, maybe Beijing, sitting in a college dorm room, gazing into each other's eyes. The word "girlfriend" tumbles from her lips; she longs to stay with me; she says she isn't pregnant; she asks what I would've done had she lied about pregnancy and asked for five hundred dollars; I laugh and feel great happiness; she really wants to know about the money; anxiety, confusion, and suspicion sweep over me; the dorm room vanishes and I'm riding a bicycle in city sunlight; she's riding ahead of me but I cannot see her; my bicycle has no handle bars and I pitch forward; I remember that I can ride a bicycle no-handed; I lean my weight back over my hips and glide; the bicycle disappears and I'm on a horse, galloping on a country road. Sunbeams push open my eyelids. The blades of an electric fan blow air and sweat across my forehead. I roll out of bed.

On a bike, I pedal through the busy boulevards in the hot, hazy Chengdu morning, pondering the dream. Immediately, intuitively, I accept its message: I'm fine, she's fine, she's carrying neither a disease nor a baby. *It was a powerful dream.* I gaze at the sky through the leaves of the trees. I lean back, no-handed for a moment, smiling around me at the avenue's healthy gaggle of pedestrians, and one by one, young Chinese women catch my eye with their beauty and innocence, their conservative dress and sweet cuteness. I'm lost in thought, and the road turns to dirt, then to orange mud, and I find myself alone, stranded in a construction site. *Is this another dream?* Turning left, then right, I finally work my way back onto a paved road. To my amazement, my destination lies straight ahead: Qingyang Gong, western China's most famous Taoist temple.

My bike fits between two others in a long rack, and I lock it there. I step past two fiercely scowling statues tasked from time immemorial with scaring off evil spirits and barbarians. At a shoebox-sized admissions window, I appeal for a Chinese-priced ticket, but the girl inside only giggles and asks more questions. I duck to look at her as I answer. She sells me the cheap ticket but won't return my residency permit. "I'm keeping this. I have to check on it." She smiles mischievously, dimples denting her cheeks. I step through the enormous front doors into a stone-floored chamber with huge, lacquered black columns, calligraphy scrolls on the walls, and incense troughs exhaling fragrant clouds of smoke. The chamber opens before me, without a back wall, onto a complex of gardens that surround a golden pagoda. Supplicants mill about, chanting, planting sticks of incense, burning piles of fake money, praying while moving. I knock on the door to the ticket office, and two different girls motion me inside. The one who sold me the ticket has more questions: Where am I traveling? Where do I get my hair cut? Why is my Chinese so bad? Her name is Shihui, and she smiles as I offer self-deprecating answers, but she won't return my permit.

I change tactics and request a tour of the temple. "I know nothing about Taoism," I explain hopefully.

She goes quiet. She rolls the sleeves of her white tunic to her elbows but finally shakes her head. "Sorry. I have to sell tickets."

"There are three of you," I say, looking from face to face. "And there's no one in line."

I suggest that one of her friends come too, and this seems to convince her. She puts her hair up in a bun and leads me and the friend out and down the stone path and into the gardens. She walks right beside me, telling me Laotse himself visited this place when he was a boy. "He was the original author of the *Tao Te Ching*, right?" I ask. She nods and grabs my forearm, talking excitedly. I barely catch a word. I just walk beside her, enjoying the sound of her voice and the brush of her fingers as she releases my arm. Around us, ginkgo trees exude their fresh floral fragrances. The friend, whose long hair flows all the way to the top of denim shorts, is less talkative, and there's a gap in the conversation. I try to think up a clever question about Taoism, but for once I have nothing to say. I remain quiet and notice myself accepting who I really am, where I really am, how ignorant I really am.

The columns of the golden pagoda are carved into gorgeous dragons, wind spirits, phoenixes, and gods. We climb to the second floor, where she introduces me to an old monk in flowing black robes. He holds a watering can, and bowing from the waist, he pours a trickle at the stems of yellow flowers until pools form in the potted earth. His presence and his quiet manner transfix me for a minute, and it's as if I'm waking from another dream.

I'm back on the ground, looking around as if for the first time. The trees and buildings flow in harmony, and the atmosphere is ineffably more serene than I had noticed, a striking contrast to the city outside. Shihui guides me past a series of nature murals, and then my eyes are drawn again to her smile and the too-distracting pinkness in her cheeks. She's lovely. It's time for a photograph. I aim the camera, but she and her friend giggle and move away, refusing to pose. Behind them, visitors insert sticks of fuchsia into a censer of spent ash, and behind the censer stands a meditation building etched with a great black and white *yīn-yáng* circle. The girls stop to sniff the long-stemmed purple orchids. They sneak a furtive glance at me, and I can't resist. I shoot. With a shriek, they spin back around and scurry all the way back to the office.

Something deep inside me smiles. I come to a knoll of plum trees and settle for a moment, cross-legged. My breathing slows, my mind releases a finger of its grip, and a tranquil peace gradually pervades everything. My eyelids drop, and I observe subtle appreciations in my muscles. My shoulders roll down off my neck, relaxing, opening space in my chest. The wind murmurs its playful sighs in the leaves overhead.

When I open my eyes, a beautiful dark brown plum tree stands before me, and I can't imagine what could be more marvelous than to study the tree and the story told by its gnarled branches. It grows upwards, reaching towards its God, but also outwards, spreading its branches and leaves into the world to explore. There is Death too, in that bark. Death and Life intertwine everywhere, harmoniously; they are partners, like the *yīn* and *yáng* of mountain lakes, like the cycle of the mandala, like trust with confusion, like solitude with yearning, like joy in the *now* with awareness of its end, like fear of the thing you long for. The openness and trust I knew in Xiahe before Michiko were beautiful, but they were mere blades of grass compared to the tree that's tall enough to see death.

The trunk forks, reconsiders, angles back, makes a tilted L into fat, healthy branches. In my dream I was scared of opening my heart; I'm drawn to this flirtation, this inclination to connect, to touch, to repel, to attract—but I am also shrinking away, terrified of this sensuous mirror trapping me, depleting me, splitting me in half.

I rise and leave, not seeing Shihui or the quiet monk on the way out. On my journey home, I pause at a row of hair salons. I've been sweating constantly under my thickening mess of hair and beard, and my next destination will be Tiger Leaping Gorge—a place Byron visited and recommended—and it lies further towards the jungles of the south.

I slide open a glass door. I'm greeted by the hot stink of hair gel. It's a minuscule space, with three women chatting on crowded stools while four children play with nail polish on a checkerboard linoleum floor.

"Do you cut hair?" I ask.

The children go wide-eyed and dart under the legs of the women. One woman breaks her stare and points to a barber's chair. After offering a greeting to the dumbstruck children, I sit and answer her questions. Very short all over, I say, showing her a little space between my thumb and finger. Seemingly amazed at both my existence and my fluency, she throws a black cloth over me and goes to work—first with scissors, and then on my face with a flat razor twice as long as my finger. I feel something grab at my leg. It's a boy, and the hair-dresser shoos him away with a foot as she brings the gray blade up to my ear, raking my skin clean. She asks me typical questions about getting used to the food and weather, and I keep my answers short so as not to distract her. Her hand shakes as she laughs at her friends' jokes, and she holds my head all the way back, pointing my chin straight up, scraping the skin of my throat. The blade burns against my jaw, up to my chin, and then it slices quickly along my Adam's apple. One false move by this woman and it's all over. Death, even at a haircut.

A bald man stares back at me in the mirror. "*Zěnmeyàng?*" she asks. "What do I think?" I reach around and feel my naked jaw. The skin is intact. "Excellent," I grin, yanking on my earlobes. "My ears are... still here!"

They all laugh.

I ride home under a sky that is taking its time forgetting the sun. No one stares at me. In the waning light, I'm just another bald man on a bicycle.

❀

THE NEXT morning, it already feels like time to leave Chengdu. I check out of the Traffic, hike to the train station, and wade into crowds that press my backpack against my back, squeezing sweat out of me like juice from an apple. The ticket woman is finally at my service, albeit curt and distracted, telling me there aren't any hard sleepers to Panzhihua. Soft sleeper? None. Soft seat? Nope. I swallow. Hard seat is the way of the *lǎobǎixìng*, the poor commoner; China still calls itself communist and "classless," so there's no "first class" or "second class," but speaking plainly, *hard seat* is the milieu of the unwashed masses. I nod. She hands me the *huǒchēpiào*, and I notice that my claim on a hard bench begins tonight at 10:10 p.m. and ends in Panzhihua, the way station on the road to Tiger Leaping Gorge, tomorrow afternoon, sometime after 1:30.

Ticket in hand, I hike through the sweltering midday to People's Park. I while away the hours in a teahouse perched on the bank of a lima bean-shaped lake. An elegant bamboo chair cradles me under a pious, many-armed ginkgo tree, and I hold a cup of green tea to my lips as the balled leaves exhale their dank fruity scent. A thin wisp of a man approaches me. "Massage, 10元?" he asks. Anton's story flashes through my mind, but to me the guy looks nothing like a prostitute. I nod. Positioning himself behind my chair, he lays his hands upon my neck. His muscular palms and fingers push my shaved head forward and down, and my eyelids fall closed as he works my shoulders in delicious circles, gripping and releasing the muscles and ligaments along my spine. Deeper, I disappear into relaxation as he lays into the base of my skull, somehow separating my head from my neck and kneading my brain. Sweet minutes or hours pass, and I leave this place, this teahouse, this empire, and float home—and I'm walking barefoot on carpet, smelling exotic things like cheddar cheese and pumpkin pie and roasting tomato soup, drinking fresh water endlessly from the tap for free. *Home.*

The hands are gone. Opening an eye, I see him, waiting patiently, but I can't even move my arm to my money pouch. I nod and finally pay him, my body buzzing.

Several hours later I leave the teahouse and the park, following my hunger and olfactory instincts for dinner. The aroma of sautéing meat and garlicky oils wafts out from an open-front restaurant, and inside, five men in their twenties laugh uproariously at a central table. They spot me. "*Wèi, lǎowài*, hello!" They gesture to their empty chair, insistently.

I join them. They are five old high school buddies kicking off the weekend: two structural engineers, a computer programmer, a chicken vendor, and a car mechanic. They ask me about America, and I tell them that, yes, the U.S. is *fādá* (developed), as everyone says, but there is more crime and people are generally suspicious of each other.

"People in America are more stressed out, more worried than people in China."

The car man nods. "So, just between you and me, why does the American army have to control Taiwan and tell the Taiwanese people what to do?"

His friends frown at him, concerned that he's brought up politics, but I offer my latest thoughts on Taiwan, as formed with Dorjee and Anton.

The chicken vendor, who has bushy eyebrows and looks seventeen, inserts a joke about Taiwanese women. He summons more cold bottles of the local beer, and to follow custom they throw a banquet for their honored guest. A waitress approaches our table, carrying a live rabbit in each hand, one black and one white. The rabbits' bright eyes dart nervously as the bespectacled computer programmer points to me with his chin. "You choose. Which one will we eat tonight?"

I point a finger at my own chin, the way everyone does here. "Me?" The waitress holds the rabbits by the ears and looks at me expectantly. The black one is kicking at the air. Do I point at the one I want to eat? Or, like an emperor, at the one I wish to spare? My eyes wander up to the brown ceiling fan circling with a dozen flies. *Everything is hungry; everything eats to live; everything dies to feed.* I point to the black one. One day I'm at swift death's mercy, the next day I *am* swift death to some other creature. At some precise, perfect moment, it will be me crossing that line and feeding trees, worms, rabbits, the earth, the universe.

We enjoy rabbit soup, rabbit skin, stir-fried rabbit stomach, and then mouth-watering rabbit leg with vicious black Sichuan peppercorns. The spices cleanse my sinuses with such vigor that my brain settles, limpid and serene. Sichuan Province is famous for this, for fighting fire with fire—for hot weather and hotter food. My nose runs as I savor the bold flavors. The succulent red-braised beef with potatoes is overpowering, but the snow peas flavored with citrus and flecks of mushroom are subtle and deliciously complex. The beer is endless. My companions' hysterical jokes elude me, but the breeze on my face is delectable, and gradually, finally, I eat and drink enough to satisfy them. Gratitude ripples through my chest, and I voice it fully to my hosts. I offer to pay, but of course they wave me off. Long after I'm gone, they'll fight humorously but fiercely over who gets the honor of paying—not because a *lǎowài* ate with them but because that's how tabs are settled here.

Outside, I glance at my watch. The hands point to ten minutes to ten! I hoist my pack and hail the first thing that comes by, a pedicab. The young driver stands up on the right pedal and lets his weight down on it, then on the left and down, then the right again, and the acceleration draws tendrils of the night like cool death across my cheeks.

CHAPTER 33

Four Sides to Every Waterfall

精誠所至金石為開

Honesty that is pure
Moves even steel and stone.
—CHINESE PROVERB

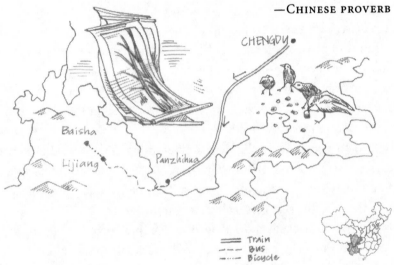

I RUSH INTO cavernous Terminal #8 of the Chengdu train station at 10:04. Hundreds of people are standing in a cone-shaped queue that radiates out from the gate, while others occupy countless conjoined orange plastic waiting chairs. I gaze at the human cone. I too have to fight for my place. Plunging into the hurly-burly, pack on my back, I'm soon hemmed in on all sides by anxious and sweaty bodies, and yet I'm smiling, wondrous at the way that this is unfolding. The delicious rabbit that I condemned and consumed—he lives still, here, now, as me. All must eat to live, and all are quickly reincarnated.

A voice echoes off the ceiling: "Train Number 356 is delayed." A frustrated surge from behind presses my chin into a man's head. Young and old jostle for inches. Time slows to a crawl. 10:10. 10:20. 10:30. 10:50. No further word from the voice on high.

My legs soon ache from holding their ground. My beer buzz disappears. Faces turn to stare at me, some curious, some annoyed. My breaths of reused air grow shallow. At 11:27, the voice breaks its silence and promises salvation. 11:50, it says. But 11:50 comes and goes. Midnight strikes. At 1:28, my entire body, numb with exhaustion, awakens to sound, confusion, fear, joy, and relief. The roar of an arriving train.

The crowd heaves forward, as if the train might never stop unless we hurl ourselves before it, and like a cattle stampede, we thousand souls ram ourselves one at a time through two small apertures. The current of humanity carries me forward, and I elbow for the left opening, and I'm there, and the man takes my ticket, and the unrelenting pressure on my back vanishes.

Floating free, my goal now is a different opening. I need to locate a seat in this chairless nation. On board, the first partially open spot I find is between a sickly woman and a PLA soldier, and I drop quickly into the gap. The seat isn't really hard, more like a bench, like a school bus's, straight-backed, and arranged so that three people sit facing forward and three sit facing backward. My pack falls between my knees just in time for a jolt to throw my torso back up and out of my seat as the train starts into the darkness. The woman beside me drapes herself over a large black lacquer box. She spits phlegm onto the floor, her contribution to an obviously ancient mélange of gum, beer, juice, grease, urine, and perhaps tears.

I avert my eyes and examine the soldier at my left shoulder. He's nodding off, beginning to snore. My spine is taut, my feet are flat on the floor, and I'm looking straight ahead, facing backwards, towards Chengdu, waiting for my own exhausted mind to release into sleep. It doesn't; I'm frozen. I mentally explore reincarnation, releasing myself, heart, body, and soul, but it feels impossible in this straitjacketed world. My legs have a non-negotiable need to straighten, my spine yearns to slacken, but my position is locked. My vertebrae have no option but upright. My neighbor's nasal chainsaw begins to roar. I hum *Aobao Xianghui*, and Lu Lan's demure smile materializes before me, her little "mm," her mischievous laugh. The train rocks monotonously on the tracks and the snoring sounds faraway then close, faraway then close...

Eons have passed, and I've been sleeping. I glance at my watch. The hands have barely budged. What seemed like hours was nine minutes and four seconds. I drift off again. Six minutes and eleven seconds. People go insane like this; I've read about it. Torturers or unethical researchers allow exhausted people to sleep a few minutes, then rouse them, then let them sleep a few more minutes, then rouse them again. In surprisingly little time the frustrated mind succumbs, goes mad.

My watch plays tricks. Its hands suddenly point to 6:37. Claustrophobia comes. Then it's 7:19, and the sun shrieks at me like a scorned lover. I rub my dry eyes, massage my sore neck, and look around. Corroding my mouth is the sour remains of beer and rabbit. Morning crawls along through farms, villages, rice paddies. At 4:17, we reach Panzhihua, a blindingly bright gravel parking lot. Buses are everywhere. I step into the heat like a ghost in search of final rest. The lot unfolds around me, and I find a bus for Lijiang, a town near Tiger Leaping Gorge, and though the bus is empty, I climb on and into a seat. I hold a hand over my eyes like a curtain. Sounds of other passengers float by my ears. A woman sits beside me with a bag of soiled laundry that smells like rotting carrots laced with excrement. It's 5:32 when a woman boards and barks orders at everyone. "You can't put that there! Don't sit on that! Pay your fare!" She snaps at me until I cough up 27元.

At 3:39 am, still open-eyed in the pitch of blackest night, as we bounce down a mountainside and through a forest, bits of light appear. The darkness morphs into a vacant city. "Lijiang," someone says. I stumble off the bus and onto an empty street. The lobby of a concrete hotel smells dank and unclean. No people, no lights, no sounds. A pummeled couch in a corner seduces me easily, and I'm asleep in less than a minute.

Double Happiness

✿

I'M DREAMING of tall Caucasian people. They are upset, shouting at a young Chinese man. They stand four feet from my head, and there's a German flag patch on one backpack. White rays pry their way past my eyelids. I'm in the fetal position on a filthy sofa, the whimsical extremities of my watch signaling 6:52. Everything feels completely wrong. I shoulder my pack and step into the street.

The town buzzes with people, bicycles, cars. In front of me, a bald old man steps herky-jerky, starting and stopping. He empties a plastic bag of yellow breadcrumbs onto the pavement, and a dozen crows descend immediately for the feast. The man regards me like a curse and continues on his way at his infantile pace. I come to a row of food stalls where pancakes sizzle and *gètǐhù* solicit passersby. The sensuous aroma of frying onions pervades the air. I hand over a pink note for one of the soft discs of toasted dough, and as I bite into it, a delicious, greasy, herbed pork oozes over my tongue.

Further down the street, I pass the glass doors of a nice hotel. I can't resist. Cold air tickles every pore of my skin as I float through the lobby, murmuring a prayer to the god named Air-Conditioning. I watch three uniformed girls behind a desk look past my deplorable grooming to my skin. Little do they know this *lǎowài* is—inconceivable!—penniless. Well, almost. I take their cheapest room, cover the sun with the blinds, and climb naked between the sheets. Oh, sheets, forgotten friends! I haven't gone insane yet.

Some time later, I awaken, and my mind somersaults into another week. The blinds stand open, revealing late afternoon. I splash water on my face and head out. Energy belatedly reaches my legs when I set foot in the town's central, miniature Tiananmen Square, where a gigantic statue of Mao Tse-tung stands. Mao offers his eternal, one-armed wave-cum-salute. Wide boulevards, concrete buildings, honking horns, red socialist banners—Lijiang feels like any other small Chinese city. But I keep walking, and when I cross a river, cut through a noisy vegetable market, turn down a winding alley, and cross another bridge, I enter a ghetto of old wooden buildings, teahouses, and artisans' shops. This is Old Lijiang, eternal capital of the Naxi people. The *LP* recounts the Naxi's descent from romantic matriarchal Tibetan nomads:

> Naxi matriarchs maintained their hold over men with flexible arrangements for love affairs. The *azhu* (friend) system allowed a couple to become lovers without setting up joint residence. Both partners would continue to live in their respective homes. The boyfriend would spend the nights at his girlfriend's house but return to live and work at his mother's house during the day. Any children born to the couple belonged to the woman, who was responsible for bringing them up. The father provided support, but once the relationship was over, so was the support. Children lived with their mothers, and no special effort was made to recognize paternity. Women inherited all property and disputes were adjudicated by female elders.

It could work. Michiko would be in a separate home, a separate country, a separate dream. I'd spend the nights with her, then go home. She'd settle any disputes.

A vendor walks by with hearty Naxi sandwiches—eggs, goat cheese, tomatoes, cucumbers, spices—and I stop him. I eat as I wander the winding streets. In a painter's shop, my eyes slowly inhale the spectacle: Hundreds of vertical scroll paintings hang from the walls and the rafters. There are butterflies, orchids, boats, and towering mountains. Scrolls of flowing poetry in an unfamiliar script, which must be Naxi, occupy an entire wall. A set of four traditional Chinese paintings depict a single waterfall in four seasons: snowy whiteness covers the perpendicular beauty in winter; tiny ships dock in the lake at the foot of the voluminous waterfall during yellow-green spring; rich flowers and a full, languid fertility infuse reddish summer; and pale pink and green hues depict the wane and quiet of autumn. I look from season to season and witness the passing of years; I lose myself in the turning of the wheel of seasons, a cycle of four so similar to the rotation of the mandala, and so similar to the flow of the body, heart, mind, and soul. There are other mysterious cycles of the universe I don't yet understand. My mind whirls, and I'm gazing again into the evanescent miracles of high summer clouds.

"Beautiful, isn't it?" A bespectacled man appears at my side. I observe his immodesty, and I decide he's probably not the painter. I ask whether the set is Naxi or Chinese. He replies quietly. "Your Mandarin is good. The set is Chinese. I can give you a special price."

I decline. "I'm a poor teacher from Guangzhou."

"Wow, that's great," he replies. "You are helping China. The set is normally 600元." He leans closer. "But for you, 400元."

I squint at the paintings. *Not bad.* I *would* like to get a gift for my family. I step away to examine two carved *zhāngs* on a long jewelry table. A woman approaches me, and in English she praises the paintings that captivate me. She leaves, and then as if on cue the salesman returns, asking for 300元, then 250元. He offers to ship them at no cost, all for 180元, and in my amazement I nearly hand over the cash. In a moment's pause, I notice an impatience rising in me, and I return to the street without making the purchase.

I walk further and cross a walled canal, examining more artwork, thinking again of the cycle, of the seasons, of the mandala. The four spheres ultimately unite, in this life or the next; that's the magic and mystery mapped by the mandala. They will unite in me too someday. What will it bring, the union of mind and body and heart and soul? Perhaps I tasted it for a moment with Michiko, or at the waterfall, but now, here, the four spheres bicker and disagree inside me: My mind wants this, my heart that.

"Hi!" The salesman welcomes me back with a smile. "Did you decide?"

I stare again at the four seasons, and they seem somehow even prettier than before. Coincidentally, the English-speaking woman stops by again and chats more with me. She's a *huáqiáo*, from England, visiting the homeland with her mother, who waits outside. The young woman lavishes encomia upon my Mandarin, and when I reuse her words playfully to praise her English, she laughs. "How much are the waterfall paintings?" she asks.

"He's come down to 180元," I reply.

"180元?" she shouts. "That's great!"

"Yes, 180元," I reply quietly, nodding, hushing her. "But I haven't decided yet."

The salesman approaches, and she tells him how great the price is. Irritated, I gesture to her to pipe down. *This is not how bargaining works.* She apologizes, but she insists that the salesman take down the paintings to allow a closer look.

"Great price!" she crows.

It's $23, or £14, not much for art. The salesman turns to me. I shake my head again. "I'm still thinking."

The woman's mother appears, and the two admire the quartet together. "It's gorgeous," they agree. "And the price!" The daughter turns back to me. "Are you going to buy it? If you don't want to, I will."

Like an earthquake, her words overturn and demolish everything I thought I knew about Chinese customs and manners. My mind runs in circles. She's trying to manipulate me—it's Western manipulation! No, she likes the paintings—it's Western honesty! The salesman wants me to buy the quartet now or let him sell it to her. *Let her have it,* comes a voice. I ask the woman again whether she likes it, and I ask in Mandarin, so she's supposed to refuse stubbornly, but in fact she declares that she adores it. "If you like it," she adds, "buy it. If you don't, I will." If she likes it, if she expresses any interest whatsoever, my polite obligation is to force it on her, and then she's supposed to fight back and make me buy it, and we're supposed to cajole and coerce each other to buy it, and then, finally, the loser of the argument buys the item and takes the winner out to dinner. That's how it works.

"I like it very much," she says. "But I feel bad. I'd like to pay you for letting me buy it."

Dumbfounded, I decline her money and turn for the door. "It's yours," I tell her kindly.

Back outside, I return to the modern city. I buy an ear of corn off a vendor's grill, sniff its green leafy husks for the scent of the nearby farmland, and bite into the browned kernels. The city floats by as I rack my brain for theories. Back in the hotel, I open my journal and reconsider everything I found strange. *It was as if in that painter's shop, I were more Chinese than someone from this country. She had Chinese features and ancestry, but perhaps nothing more.* And how did it end? I walked away empty-handed, but with more Chinese "good" feelings—face, honor— and fewer Western "good" feelings—none of the delight of acquisition. Yes, my mind wants to judge. "Good," "bad," "Chinese," "Western." It puts everything into boxes rather than consider anything new; it will make more boxes if necessary, but it never releases its grasp. That's the mind. But here, along with the shreds of corn in my teeth, is a new idea from somewhere else, from my heart, or from my soul: *There is no judgment. There is no right answer.* It would have been partly "good" and partly "bad" buying the paintings, or choosing the white rabbit, or chasing Shihui in the Taoist temple, or saying no to Michiko. There is no *wrong*. When the parts of me conflict—no choice is wrong. I learn from either decision. Both paths take me home.

❀

IN THE pale, dusty light of the next morning, Tiger Leaping Gorge beckons me. I rent a bike and ride towards it, out of town, into Naxi country. Endless beige prairie wilderness unfolds between me and the peak of Jade Dragon Snow Mountain at the horizon—the peak that attracts everything to this realm, this place where the eternal Yangtze River forms. Weeds grab at my legs as I pedal towards the peak. The sky hangs thick and low, brushing the dark mountaintop.

A half dozen figures appear on my right, running over the low brown vegetation, and I stop as they come closer. Eight children rush up and stop in a tight huddle. They are filthy from playing in the dirt, and more carefree than my Peizheng students ever seemed to be. I greet them in Mandarin, and they smile and laugh and whisper. A boy in a blue jacket asks me the usual questions. They're Naxi children, children whose schooling is in Mandarin—and only in Mandarin— but who still speak Naxi at home. We compliment each other's use of the Mandarin language, and we laugh and teach each other words in

Naxi and English: *bicycle, friend, prairie, mountain.* Before they dash back across the field, they tell me that I'm on a path: I'm on the road to the village of Baisha.

Sure enough, I pedal through a river and then the suggestion of a path merges with a dirt road and carries me into a village of adobe and garlic-gray stone. Birds sing in the trees, people stroll about on pale, khaki streets, and I let the word *Baisha* (white sand) trip a few times through my lips; the town does seem to be made of strange, cloud-colored sand. In a painter's shop, a place as cluttered with paintings as the gallery last night, a saleswoman asks me where I'm from. She also asks whether I like the painting that has stopped my eyes: a towering pagoda that seems to climb a mountain behind it. I relate my indigent teacher's pay, and she offers discounts.

Her price keeps dropping. Finally I ask, "How can you go below half the listed price?"

"They're on sale," she says cheerfully.

Peering more closely at the pagoda, I notice something odd about the brushstrokes. I ask about the painter, but she says he's not available. "Will he be around later in the day?" I ask. She shakes her head. He's out of town. "What's his name?" I press her.

She sighs. "He's...these are fake."

"Fake?"

"In Lijiang too," she nods. "They're all copied in Guangxi province or in Singapore, and then we order them cheaply from a catalogue. I can look up the painter's name if you want."

"But everyone thinks this is an artistic area. They think they're buying genuine artwork."

"Mm."

I look at the paintings again. They're pretty, but they're no closer to works of art than a Mona Lisa mousepad. I thank her for telling me that they're just posters, and she thanks me for helping China. "If you want to support local painters," she adds, "walk down the alley to the home of Li Pengjun. He's a Naxi artist. His place has a painting of a tiger on the door."

Double Happiness

I leave the shop slowly, feeling odd, insubstantial, uprooted. A lightness builds in my limbs, a gratitude for the blessing of her honesty. Minutes down the street, set in a wall of ash gray stone, I find a door decorated with a painting of a tiger in a tree. The door is ajar, and I step into a large courtyard where a young man sits at a table of wooden masks and figurines. He shows me to a small gallery with walls of rough-hewn wooden planks, upon which hang watercolor paintings—paintings far simpler than the posters in the shop, paintings that depict recognizably local scenery. In one sublime work, men drive oxen over a misty bridge against a backdrop of delicate, almost invisible mountains. I gaze at it, and a tall man in a white shirt and black vest descends a staircase and smiles thinly at me. He stops to look at the painting with me for a moment.

The price turns out to be high: 350元. A painting of fat, old men in a dark tavern playing flutes and stringed instruments called èrhus fetches 400元. "If I buy both," I ask him, "is there a discount?"

He thinks for a moment. "700元." He's silent as I wait for him to go lower.

"Can you go any lower?" I finally ask.

"I'm sorry."

"I'm a poor teacher from Guangzhou..."

He listens with interest to my story but doesn't drop his prices; he even endures my attempt at the hungry-white-man paradox. I ask who painted them, and he replies that he did. He is Li Pengjun.

Admiring again the serenity of the oxherders on the bridge, I praise him solemnly. "You are a master painter."

We discuss the scenery—mountains and prairies—and then I tell him that I'm going for a walk, to think it over. "Please come back" is all he says.

I do. He invites me to tea, and we exchange stories. He studied painting in Kunming, the provincial capital, and now lives in a house down the street with his wife and children. When I ask about the poster swindlers, he nods sadly, calling them dishonest. "They steal many customers. And the art isn't always of a high quality." He asks about

288

America, and I tell him that it's the same, that we too have painters, merchants, travelers, and thieves.

I look at the two paintings again—the oxherders and the musicians. They'd be superb gifts for my family, but I can't pay any more than 400元 if I want to get to the gorge. I offer 350元. He comes down to 650元. I can't believe he would let 350元 walk out the door, but he doesn't even say 600元. We regard each other, and he smiles kindly. He hasn't haggled, he hasn't mentioned food, and he hasn't even considered slashing the prices of works he clearly knows are valuable. He tells me that he has a smaller version of the painting of the musicians, one that he painted the same day, and he takes me to it—points to the brushstrokes and the black calligraphy to prove it isn't a facsimile. I fall in love with it, and we quickly settle on 450元 for it and the oxherders. Just like that, business is over. He wraps up my paintings.

I gaze around me as I pedal out of the village. *Thank you, dear, honest, little Baisha. Thank you.* Honesty is the name of the quality that a thing possesses which is what it is, nothing more, nothing less.

❁

To SAVE money, I switch into the hotel's dormitory. I claim an empty bed and set my oblong box of paintings on a windowsill. The only other person in the room is a dark-haired *lǎowài* woman reading on another bed. "Excuse me," I venture, "do you speak English?" She looks over at me. She's in her early twenties and apparently just out of the shower, her face flushed and her dark hair wet.

"A little," she says. I ask her if she knows where the town's post office is, and she gives me directions, fluently, with a French accent. "Don't hurry," she says. "They are slow with everything." I thank her and inform her she speaks more than a little English. She turns back to her book, looking pleased.

The post office is where she described, and she's correct about their efficiency as well. Two hours after I arrive, a lady in an olive green uniform charges me an exorbitant fee to send home the paintings and some excess clothing. I wander out, essentially broke, following my footsteps along the river back into Old Lijiang, wondering whether I should still try to go to Tiger Leaping Gorge. The people in line warned me about avalanches after I told them my plans, and now I'm nearly penniless. I sit at the last open table in a restaurant on the river's edge. Sipping tea and gazing into the stream, I hear familiar sounds inside me—dreams and fears—and there's also the voice that has been whispering to me now for days, for weeks, that perhaps has been there my whole life and only now I can hear. In any event, the choice is obvious. I am to follow my intuition. I am to go to the gorge.

Three young Americans sit in the other three chairs at my table. "Are these taken?" they greet me. I welcome them. One, a tall, blond guy with a loud voice, eyes me. "God, the crazy things these Chinese people do! You know?" Another, a guy with dark curly locks and a necklace of fat orange beads, agrees. "I can't believe that one fucking guy charged us eighty bucks for the train ticket to Kunming!" The third, a pasty-skinned woman, sighs. "I still can't believe I bought that fake silver box from smiling-man!" They complain for a while, ordering food, eating, chatting, and I sit there, adjusting to their presence, wondering why people voluntarily ruin their experiences by focusing on grievances. The tall guy tells a bitter anecdote. "God, that whole district sucked, but at least the Belgian dude sold us that good weed." They laugh but seem unhappy. They're skipping Tiger Leaping Gorge because of the avalanches. I'm about to leave when they order miniature apple pies. The woman smiles at me. "I've heard these pies are awesome. Don't miss out!" I release my thoughts for a moment and chuckle cynically with them about where the apples could possibly have come from. Warm little pies chock-full of softened cubes of *pínggŭo* arrive, and their sweetness is pitch perfect. My body rejoices.

The warm twilight disintegrates into an alpine chill as I walk homeward. Crowds throng the central plaza for a fire festival. Huge, roaring torches illuminate hundreds of faces and throw macabre shadows onto the statue of Mao. People hold hands and dance in giant circles, around and around, swinging out near me. Thumping drums and tinny flutes keep time. I step nearer, and then a young woman waves at me. She shouts in Mandarin: "Come on!" I go for it, rushing after her. "What is this?" I interlock arms with her and her friend. She shouts over the din, "The Naxi Torch Festival!" Their cheeks are flushed and they giggle with delight. The beat and the screeching melody accelerate, and I quickly learn the left-left-right-left step. The girls grin and exclaim their approval. We go around and around, four times, five times, and I'm completely exhausted in short order. Before they actually hand me a torch, which would happen on the next lap, I release their hands and say good night.

In the dormitory, I extinguish the lights and collapse on my bed. The door swings back open, and two silhouettes appear, flipping the light on and back off. One is the French brunette. "I'm still awake," I startle them. The light comes back on, and they apologize. Propping myself on an elbow under my blankets, I ask if they've been to Tiger Leaping Gorge. The other girl, a blonde, confirms that she has, so I should be interested in her advice, especially as she sits down like a travel agent and dispenses it freely; but my attention moves like a magnet to the brunette. There's something about the tan on her cheeks and nose that I didn't notice before but now find unbelievably pretty. I can't look away.

"...one of the deepest gorges in the world," the blonde, a New Zealander, is saying, "but like idiots, they're blowing dynamite to build roads..."

The brunette's name is Chantal. She hasn't been to Tiger Leaping Gorge yet—the two just met yesterday—so I voice my new wish and ask if she wants to go. She has long brown hair, sparkling brown eyes, and when she explains that she doesn't have time she sounds contemplative and intelligent. Her journey is nearly over, she says, she has to be in Kunming in three days. Oddly, this more or less matches my plan. I don't know when or if I have a ticket home, but I need to start turning towards the coast to renew my visa, at the least. The Kiwi speaks up. "Chantal, it's glorious. It'd be a real shame to be this close and miss it."

Chantal climbs under her covers. I tell her she can let me know in the morning.

"Any time before 7:30?" she asks, with a hint of sarcasm.

"Right. Don't be late. That's when the bus leaves."

Closing my eyes, both adventures, like freshly finished paintings, stand before me: trekking the gorge while exploring this magnetism, or going it alone on intuition.

CHAPTER 34

Tiger Leaping Gorge

明知山有虎偏向虎山

Go deeper into the mountains
Even knowing there are tigers.

—CHINESE PROVERB

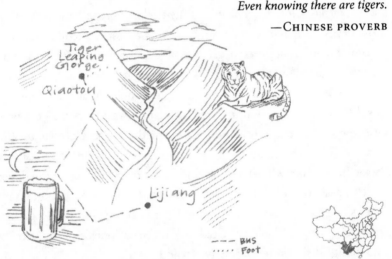

THE ALARM shrieks. Chantal, bleary-eyed, sits up and leans on an elbow. "Tony, I'm coming." Minutes later the two of us are out the door, down the elevator, and on the street. We climb aboard the bus and share a Naxi sandwich and a bag of pork biscuits. She laughs about the odd smell of the biscuits, which she bought yesterday, and I tell her that they must be good for some aspect of our health. "I ate snake in Guangzhou," I say. "It was supposedly good for my... manhood."

She laughs and tells me she's been traveling for six weeks. Waiting for her in Montreal, her hometown, is a drummer in a rock band, her boyfriend. This news is like cold water on my face. Her accent hails from Quebec, not France, and now her English suddenly seems poor, and francophone Canada is a new, frustrating concept—so close to home, yet so far. She was an English major, she tells me, and were she Chinese I know I would find her English amazing, the way everyone here praises my Mandarin to heaven while criticizing fluent *huáqiáo*.

The bus chugs up into the mountains. Chantal and I give our seats to two old women. She stands in the aisle, facing me, holding onto the luggage rack, our arms touching repeatedly. We're practically embracing. I can see a freckle on her long, narrowish nose. I can count the moist strands of hair on her forehead and the flecks of green and black in her brown eyes. I feel her breath on my neck. She flashes a smile and a nod at something I'm supposed to get, maybe that this is fun, that this is what it's like to rough it on the back roads, but as I nod back what I feel is more remarkable, a thrill at something inside me melting, and I balance on this dissolution as we bounce over boulders. I wonder if she's the prettiest woman I've ever seen, or if this is something else. Companionship, solitude, they come and go. A bead of sweat stands on her chest, just above the V of her white tank top, and I can't help watching it roll down.

Two seats open up and we settle into them. A wrinkled man on my other side starts talking to me about Tiger Leaping Gorge. He's pleased we're going there. "You'll see Golden Sand River, our favorite river. She runs alongside her sisters, the Salween and Mekong Rivers. Do you know the story?" he asks me. I shake my head. "Her sisters were happy running south," he explains, clearing his throat. "That's how it was. But Golden Sand wanted to marry the eastern sea. A dream told her to. Therefore, she made a sudden turn east to meet the sea, but her jealous brothers, Gold Flower Mountain and Jade Dragon Mountain, blocked her way. They guarded her passage day and night, until one night Gold Flower fell asleep on duty, allowing Golden Sand to slip past, leaving the deep Tiger Leaping Gorge behind her speedy escape." He grins at me. "That's why today it's the tallest gorge in the world! The towering snow mountains are still there, and it seems impossible that such a huge river could find its way through—the mountains are six thousand meters high!"

Chantal gazes out the window, not following the story.

The man changes gears, starting in on *fǔbài* politics. "These days, politicians and businessmen here—it's all about the *guānxi* and corruption. Except for the princes, they do whatever they choose, marry whomever they like, have all the kids they want." He shakes his head in disgust and blows his nose.

Chantal apologizes that she hasn't learned much Mandarin as she lights up a cigarette.

"You don't get enough second-hand smoke?" I ask her, joking. As always, half the passengers on the bus are puffing on *xiāngyān* (cigarettes).

She nods without looking at me. "You'd think so."

When she's done smoking, she asks me about the story, and I translate it for her as we circumnavigate the first of the great snow-clad peaks, Jade Dragon Mountain. She smiles and listens, and calls it a story of female liberation.

The bus rolls to a stop in Qiaotou, a tiny mountain village nestled at the foot of the gorge. Skyscraping peaks surround us, and the river runs alongside the road. We climb off, leave our hefty backpacks at an inn, and take only water, cameras, and a warm change of clothes.

Golden Sand River might be the man's favorite because it transforms itself into China's greatest river, the Yangtze, the river the Chinese call simply *Cháng Jiāng* (Long River). But here, by our feet, the cute stream gurgling by is actually only one of Golden Sand's many tributaries. Tiger Leaping Gorge is the vast canyon where Golden Sand appears from Tibet, gathers the strength of a hundred contributors, and with her new, heady unison metamorphoses into *Cháng Jiāng* and gushes down tall peaks on her way to hydrate the countless realms of the vast kingdom, to irrigate thousands of terraced hectares of ancient farmland, and to run all the way to Shanghai before swimming with her beloved eastern sea, the Pacific Ocean.

We take one step at a time. We cross a small bridge over the tributary and continue on a dirt road upward. Chantal hikes strongly, and we find a pace that soon leaves the river far below us. Another mountain rises across from us, forming a deep, green-walled gorge. Two monks in burgundy robes approach and stop us. "You should take the steps," they turn to point to a wooden platform fifty yards ahead. "Go down to the river. Walk on the famous stone." Here we learn another legend: Many centuries ago a tiger wished to leap the gorge, to cross Golden Sand, but he was unable to jump across it. The tiger spotted, with his acute tiger eyes, a stone down in the middle of the river. He leapt out onto the stone, and then a second leap took him all the way across.

I crane back at the peaks. "Must've been a big tiger!" I say.

They laugh and wish us luck, telling us that they have to fix a bridge that was taken out by an avalanche.

I translate this second legend for her, and Chantal remarks that we're entering a place full of mythology. At the wooden platform, we peer together down the steep staircase and spot the big boulder amid roiling torrents of the river. A dozen tiny people walk about on the stone, but she wants to skip it, telling me that there is a higher road than this one, with harder, prettier hiking, and we need to save time. The rock piques my curiosity, but I accede. "OK, you're the boss."

She smiles at me. "It'll be good for your manhood, like the snake."

We tread along the mile-high shelf of shifting apple-sized rocks. It narrows and we have to pause as two local women carrying leafy baskets of corn approach and pass us. Chantal spies another path branching off straight uphill, and she suggests it could lead to the high road, but when we draw closer we see that it's not a path at all, but a river—a waterfall dancing down the mountainside. It washes out our path and continues down, plummeting through sideways-lolling bushes and outcroppings of stone all the way to the river. We stop in front of the waterfall, and its frigid spray wets our faces. We remove our shoes to cross the shallowest part on bare feet.

I go first, treading carefully, but I slip on a rock halfway across and slam my hands-in-shoes onto a boulder to halt my fall. Chantal slips too, and she catches hold of me. We proceed so slowly that we're laughing when we safely reach the other side.

More waterfalls lie ahead, decorating both sides of the gorge, cascading down like rivulets of white tears. I press her about this so-called high road, but she doesn't know much. She says the New Zealander told her about it but spoke vaguely since she hadn't been able to hack it and gave up. I ask her about her energy, her physical condition, and she lets out a sigh. "It's been a long trip," she says. "So long. Not that I'm ready to go home yet. I'm OK." This is her first major sojourn abroad. I tell her it's mine too, and call us "globetrotting virgins," but she doesn't like this name much, and she walks ahead of me. I ask her about her thoughts on Québec's independence movement, and she turns on me, like I've slapped her, but maybe it's how I phrased it. "All right, Mr. America," she says. "When you're finally ready to let Hawaii go free, and Puerto Rico, let me know. And when you're about to go crazy and shoot everyone," she stops and laughs, glancing at me sideways, "give me a good head start, OK?"

I make the promise. "At least ten seconds."

Warm winds caress our faces, and we hike silently a while. We're surrounded by magnificence on all sides and there's really nothing to wish for. A path diverges downward onto a bare rocky knob that protrudes from the mountainside, and we sidle down onto it in order to rest. We sip our water and feast on the view. Stretching out in every direction, upwards into a sublime cloudless sky, downwards to the rock-pounding brown waters, and forwards and back between tight mountain walls of emerald, the beauty is endless, jaw-dropping, ineffably grand. My spirits soar upward with the geology into the cerulean unfolding of the sky.

Beauty. It is this thing that draws us, that attracts us, that makes us open our eyes.

Chantal sits near me and my eyes are drawn to her anew, as if I hadn't even noticed her. Strands of her dark hair fly in the gusts, her cheeks glow, and there's a brown smudge on her nose. I wait for her to meet my gaze, to smile at me, to say she loves all of this too, but she doesn't, and I realize that I'm staring.

"Ready to go?" she asks when I finally look away. I look at her again, wondering if she appreciates any of it. The view is amazing, she says.

The road carries us further upward. A towering, snow-clad cone comes into view far ahead, and it's so large it must be Gold Flower, brother to Jade Dragon. My eyes rest upon it, and it is that beauty that I have longed to see, to feel, to understand. The peak's majesty breaks me open, and I begin to make promises. *I will be true to my own beauty. I will live with complete honesty. I will be what I am and trust my own inner knowing. I will look and find beauty everyday, forever.*

The peak, like a mirror, reflects sunbeams at me, asking me questions, and I wonder whether I will forget all of this if I don't see such beauty every day. Is this beauty in all of nature, in all of life, available everywhere? Is it only human creations—the concrete cities, the metal machines, the plastic desks—that are bereft?

BANG! Men come running towards us, as if fleeing that mythic tiger. They sprint at us. CRACK! CRACK! Explosions erupt out of the mountainside behind them, hurling careless volumes of dust, dirt, and rocks upward and outward. The men stop and walk back into the billows of smoke and pulverized earth. We wait until the clouds have dissipated before cautiously advancing. The men admire their handiwork. Enormous cubes of rough-hewn black rock overhang the newly widened, now-eight-feet-wide, shelf-of-rubble path. They heave, one by one, large shards of rock to the edge and shove them over, smiling at us as we pick our way past them.

"You can walk in front now," says Chantal.

"The American isn't the one with the bombs this time," I reply. She chuckles, shaking her head. What I know is that we still haven't found the high path, that cataracts periodically wash out our route, that avalanches can be triggered by explosives, and that the sun is dipping languorously toward the peaks. We need a destination. Just as all of this dawns on me, a small path diverges upwards, towards a house on a little plateau. I share my thoughts, but Chantal doesn't need to be convinced. We take the path.

A leather-faced man stands in a small garden and thrusts his shovel into the dirt as we approach. He wears a communist-era navy blue coat—a "Mao Suit"—and examines us with sunken eyes. Mao Suits became politically incorrect sometime around 1982. I pull out a map that I found in a Lijiang restaurant and point to a guesthouse called the Halfway House. He takes the map in gnarled hands and peers at the scrawled Chinese, knitting his brow and hopefully ignoring the distortions and advertisements. "Up there," he points up the mountain. His Mandarin is thick and choppy. The door to his house flies open, and a lanky, shaven-headed 12-year-old shoots out, stopping at his father's elbow and firing "Hello!" at us in English. His father waves upwards and says something incomprehensible. The two of them lead us around the house to a path that cuts up through dense undergrowth. "Do you know where the Halfway House is?" I ask the boy, who's wearing a red turtleneck. He sneaks a peek at the map. It's hard to imagine what there is to do up here besides explore. He nods: "When you reach a bigger path, go left." His name is Baobao and his Mandarin is clear, so I ask him to be our guide. I promise 5元, and he and his father agree. We shake hands with the father, who resumes turning soil before his mountain panorama.

Baobao darts up the steep path. A rich diversity of weeds and bushes scratch our arms as we follow. He bounds like a rabbit up and around sharp switchbacks, stopping to wait for us only every few turns. My legs quickly turn to rubber. "Do you go to school around here?" I call after him, hoping to slow him down.

"Yes, classes start in two weeks."

"What grade are you in?"

"Sixth."

"Where is the school?"

"Gaohan."

"That must be a long way." I pull myself up onto the rock where he stands, then turn to help Chantal.

"Do you like American movies?" he asks. "Do you watch American movies often?"

"Sometimes," I reply. "Not very often these days."

"I've seen them," he says.

"Let's take a little rest," I suggest, when we reach a clearing.

"I like *Predator.*"

There's a sucking feeling in my calves as I sit on a boulder. The sun is absconding with every last shred of azure and warmth, leaving the sky violet blue and chilly. "It's not much farther," Baobao says. "Ready?"

Thirty seconds will have to do, since this ascent will be a nightmare after dark. Chantal hops up and starts after the boy, scaling a dry riverbed; less energetically, going mostly on will-power, I take the rear. We don't see Baobao for a long while. Finally we spot him atop a broad horizontal path. He's smiling and pointing left. "One hour to Halfway House!" he calls. Reaching him, I offer gasping thanks and a brown note. He bounds back down, disappearing around a tall rock.

"That's one of *his* hours," Chantal inhales a gallon of air. I nod, stretching my calves, standing on tiptoe to get the blood flowing. We start up the path in the fading light, seemingly back towards Qiaotou. The narrow trail takes us through sloped cornfields, sloped spinneys of walnut, and sloped glades of azalea and rhododendron that seem to rustle with small creatures. We wend up and down the mountainside, over rocks and between tilted fir and cedar, and we realize something—this is the "high path." The trail here makes the TNT-fashioned route below seem smooth as glass.

Two hours labor by, and then in utter darkness we come upon a village nestled into the mountainside. A wooden sign in front of a stone farmhouse reads "Halfway House." Exhausted, we knock at its gate. A gaunt man appears with a lantern and guides us to a room with two beds. I watch Chantal collapse like a dynamited mountainside onto one. The man asks about food and beer, and I nod.

Minutes later, we're dining out on the porch in delicious, private bliss, toasting beers in the moonlight. The central courtyard of the inn is bounded, on one side, by a barn, on another by our porch, and on a third by the innkeeper's living area; directly before us stands the mountain face. The river murmurs far below.

When we've finished eating, I visit the open living room, where I find a whole family gathered around a television. The grandparents are in chairs, the parents on wooden crates, and the children sit cross-legged on straw mats. They stare at me. I smile and they smile, and delightful moments pass by in the ancient pleasure of observing something unusual. I ask about showers, and the innkeeper points through a dark doorway, promising to bring water. Three stairs lead me down into an outhouse where cold boulders make an uneven floor. I strip naked, and the slosh and gush of water overhead announce the arrival of, first, just a few drops, then a steady sprinkle, and finally a hot storming stream on my bare neck, shoulders, and legs, massaging me like a heaven with fingers.

Dressed, relaxed, feeling sublime, I sit again on the porch as the evening temperature nosedives. The wife is pouring water for Chantal. The innkeeper takes a seat beside me and compliments me on my Mandarin. He asks politely for my help in making a map for this place, showing me an indecipherable drawing that he started. "Halfway House" is scrawled in the middle, so I begin with the name. "It has a bad meaning in English..."

He looks confused.

"A better name might be Halfway Hostel or Tiger Leaping Gorge Hotel."

Chantal yanks my eyes away when she returns from the shower covered tightly in a towel, and the perfection of the notion of being near her as the world darkens pushes everything else from my mind.

"I think I have a sore throat," she says, without sadness, coughing as she passes into the room. She's going to read and get in bed, she adds. I almost joke that she should have a smoke, but I hold my tongue. Fitful coughs emanate from the room before the sustained silence of her sleep prevails.

I stay up several hours with the innkeeper. We devise directions, translate food listings, make new sketches, and add advertisements for "cold beer" and "exquisite showers." By the end of the night, when I'm hugging my blue wool sweater closer to my sides, his map is surely the best in the Gorge, better than anything I saw in Lijiang. I tell him to put copies in restaurants in that city, but he seems aware of the benefits of advertising. He's a shrewd man.

"Since I've helped you," I yawn. "Perhaps you can give us a discount."

Double Happiness

He gushes that it's obvious and proper. Grateful to him, pleased with existence, comfortably shot, I withdraw, check on Chantal, and climb beneath the thick blankets of the other bed. Like a waterfall grabbing a green gingko leaf, sleep swiftly whisks me away to another world.

CHAPTER 35

A Tiger and a Butterfly

天外有天人上有人

There is a man beyond every man.

There is a heaven beyond every heaven.

—CHINESE PROVERB

S TEAMY BREATHS of morning fog clothe the mountainsides. Chantal and I share breakfast on the porch of the renamed Halfway Hostel, and I tell her why we might not have to pay for our stay. She stretches her arms, pulling on her elbows in turn, content, knowing as I do that between us we have 242元 ($29.13), no way of getting more, and no ticket onward to anywhere. The innkeeper greets us with a smile, holding a scrap of paper. "75元 for everything," he announces.

I give him a meaningful look.

"Of course. I've included a discount!"

"75元?" I ask, to ensure I've heard right. It's high, especially for the middle of nowhere, especially because I've helped him, especially because it could strand us here in the hinterlands of Yunnan Province.

"Your showers are *free!*" he announces.

"Showers?"

He shows me his list, which includes meals, drinks, beds, and showers. Two 3's under "showers" are dramatically crossed out. He nods at me proudly. A bitter taste rises in my mouth. I refuse to pay. Chantal looks mystified by my anger, and I finally hand over my share, throw on my backpack, and stomp off down the path.

"You think he took advantage of you," she says, following me. She's not trying to make things any better. "People lie in China, like everywhere. That's how it is."

"It's bullshit." I turn and look at her. "Here, surrounded by this truth and beauty, still we lie?"

"People always lie. Or maybe it wasn't a lie. Maybe it was miscommunication. Maybe it was a lie. Who knows?"

"Why isn't this—heaven's honesty all around us—enough to inspire us?"

"Heaven is honest?" She looks past me. "Even if it is, not everything else is, not everything is pure like this."

The breezes brush my cheek, and I take in the yellow sunshine glinting fresh through fir boughs. I remember being ripped off in the Guangzhou markets, deceived on the way to the Great Wall, and surrendering to wild cultural misunderstanding about those paintings in Lijiang. "Fine. Why be so angry, right? Why shut myself off?"

"You think you're going to win one before God? Be angry, see if it helps."

"Be angry." I turn, feeling her strange advice bore into my back as we continue on the path.

"Sometimes it does help," she murmurs.

"Be angry," I say it to myself. "Be angry! Yeah, I'm angry. I'm pissed off!" A wave washes over me, opening a soothing spaciousness in me, and I laugh as I witness again the cascading waters above us.

304

"This time here is short," she says.

"Real honesty isn't avoiding anger or bitterness—there are avalanches and thunderstorms. Honesty is letting it come and letting it go."

"Even if we think we're poor, they probably need the money more."

"Letting it come and letting it go."

Our path weaves through knolls and groves of fragrant pine. She starts talking about her private Mandarin class in the countryside of Hunan province, where she was isolated in a dorm with a Chinese guardian and rarely interacted with locals. Her one classmate, who happened to be another young Québécoise woman, didn't seem to mind and lived in the created world of the myths offered by Anton's CNN—that China is dangerously poor and backwards. "Her idea of enjoying China was staying in the Changsha Holiday Inn," she laughs. "As often as possible, almost every weekend! She'd just go eat sandwiches and pancakes. That was her China. Neither of us was learning a thing. After a month, I just left—to travel and—" she stops. I follow her eyes. Two wings of orange and purple dart a drunken course through the wind, flitting beside a bush, and then fluttering to her, alighting on the end of her finger. A butterfly. Smaller blue and white ones play like tiny winged angels above the bushes. She's transfixed, overtaken for a moment by awe at creation. The miraculous beings draw me in too, and whole minutes pass.

An urge grabs me—to go all the way to the top, to leave the path and to forge as high as we can up the wooded slopes. My enthusiasm wins her. We cross sun-dappled beds of pine needles and summit one crest, then another, and everything turns vertical, reaching upwards through the crystalline morning. Way down below, ten thousand feet away, on the river, in the very crease of the gorge, the rapids rush with the wind. The gusts sweep up the slopes, through the pine, into my nostrils, and I ask the water, the mountains, the trees for their captivating secret: What is this eternal beauty, this honesty? What is this unnamable quality? The natural world is what it is, it releases itself entirely, it knows no fear. The answer has always been to choose trust.

The ground suddenly ends. I drop to my belly and creep forward to peer over the edge. A yawning abyss is carved by a tributary that feeds

Cháng Jiāng. It seems incredible that such tiny streams could carve through three vertical miles of rock. Chantal steps back, but I stand up, right at the edge of the precipice, overcome with wonder, watching birds swoop and dive, suddenly knowing that I too could jump, throw myself into the wind, and leap this gap; I could release all the way into this universe; I could fly. I look back at my earthly companion, and limitations return to my brain. It's three hundred feet across, and if I don't make it… I die, Chantal is alone, and no one else knows. I sit on the ground beside her, and together we bask.

Raindrops sprinkle on our wondrous contemplation. We hike down on our own new path, on a diagonal, so as not to waste time retracing our steps. The precipice hems us in on our right and the slope steepens. Rain slicks the clumps of dirt and grass beneath our feet. Chantal loses her footing, slips, lands on her back, and slides five feet before catching herself. I fall too. Mountain goats chew calmly and watch us filthy, ungraceful animals. We scramble, foot by foot, down, farther, finally all the way to the high path, and it feels like a triumphant return to civilization. My relief turns into euphoria, but Chantal looks shaken and is coughing and wiping mud from her cheek. "I should stop smoking."

"We should've taken the easier way down," I say.

She smiles weakly.

We gulp from our water bottles, and the sun reappears more glorious than when it left. The path takes us up onto a sharp ridge atop tall boulders, letting us walk there atop the world's praying fingers. The view is spellbinding and a thousand photographs beg to be taken, but their voice is a whisper. I let everything go and walk in the beauty unhurried, undesiring, undefended. The sensations penetrate my being, and my billion molecules relax, soften, and dissolve. My eyes open to Chantal and I am overcome with admiration and joy. A vast freedom opens in me, and I realize I have no expectation of anything in return from her. I realize I have no expectation of anything in return from the planet. My heart drops open like a door, and I laugh and live naked with the abundant beauty around me. It too is naked with me. I honor and praise it, and I feel myself give into it—give in with all of me, my heart, mind, body, and soul. This truth, this wholeness, this absence of any need for perfection defines beauty and honesty. It is love. The act of making love is to release all of our personal words and needs and hopes and dreams and just to be beside beauty, to forget oneself, to remember that we are not separate beings. My breaths source behind my lungs, deep in my heart, and my mind wanders through a parade of visions: the whiteness of the students' uniforms on the first day of school, the red flags and lanterns when I first arrived at Tiananmen Square, the ripples in the pool at the Forbidden City, the heavenly summons of the clouds on the mountaintop in Xiahe, the wet tears on my cheeks at the waterfalls, the softness of the red cushion beside the mandala with the monks. And there are the two happinesses, standing, waiting, smiling, as simple and obvious and sacred as twin mountain peaks: the happiness of my desires fulfilled, and the happiness of my pure awareness. They've been there all along, waiting for me to dance between them like a river.

The path bends deep into the mountainside. Our footsteps stop. Before us is a river blocking our way. A ferocious waterfall, a liquid avalanche twenty feet wide, pounds down from above, landing on the rocks just to the right of where our path should be. The water then completely takes out our path as it rushes to the edge, flies over the edge, and then drops hundreds of feet to the next outcropping. We stare at the waterfall and river, at their beauty, at their ferocious power, at their impossible breadth. Planks of what yesterday may have been a bridge stand akimbo, in splinters, to one side. Chantal takes off her shoes, but we can't walk across this river.

"What's the other plan?" she asks.

There's only one. I take a deep breath and retreat several steps. If the universe had planned to kill me this week, I'd already be dead. "Let's jump."

Her eyes widen.

I dash towards the water and vault off one foot. Below me, the current gushes over the edge. I'm floating, stretching out through the air. With one foot I alight on a rock halfway across, then, using my momentum, I leap again, lunging towards the other side. I land a toe on the bank, my heel splashing in the water.

Chantal cries, "You're like the tiger!"

I catch my breath. "Can you do it?"

She backs up, checks her pack, and reties her shoes. "I'll try."

She takes one look, runs, and jumps. Her foot lands on the same rock in the middle, but her second jump falls short and she lands in the current, barely a yard from the cliff's edge. The water pulls on her. She struggles towards me, and I step into the river and reach out for her arm. Our fingertips touch. Her hand is in mine. She's in my arms, her shoulders shaking. We fall to the solid earth and stay there a while, watching the gushing currents soar chaotically over the edge, spraying us with drops of whiteness. Tears melt on her cheeks. The towering walls still yawn beside us, beneath us, around us, whispering about life and death, offering no apologies.

"Thank you," she says, touching my knee.

I nod. "We made it."

"I don't think you had to grab me."

Our eyes meet. She seems worried, scared. She looks away, but her eyes return to me as I get up.

We walk onward, and the path grows more difficult, winding around higher and steeper chasms. Overhead, the sun burns. Fatigue touches me, a gentle hand on my chest, and I can't help swallowing the last drops from my water bottle. Walking faster, I feel the last fluids begin to flee my pores. We hike for what feels like several hours.

At one point I realize that fifteen minutes have passed since I last saw her. I stop and wait, but too many minutes pass, and she doesn't come. *She was right behind me.* I walk back a bit and look for her, then forward, more slowly. No sign. I strike off the path, into thick bushes, pushing through. I don't see her. *I can't risk getting lost myself.* I stare into the gorge, listening to it. A calmness comes, and I sit on the path and rest.

She appears, tears on her cheeks. We hold each other. She says she walked backwards and forwards. She thought I fell; she thought I was gone; she thought she was alone.

I feel her heartbeat beside mine, and I wait for it to slow.

When we continue, we stay close to each other, sharing a deepening gratitude. We reach a crest where the path descends steeply through colossal boulders. Step by step, as if on a staircase, we go down, realizing that this is the big descent, the one we've been waiting for. Two other people climb up towards us—the first souls we've seen since the Halfway Hostel. It turns out to be a French couple, and Chantal speaks with them, learning it's still two hours to Qiaotou. Chantal tells them about the waterfall, but they forge on. "*Bon chance,*" Chantal says, to them, then to me, with a shrug and a smile.

An hour goes by, and the path leaves the woods and meanders downward, and it's just the right steepness to release our bodies into a run, to gallop in freefall through pastures and meadows. The spirit of the gorge pushes us from behind, doing all the work, sending us off back into the world. Soon we're on a gravel road and the village of Qiaotou lies nestled below us. A *Cháng Jiāng* tributary near the road lures us like paradise, and we kneel on its banks in delight. Into the gelid water we plunge our heads, to the eyebrows, to the cheekbones, to the chin. The river washes through me, swimming across my face, drenching my scalp, running up my spine. I throw my head back and gaze gratefully into the sky.

CHAPTER 36

Homecomings

We shall not cease from exploration
And the end of all our exploring
Will be to arrive where we started
And know the place for the first time.
—T.S. ELIOT, *LITTLE GIDDING*

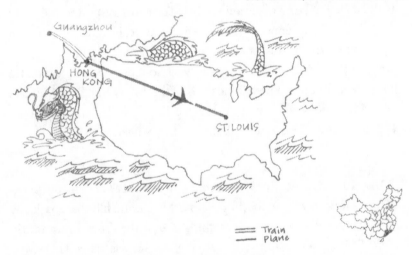

GUANGZHOU. IT'S been exactly forty days and forty nights. A man squatting in an apartment doorway stares at me as the train from Kunming completes its cross-country journey, having hauled me all the way across the vast south of this empire. The train screeches to a rest inside the *Guǎngzhōuzhàn* station.

I shoulder my pack and step out into the City of Five Rams. On the sidewalk I hail a shiny red taxicab, but it accelerates past me and stops beside two businessmen. It all returns to my mind in a flash: the incessant worship of wealth. The way a younger brother imitates his older sibling, this city idolizes Hong Kong. The wild and worrying political uncertainty exacerbates the craving and imparts a flavor of frenzy—everyone yearns for a piece of the sweet new prosperity *now*, before it's gone.

A taxi finally stops, and I climb inside. I'm greeted by the heavenly breeze of air conditioning, and for the first time in what feels like forever, I stop sweating.

Home sweet Peizheng. The gate welcomes me with anonymous generosity. A half dozen students play basketball on the court beside the big tree. The athletic field waits, deserted.

The dorm is unlocked and vacant. I climb the stairs, and my key fits the lock. Greeting me is a thick new layer of dust on the walls and tables. Everything remains where I left it, physically and mentally. An irrepressible frisson runs through me like lightning, and in an instant I strip off the ragged clothes that I've worn for eons. Naked, exultant, I shout my triumph and joy off the walls of the empty building. My fears showed me the way to every single step that I needed to take. I only needed curiosity. I only needed to look. I only needed to listen.

❧

T HE SUN rises slowly, hiding behind the haze of a Guangzhou morning. I leave my dorm for the last time. My faithful blue backpack, my excess clothes, the rice, and everything else in the dorm I give to Mr. Chen and Bo. They're surprised to see me, and surprised that I'm leaving again. I bid them a final goodbye and then bid everything on campus a final goodbye. Goodbye Peizheng, you were my most important teacher.

Onboard the train, I witness the other passengers. So many months ago this ride seemed wild and exotic; today it seems efficient, plush, streamlined, and blindingly clean. I gaze out the window at the fertile cropland, and it looks so utterly different, opposite from the spent, stretched farmland up north: The browns in the earth streak richer and sweeter, the greens in the stems and leaves unfurl more deeply. Hong Kong coalesces its grand spectacles around me, and I step off the train into a modern metropolis, realizing that the last time I was here this island kingdom was part of Great Britain. Elevated sidewalks ferry me between towers of black steel and glass. Anxious people in dark suits thrust my luggage aside without looking. The straps of my duffel bags saw into my palms. Overhead, a bright purple and lime billboard advertises cell phones in screaming characters that I can now read: "Convenience, Pleasure, Freedom."

At the airport, my bags disappear on a conveyor belt. Weightless as a mountain wind, I float onto a plane. Cloud-like carpeting and luxurious seats expand around me. Have the seats always been this big? Is this "class" really "economy?" The plan is impossible—to go six thousand miles in eleven hours.

The stewardess bends over me to help the little boy in the seat next to me, and her perfume furtively yanks my brain into another galaxy. Some sensual rule inside me dissolves. *In this world everything smells good.* She leaves, and we're left with no odor whatsoever. The fragrances of Asia—the tea, the incense, the cigarettes, the garbage, the constant body odors, the piercing fish sauces, the spry ginger, the tonifying garlic, the hefty braised pork wielding dark plum sauce—it's all gone.

Engines roar, wheels accelerate down a runway, and our wings lift us into the air. We float off over the sea. Out the window, the continent crawls away.

August 6

Yes, it is here, the levitation home. So many journeys, so many hours, so many rides, so many waits, so many days, and here it is. Now. It's unbelievable, but everything is unbelievable. We believe whatever we open ourselves to see. But this very moment—now—I've thought of it forever—it's impossible! Are sheetless beds, filthy floors, rude vendors, and densely polluted air all behind me?

I just watched a movie. I've eaten more food than I often do in two days. What a sweet comfortable life it must be back home. How are we stupid enough still to be unhappy and fearful and greedy and envious? Or is that a mistaken memory lodged in my mind? With all the variety of experiences on earth, the homeland I remember is superficial, incomplete, unreal; so too is the me who last lived there. Now I'll see it all firsthand once again. Home, here I come.

CHAPTER 37

South of the Clouds

將欲歙之必固長之
將欲弱之必固強之

To shrink something, first allow it to expand.
To remove something, first allow it to flourish.

TAO TE CHING, 36

M Y HAIR stands on end, still wet from a shower. The bus came through Qiatou so quickly after we arrived from the gorge that only one of us got to bathe. "Sorry," I grin, feeling my heart pump the blood fast through my veins after the frenetic rush to board. Her knee rests against mine. "But that's what you get for always making me go first."

"Americans always do that," she says, with a sidelong smile. She got to change clothes. "You owe me. I'll be first next time."

The bus, a sleeper to the city of Kunming, is beyond full. I'm sitting on the edge of a bed on which two men lie; Chantal sits across the aisle, on the edge of a bunk occupied by two teenage girls. The bus rumbles out of town, and we ride down, down from the mountains, down through forests, down into rugged farmland. My view remains mostly her profile. "You're the most beautiful woman I've ever met," I say. "I've seen women in magazines, but that's nothing. You're beautiful and you're real."

"You've been in China too long," she replies, blushing slightly.

I consider her words, and I speak from the part of me that walks selflessly, honestly, that channels the energy of waterfalls. She doesn't have to do anything about it, I just want her to hear me, to hear about hiking amid great beauty, about not knowing where to stare, about being swept away.

Her brown irises lock on mine for a moment. She listens, considers, but she seems to refuse the premise, the logic, the whole idea. For a while we say nothing. The girls behind her on the bed are giggling... at me! *They understood.* Chantal catches on, and she laughs at me too. Now I'm the one blushing. It's too ridiculous, and I just give up and laugh.

Further down, in the coffee-colored Yunnan lowlands, we pull over at a bus stop for dinner. Spicy chicken and green peppers steam over to our table like manna from heaven, and the food is cheap enough for us to feast like the ravenous beings we are. She seems self-conscious and distant, thinking about something far away, maybe that boyfriend; then something shifts, and she laughs and jokes with me and asks about Peizheng and playing guitar for my students and the songs I played. She climbs back onto the bus ahead of me, and the driver grabs us with his eyes. "140元, you two!" he barks. We can't risk anything, so we give him only half the amount, promising to pay the other half if we actually get beds. An hour later, two men get off, and the driver calls to us. We fork over the balance, leaving ourselves with but a pinch of colorful paper equivalent to $2.49.

The whole journey I've been wondering if this could happen—if she and I could share a bed—since every other bunk holds either two men or two women, and since even married couples rarely touch in public. Yet sure enough, this captivating creature I admired and released and drew into my adventure and still don't quite understand— she and I climb into bed together. *Lǎowài* are different. Perhaps to everyone she and I are the same gender—a third gender, off-limits to all. Or maybe we're just perceived as incurable freaks, barbarians to be indulged and humored, because, God help us, we didn't grow up in Central Nation (the literal translation of the word *China*), and we don't know any better. This is why Byron and I were locked up on campus for a year.

To me, it doesn't feel like we're the same gender. Our hips touch as we gaze out into the indigo quilted sky and witness its bashful stars. We shift beside each other, trying to stay cool in the lazy sticky air, remarking how good it feels to relax. We discuss the highs and lows of this seeking, losing, and finding called travel—its treats and traps, its sometimes forgotten role in spawning the demon named "tourism," which is defacing this land with plastic ski lifts and concrete promenades. Her foot brushes mine, and I apologize for embarrassing her. She glances at me, laughs, and elbows me in the ribs. "You could stop staring at me." She doesn't seem upset, and my body aches to embrace her, to hold her, to comfort us, to share this pleasure and physical exhaustion. My mind intervenes with more serious considerations. *I can't, here, on the bus. It's too aggressive when there's nowhere for her to go.*

I lie back, alone, and look out into the billion minuscule pinholes twinkling silver. I focus on just one star, feeling its distance and then feeling her closeness: the tingle, the gentleness, the curiosity. I hear her breathing soften and deepen. Memories of people I've pushed away float by my heart like clouds, and then memories of the gorge dart through my mind like mountain sparrows. The bus rolls to a stop in the darkness, and we sit motionless in a caravan of buses and trucks stretching across the barren plateau like a Great Wall. Stranded in the heat and silence, in this tight space and taut magnetism, my mind longs to wander. A voice whispers. *I can choose my experience in this moment, and in all moments.* Liberation unwinds. She rolls over towards me, naturally, into my arms, and we're finally united, together. So much needless anxiety melts. Gently I kiss her warm neck and we relax, but a jarring bounce in a pothole wakes me up. A bead of sweat rolls into my eye and the mattress beneath me feels hot, unbearable. Chantal is on the other side of the bed. It was a dream.

A horn blares into my ear, sunlight pours through the window, and out there in the brightness stands a sign with the characters *Qìchē Xiūlǐgōng* (Automotive Mechanic). We're in industrial suburbs, and the riotous cacophony is the city of Kunming. My back screams its soreness. I tap her awake, and we unload our packs onto the white concrete and squint at the pollution and construction. With our final mao pennies we hail a cab. I want to ask if we ever kissed, because I'm really not sure, but she's sitting over by the window, too far from me, so I let it go. At a bank, we get out. We negotiate with a teller, and insistent in the face of hostility, I find my bargaining paying off like never before: For the first time I'm able to withdraw Chinese money from an American account. Chantal scores too.

We part ways—she to a travel agency, I to the train station. She needs a plane ticket to Beijing, since she goes home from there in two days; I still need to discover whether I'm going home at all, and if so when. We pick a café listed in the *LP* and agree to meet there at 3, in four hours. "Let's not say goodbye now," she says, standing at my shoulder, watching me write my address in her little book.

"Just in case," I say, and I take her into my arms. The quick, perfunctory closeness melts into a moment of warmth, and the world around us stops, and then she boards a bus for the airport.

At the Telephone & Telegraph Office, I decide Kunming agrees with me. The god of telecommunications grants a connection, and my mother's voice is like a light at the end of a long tunnel, a faraway sound arriving like a vision from the wrong end of a telescope. She says I'm coming home. I have a flight out of Hong Kong. In five days. I thank her twice and tell her I love her.

Home. The word trips off my lips, clumsy, unfamiliar, exotic, like "gorgonzola." It seems illogical, impossible. I pay, but as I head for the door, a bizarre vision from a corner of the room seizes my eyes: a row of five brand new computers. They're part of a new government experiment with the *yīntèwǎng* (Internet), I learn, and I'm actually able to log on and access my college email program. Dated yesterday, something atop my inbox hails from a Japanese address. *It's Michiko.* She's seeking me, writing in English. She's cheerful, using exclamation points and a smiley face. She's back in Kurashiki, finishing college, spending the rest of the summer there. She wants to know about my travels; she hopes to see me again, someday, soon. She thanks me for my letter. She waits two paragraphs before telling me. She isn't pregnant. She isn't pregnant. She isn't pregnant. It wasn't that time of the month for her. My exhalation pushes me back from the plastic, up from the chair, across bumpy linoleum, to the window, where a breath of sunlight falls on me, touches me to the core, whispers gentle words.

Treading the sidewalks, stepping on the suitcase-sized stones of the city's central plaza, I witness the world dumbly, believing nothing. All of this was meant to be. She's doing fine. I'm going home. The answer has always been to trust. *I was meant to open my heart.*

A martial arts exhibition blocks my path. Young teenage boys in white robes wave black wooden swords over their heads and then stab right, left, and finally down, in choreographed uniformity. Dozens of them prance about the plaza, mirroring each other, approximating military precision.

I continue on, reaching the enormous central train station. Men fling fragments of English at me like frogs licking for gnats. "Tickets! Cheap! Fast!" They look leaner and more aggressive than their counterparts in Chengdu, so I expect the worst. I need to get to Guangzhou, to get to Hong Kong, to cross this kingdom quickly. Standing in line for an hour, I reach the front just as the ticket windows slide shut for lunch and the two hours of *xiūxī*, Chinese siesta.

Frustrated, I comb the nearby blocks for a cheap hostel where I can drop my pack. Up and down the streets I go, but there's nothing, nowhere that accepts *dà bízi*. Two hours drift by, and with nothing to show for my time, I return to the train station and again wait in line.

This time I do reach the front of the line, and I speak with a surly lady who snaps at me as if I'm her least favorite, most impetuous child. I ask for a hard sleeper to Guangzhou. "*Yìngwò dōu méiyǒu!*" Nothing.

I allow a man to nod at me on the way out. "Where you go?" he asks.

"Guangzhou. Hard sleeper. Tomorrow."

"Of course. Come with me."

"How much?"

"400元." A smug smile darts across his face. "At the most. Come with me." He wears a black jacket and a Puma cap, and he points to an alley beside the station. "Our office." I consider a moment, then warily follow him down a crowded alley redolent with pungent herbs that summon memories of my hospital nightmare. He motions for me to wait and darts inside a tiny café. I back up against one wall as a shirtless peasant pushes a wheelbarrow of coal past my toes. Huffing and puffing, the peasant narrowly misses a suave man with sunglasses and a cellular phone. His wheelbarrow then grazes a table of toy plastic airplanes and Bugs Bunny figures, and he knocks some toys to the pavement. A salesman unleashes a furious invective at the peasant, who freezes in place and stares penitently at the ground.

The man emerges from the café and asks whether I can leave on the 4th. I say it has to be sooner—I could leave tonight. He regards me a moment, nods. "Come with me."

"Are the tickets real?" I ask, following him around another corner and into a fish market.

"Of course," he picks his way between busy stalls, around puddles, and I have to hurry to stay close. He glances over his shoulder at me. "My name is Wei."

Down a still narrower alley, he leaves me in a minuscule office where a different man, one with a thin mustache, who smokes and leans back precariously on two legs of a chair, advises me to be patient. "Wei will return soon. He's good." A fleck of ash from his cigarette falls onto his red tie, and he leans forward as I sit down. His chair crashes to the floor. He mashes the cigarette out in the ashtray and lights another. "It's difficult to work on such short notice."

The sweaty little room looks, I suppose, somewhat like a travel agency—train schedules and tourist posters cover the walls—but it seems unlikely many travelers solve the maze to get here. A rare obese Chinese man tries to sit at the other desk, but he's too big for it and gets comfortable instead by turning the chair sideways, loosening his tie, and undoing a top button. Two other men come and go, as if taking turns standing guard outside. They chain-smoke and talk fast in dialect. I tell them many times where I'm going, that I'm a teacher, that I'm American, not mentioning why I need to leave so soon—international air travel would imply riches and they might gouge me harder. The man with the red tie stares at me. "You speak Mandarin well." He turns and speaks with the fat guy in dialect, nodding at me and laughing. I look at them all. Yes, it's a den of thieves.

He turns back to me with a smile. "You'll get your ticket. It's Wei, he's good." I glance again from face to face and see something, or rather the absence of something—the coldness that turns mischief into malice. It's not here.

A new man enters and shuts the door. The man with the red tie turns to me, holding a slip of paper. "Here's your ticket. 12:30 pm. August 2." He puts it down on the desk between us and lights up another cigarette.

"Hard sleeper?" I ask.

"Mm."

"Express train?"

"Special fast."

I nod and reach into my money pouch.

"500元," he says, tapping his cigarette.

I look around, but still no sign of Wei. "Wei said 400元."

"It's difficult to get a ticket like this," the man explains.

"He said four hundred," I repeat. "You probably paid two hundred, so it's a fair price. Don't try to trick the foreigner."

"500元," he insists, throwing me a smile, gesturing to the others. "There are five of us. One hundred each." *They want a banquet tonight.* But now I know what this is—bargaining.

"I'll give you 450元," I say. "That's fair. I still need to eat dinner myself. The ticket was probably 200元, so this is 50元 for each of you." I put the money on the table and read the ticket carefully. He puts his hand on the cash, and I'm out the door faster than Sandoh ever darted out of my classroom.

A bus ferries me across town to the café, forty minutes late, and it's not a sweet "oasis of French pastries," but a dark, narrow Chinese bakery where they probably put the red bean paste in everything. Wrong again, *LP*. Chantal is nowhere to be seen. I buy a coconut bun, take an outdoor table, and survey passersby: bankers, mechanics, saleswomen, shoe-shiners, schoolboys. My watch gestures towards 4, and I realize that she's not coming, she never came, and she never was going to come. She was through with me. I bite into the middle of the little cake, and red bean paste squirts out. At 4:30, I stand, leave, forge down the pavement, and make the hour-long hike to the Camellia Hotel, Kunming's main backpacker joint. The last bed in the dormitory was just rented, I discover, dashing my hopes of saving money. "To a Canadian girl," the attendant apologizes. I ask for the name, and sure enough my heart somersaults into my stomach. After a moment, when no one's looking, I steal into the dormitory on my own. It's empty—those smart brown eyes, that smile that made everything richer, more complicated, more fascinating—she's nowhere to be found. The room is vacant save for standard-issue, bulky *lăowài* backpacks, some typical porcelain souvenirs, and ten hard empty beds.

The hotel flees behind me. In a hole-in-the-wall diner, a family bickers at the table beside mine. A bowl of spicy noodle soup—Kunming's famous *guòqiáo mĭxìan*—shows up before me, and I disappear into sip after sip of the broth, slurping up the long white *lāmìan* (hand-pulled noodles), letting the fiery flavors cleanse my sinuses and caress my brain. Cleansed and massaged, my brain knows what it knows: Companionship is temporary, solitude is temporary, and anything that can disappear will. A spicy lump of chili, tripe, and egg slides into the belly. My heart marches to a different drummer, however; it laughs in the temporary, cries in the temporary, draws me into the temporary, savors the temporary, and then languishes in the narrow, barren lands of fear and confusion brought by the temporary. *I was never meant to open my heart.*

❀

THE SUN fires brilliant morning spears into a dank, double-occupancy room. I arise, feeling a sweet serenity in my limbs. I leave the room and wander through the streets, feeling happy with every shop and face I see. I climb onto a bus headed to Lake Dian, which lies far outside the city. The scenery fades from city blocks to paved industrial sprawl, then from moist, fertile farmland to broad, rolling, forested hills. An enormous expanse of lapping blue water appears in a bowl in the contoured woods, and the sun's magnificence ripples on its surface. I step down and walk along its banks, letting my lungs open and relax. My torso ascends in the broad beams of light, and I feel the inhaling and exhaling pass through my heart. The light pierces deeply into me, releasing knots between my lungs. The exhalation is vast. The next breath carries into my being hopes, lessons, beauties, discoveries, disappointments, and strands of tingling things that remain incomprehensible.

I hold out a thumb, to hitchhike, and eventually a towering truck picks me up. The driver is a chubby-faced man with a little cap that makes him look like Mao Tse-tung. He curses in torrents as his vehicle stutters its way up a slope. Between choice phrases, he tells me that these hills are often called "the Dragon Hills," since they look like a dragon, but that some other people call them "the Sleeping Lady," since the flowing contours of the hills also appear to be hair falling into the sea. It's Kunming's organic Rorschach test.

He lets me off when I spot a path threading higher into the wooded hills—into the sleeping lady's breasts or over the scales of the dragon's back. I hike up along the path, my feet scratching a rich scent from soft beds of yellowed pine needles. A grove of huge, smooth, black stone boulders carved with writing and dates make me stop, and I run a hand along their inky coolness. Gravestones for Kunming's rich and famous, I decide, resting, sighing, turning to absorb their breathtaking view of the lake. The sails of several junks dot a distant bay. Continuing higher on the path, I pass through a grove of erect, smoke-colored birch trees, and I reach a meadow at the small mountain's summit. Wind rushes violently through the meadow, bending beige grasses. Far below on one side lies the lake, shining like a vast blue mirror; far below on the other side lies endless countryside with villages of white specks. I take in the view on both sides, pausing, contemplating. Yunnan, the name of this province, literally means "South of the Clouds," and from this point China's southbound rivers, which form in the Himalaya, flow down into Burma and Vietnam. My journey too now takes a new direction.

Yes, this is how it ends. Traveling, life. It begins unusual, surprising, and exciting, even though we know that it will end, and that when it ends, we will return to where we came from. Still the suddenness is shocking. The now *comes unexpected every time.*

Unquenchable gusts rush through my hair and drive down a yellow flower at my feet, making it bow to me. Instead, I drop to my knees and bow to it, living alone with it atop the world, closing my eyes. Overcome with the arrival of gratitude, I revel in the sensations of the wind, the spontaneous kiss of the wind, the fickle intimacy of the wind. Gusts blow through my ears, through my head, through my chest, and I release further, and everything disintegrates, and I am blown apart, scattered like dandelion seeds. Nothing is solid, nothing is permanent. There is only a singular presence, the earth beneath me, firm and fertile, calm, everlasting, singing one note, one hymn, one rhythm, one command, one order, one word that goes out to everything: *Grow.* The grasses, *grow.* The rivers, *grow.* The canyons, *grow.* The plants and animals, *grow.*

My eyes slowly open. A blue-orange butterfly alights on my knee. Gazing at it, I sense Chantal and feel exquisite delight with her visit to my life—her companionship, her smile, her bittersweet choice. Her departure was a small death for me, an invitation to suicide for some corner of my heart, and last night I let it die. I let it go. Now something new there may grow.

The lake and the hills and the sky spread out wide around me. I pray to them for acceptance of all that has passed. I pray for beauty and honesty in all that will pass. Now, *now*, another small death. I exhale, and I die. I leave this trip, this life, this time. I leap into the breezes and fly.

Epilogue

活到老學到老
還有三洋沒有學到

Live to old age, study to old age,
Still there is much you will never learn.

CHINESE PROVERB

TODAY I'M in San Francisco. After leaping home to St. Louis and living there several years, I followed my intuition here. It's now been many years. The lessons that I learned in the classrooms and mountains of China remain with me. They are the inspiration for how I create my life today—trusting and grateful, choosing love, curious about every fear, dying every necessary small death, open to the eternal growth around me and within me. I long for every one of us to discover what we truly want, and to create it, to live it, to be what we long for, to do what pleases us most deeply. I long for us to connect with each other, to inspire each other, to open ourselves to the depths of our every experience.

There are always many deaths, big and small. I fell ill with persistent sinusitis shortly after returning home. My recovery was slow. A friend, Mark Schulte, contacted me about writing a small article on teaching English in China. I declined; I didn't consider myself a writer. But he insisted—he was launching a new magazine and its first issue remained thin—and finally I acceded. A mass of prose effortlessly poured forth. Writing proved essential, and writing restored me. I still had so much more to learn, as it seems we always do. China was but the beginning. And yet that beginning revealed to me the path that I needed to take to reconnect deeply with my parents, my brother and sister, my friends, and my own body. May we all grow, as the universe does, continuously, everywhere.

I did go learn about Nicaragua, Chile, and Iran, as I promised myself in Xiahe, and what I discovered primarily was my own naiveté. My research often led to a discomfiting discovery and a heavy heart. The critics of the U.S. are largely correct: American intervention in countries around the globe has almost never been intended to spread democracy or fairness or the values that American citizens share, but rather to expand the wealth and power of America's military and to advance the interests of its biggest corporations and wealthiest people. We Americans are propagandized to believe otherwise, and many do, as I did. The events of 9-11, about which there remain many questions, produced an enormous opportunity for goodwill towards and among people of all nations; that we responded to that opportunity for growth as a nation by launching more interventions of the same kind saddened me deeply. But still I hope and expect that we as a country will grow.

On the question of how to affect China—how to make it more peaceful, more democratic, more environmentally sensitive, more politically friendly—I've come to see that we as a nation need only to demonstrate the behavior we advocate. China wants, more than anything, to be a "superpower"—and a respected one—as it was a short five centuries ago. The way it is going about becoming such a power today is by following the example, like a son would a father, of the nation to whom it looks up: the United States. It takes its cues from us.

Today I write about the media and politics as an avocation, as well as play guitar and compose songs in Chinese and English. I make my living primarily through website programming.

My parents remain in St. Louis. My father's career—suit, tie, and all—took my family to several cities and eventually made them wealthy when his St. Louis telecommunications company built a network of fiber optic cables that became a backbone of the internet.

Byron is near me, across the Bay in Berkeley, California, pursuing a

Ph.D. in Political Science. His area of focus is East Asia, and as I write this he is in Beijing doing research on labor law and reality at two rural Chinese factories.

Lauren lives in Washington, D.C., working for the Department of State, focusing on trade, and international development in Southeast Asia.

Paige, living in Seattle with her husband Travis and two children, does children's programming at radio station KUOW, an NPR affiliate.

Anton is in Boulder, Colorado, lecturing as an Assistant Professor of English. He enjoys mountain climbing and kayaking.

Michiko and I wrote back and forth for nearly a year in both Chinese and English, but the conversation eventually went quiet, and I've lost track of her.

Chantal worked for several years with the Canadian consulate in Abidjan, Ivory Coast, in West Africa. Now she lives in Ottawa, working with the Minister of Foreign Affairs and International Trade. She sent me an email one day, remembering the night on the bus to Kunming. "I remember a fabulous sky. There were so many stars; the little spaces of darkness that I could find were deep black. Wow. I was feeling very good and must admit that the temptation was strong. I wanted to put my head on your shoulder. But after those two days of neglecting your nice attention, I could not change my mind so easily!" She is planning a trip to California.

I am planning travels to South America.

A Glossary of Chinese Terms

1元 = 1 Yuan = 1 *Rénmínbì* (RMB) = 10 *máo* = $0.12

$1 = 8.30元

白酒	*báijiǔ*	Baijiu, China's famous sorghum vodka (literally: "white liquor")
包宁同	*Bāo Tóngníng*	Tony Brasunas ("common peace")
长江	*Cháng Jiāng*	Yangtse River ("long river")
大鼻子	*dà bízi*	Foreigner ("big nose")
单位	*dānwèi*	Work Unit ("single position")
独立	*dúlì*	Independent ("sole stand")
风水	*fēngshuǐ*	Ancient Chinese geomancy ("wind water")
腐败	*fǔbài*	Corrupt ("rotten decay")
干杯	*gānbēi*	Cheers! ("dry glass")
广州人	*Guǎngzhōurén*	Canton resident ("Guangzhou person")
共产党	*Gòngchǎndǎng*	The Communist Party ("shared manufacturing political party")
个体户	*gètǐhù*	Street vendor ("individual body door")
狗屁	*gǒupì*	Bullshit ("dog farts")
关系	*guānxì*	Social connections ("closed system")
鬼佬	*gwailo*	Foreigner ("devil man") [Cantonese]
很好	*hěn hǎo*	Very good ("very good")
华侨	*huáqiáo*	Overseas Chinese person ("brilliant abroad")
回归	*huíguī*	The Return to the Motherland [of Hong Kong] ("return converge")
胡萝卜	*húluóbò*	Carrot ("barbarian radish")
胡同	*hútòng*	Winding narrow city alley ("barbarian share")

国民党	*Kuómíntǎng*	The Nationalist Party ("nation people political party")
老百姓	*lǎobǎixìng*	The masses ("the old 100 names")
老师	*lǎoshī*	Teacher ("old master")
老外	*lǎowài*	Foreigner ("old outsider")
没关系	*méi guānxì*	It doesn't matter ("doesn't have any connections")
你好	*nǐ hǎo*	Hello ("you good")
旗袍	*qípáo*	Traditional Chinese woman's formal gown ("banner robe")
人民币	*rénmínbì*	RMB, the Chinese currency ("the people's money")
市场	*shìchǎng*	Market ("city site")
我听不懂	*wǒ tīngbudǒng*	I don't understand ("I hear but don't get")
休息	*xiūxī*	Rest, midday siesta ("rest breath")
习惯	*xíguàn*	Become accustomed to ("practice repeat")
一路顺风	*yī lù shūn fēng*	Bon Voyage, Safe Journeys! ("a smooth breezy road")
再见	*zàijiàn*	Goodbye ("again see")
早安	*zǎo ān*	Good morning ("early peace")
中国	*Zhōngguó*	China ("central nation")
粽子	*zòngzi*	Steamed rice dumpling wrapped in bamboo leaves ("palm piece")

Acknowledgments

感謝您們

Thank you.

I WISH IT were possible to mention all the friends, family, colleagues, and strangers who provided assistance along the way to creating this book. Writing coach Tom Bird dropped the first seed of this book into my brain, and wise book designer, Joel Friedlander, and talented cover designer, Laura Duffy, together put the final touches on the finished product you have in your hands. In between, I crossed paths with dozens of people who proved essential in completing this labor of love, and I am ineffably grateful to every one of them.

I would like specifically to thank: Jim Brasunas, Lynne Michelson, Pamela Mendoza Brasunas, The Heilbut Family, Maurine Heard, Joshua D. Bruzgul, Lainie Fairbanks, Ellen Brasunas, Jenifer K. Chan, Sir Gemmers, Jerome Michelson, Mark Pinto, Christine Schutz, Rev. Ritter, Robert Arnow, Joan Elizabeth, The Awaken Cafe, Michael & Sanda Brasunas, Chris Ross, Al Mendoza, The Bacon/Mulder Family, MD, Emile Litvak, Michael Park, Jon 'J-Stick' Ayers, Brian & Tamara Lemesh, Peggy Duffield, Jeddy Azuma, Mike Simpson, Reijo Oksanen, Susan Hollingshead, Phil Pusateri, Omar Cuellar, Jessi Callihan, Amanda Joost, Kevin Christaldi, John C. Brasunas, Greg Christoffel, Chris Chromey, Anna, Steve Atherton, Anne Buzzard, Maria Bucaro, K.C. Cavanagh, Elliot Cahn, Stephanie Smith, Jonathan Bloch, Angie & Chuck Becerra, Jack & Roberta Chromey, Kate & Howie Cockrill,

Jon & Edie Michelson, Wesley Hedden, Andy VanSickle-Ward, Robin Cahn, Danny, The Sandler/Michelson Family, Elizabeth Amideo Watson, Walter Schweikert, Benjamin Robert Freidenberg, and Jonah Larkin.

I would also like to thank Lara Ortiz-Luis for making a superb Kickstarter video, Nicole Francois for her editorial insights and expert proofreading, and Estelle Kim for creating the gorgeous maps and illustrations in this book.

Finally, and most of all, I would like to thank my wife Pamela, whose amazing love inspires me daily to keep growing, to keep learning, and to keep opening my heart.